EXPANDING ARCHITECTURE
DESIGN AS ACTIVISM

**EDITED BY
BRYAN BELL AND
KATIE WAKEFORD**

**FOREWORD BY
THOMAS FISHER**

METROPOLIS BOOKS

By expanding the population we serve and the services we offer, designers can play a significant role in addressing the most critical issues we face in the world today.

CONTENTS

FOREWORD

Architecture and all the design professions are undergoing a major transformation that is both pro-active and reactive: proactive as a search for roles with greater rele-vance, and reactive as a response to the humanitarian and environmental crises facing the world.

Public-Interest Architecture:
A Needed and Inevitable Change

THOMAS FISHER

This book provides an exceptional overview of the diverse and growing practice of community design and public-interest architecture. Some architects may consider these activities to be marginal within the field, but this form of practice promises to open up whole new areas of service for design professionals; and, given demographic and environmental trends, it may eventually become a primary career track for many people. That may sound odd to those who currently work in this area, given the occasional sense of embattlement and the number of obstacles that many of the authors in this volume have encountered. But the gap continues to grow between what millions of people need and what the current system of housing and building provides. For that reason, change is inevitable.

Consider the metaphor that Sergio Palleroni uses to describe the situation most North American architects find themselves in: "I often compare the situation of living in the United States to being in the eye of the storm. When you are standing in the eye of the storm, everything seems calm. But as you step away...you realize that this storm you're at the center of is changing the rest of the world dramatically."[1] Millions of American citizens, as well as billions of people around the world, battle the storms of inadequate services, unaffordable housing, and unsafe neighborhoods on a daily basis. It is only a matter of time before the winds of unrest and a rain of violence descend upon everyone, including those who may think their money and power can keep them permanently safe in the storm's eye.

The architectural profession reflects this dichotomy. Most architectural practice is similar to the practices of physicians and lawyers, in that professionals work mainly with clients—wealthy individuals, corporations, institutions, and governments—who can afford to pay professional fees and who receive, in exchange, highly customized responses to their specific needs. In architecture, this form of practice has led to the design and construction of many visually powerful and functionally successful buildings, but it also greatly limits the number and types of people served by the profession. As several writers in this book tell us, architects directly affect only about 2 to 5 percent of all that gets built, which hardly makes a dent in the requirement that we, as licensed professionals, attend to the public's health, safety, and welfare.

As Palleroni observes, things may seem calm now to many American clients and their architects, but the storm clouds are on the horizon—and they are rapidly approaching. If you want proof, look at the housing situation in the United States. One-fourth of all American households—some 30 million families—lack adequate housing or the funds to secure such housing, as Kathleen Dorgan and Deane Evans note in their essay, and subprime mortgage lenders have created a financial tsunami of foreclosures around the country, which have increased 90 percent since mid-2006.[2] Tighter regulation of the mortgage industry may help reduce the size of future foreclosure tidal waves, but the failure of creative financing to get more people into their own homes highlights the growing hopelessness among a substantial number of Americans, whose inflation-adjusted incomes have remained essentially flat for decades even as the cost of housing has risen faster than inflation in most areas of the country.[3] The United States is becoming divided, like many developing countries, into a small number of the super-rich and the majority, whose relatively stagnant incomes place the American dream permanently beyond their reach.[4]

1 Sergio Palleroni, "Building Sustainable Communities and Building Citizens," in this volume, 275.

2 Kathleen Dorgan and Deane Evans, "Mainstreaming Good Design in Affordable Housing," in this volume, 149; John Schoen, "Mortgage Foreclosures Rise to Record; Delinquencies Jump among Riskiest Loans; California, Nevada Hit Hard," MSNBC, June 14, 2007, www.msnbc.msn.com/id/19225568/.

3 "Median Income and Housing Cost Index vs. United States," Swivel, www.swivel.com/graphs/show/1170178.

4 Roger Lowenstein, "The Inequality Conundrum," New York Times Magazine, June 10, 2007, 11–12, 14.

However socially and politically divisive that gap may be in the United States, it doesn't come close to the extremes of wealth and impoverishment or the depths of desperation experienced by billions of people elsewhere in the world. With the global population anticipated to increase to about 9 billion by 2050, the United Nations expects the number of people living in slums to reach 2 billion by the same date.[5] The conditions in what Mike Davis has called "a planet of slums" may seem far-off and abstract to most Americans, but such concentrations of human misery will eventually affect us all.[6] It is almost certain, for example, that a devastating disease will originate in one of these slums because of terrible sanitation, and that unsuspecting people on airplanes will spread the disease to the entire human population, rich and poor alike. We have already seen how the sense of hopelessness and anger that young people feel in such situations can lead them to embrace various kinds of extremism, providing fuel to terrorist activities that disrupt economies and undermine democracies. Add to this the prediction that as many as 200 million environmental refugees will be on the move over the next several decades because of global climate change, and we have all the makings of a human hurricane from which no one will be entirely safe.[7]

As such calamities come to our shores, there will be urgent calls to correct their causes, which will place community design and public-interest architecture at the very center of public concern. This will, in turn, transform the profession, for we may soon find that we have too many architects skilled at designing museums and mansions and too few able to work with indigent people and communities in need of basic housing, sanitation, and security. Licensure may push this change as well. Right now, we assume that architects' responsibility for public health, safety, and welfare remains largely confined to those who commission and use our buildings. But with the human storm gathering force around the world, architects may well see the definition of "architecture" expand to include the health, safety, and welfare of all people, wherever they live and whatever their ability to pay.

Changes in education and practice will follow these changes in demand and expectations. Currently, architectural education mostly prepares students to meet the building needs of relatively wealthy individuals and organizations, even though most of the growth in population and most of the need for architectural services exists among billions of impoverished people across the planet. In some ways, architectural education occupies a place similar to the one it occupied in the nineteenth and early twentieth centuries, when schools still taught the design of classical monuments even as newly industrialized cities grew up around them. The schools changed their curriculums in response to that transformation, and a similar change will occur again in the coming decades.

The same sense of overdue change exists in the delivery of housing and other essential services. As several of the essays in this book attest, practitioners of public-interest architecture and their nonprofit clients must continually struggle against the resistance of conservative lenders, unwilling to invest in anything different from what they have funded before, and cautious regulators, reluctant to approve anything they have not seen before. This approach may make sense to those who think they can stay in the eye of the storm forever, but once the tempest arrives, we will look back at this resistance in disbelief, as we now do at those who, charged with protecting us, acted as if we were immune to international terrorism.

What might a whole new profession of public-interest architecture look like? Precedents exist in medicine and law. Although the traditional practice of architecture parallels those of medicine and law, architects do not have the benefit of an insurance system that protects patients from paying the high fees of doctors, or the contingency-

5 "World Population Will Increase by 2.5 Billion by 2050," United Nations Population Division, www.un.org/News/Press/docs/2007/pop952.doc.htm; "UN-HABITAT Report on Global Slums," InfoChange News a Features, Oct. 2003 www.infochangeindia bookandreportsst48

6 Mike Davis, *Planet of Slums* (New York: Verso, 2006).

7 Norman Myers, "Environmental Refugees: An Emergent Security Issue," lecture, Thirteenth Economic Forum of the Organization for Security and Co-Operation, Prague, Czech Republic, May 23–27, 2005, www.osce.org/documents/eea/2005/14488_en.pdf.

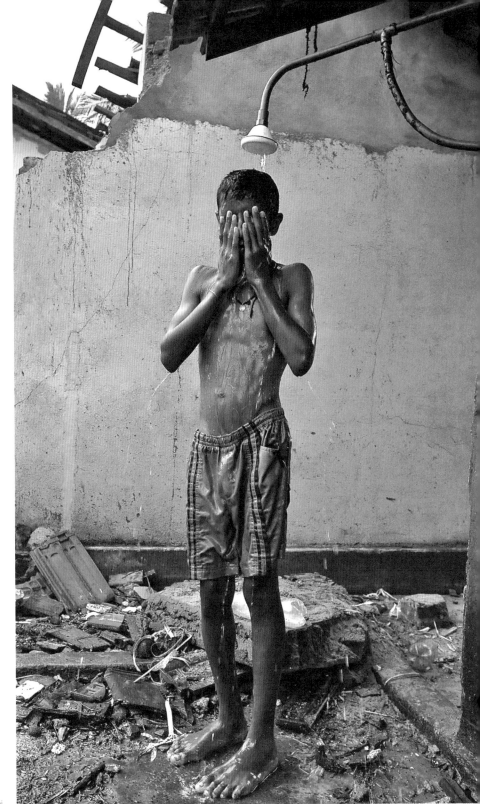

Right
In Piyadigama,
Sri Lanka, a boy
takes a shower at
his grandmother's
home, which was
destroyed by the
2004 Asian Tsunami.

based fee agreements of lawyers who get paid only if they win the case. Nor do most architects have the ongoing relationships and repeat business that many doctors have with their patients or lawyers with their clients.

In the area of public service, medicine and law have created an infrastructure within the profession that allows its practitioners to provide services to the needy, but architecture has no such infrastructure. Of course, doctors and lawyers (and architects) do pro bono work in legal aid clinics or as part of organizations like Doctors Without Borders. But medicine has spun off the field of public health, and law has created a public-defense system. These are vocations in their own right, focused on serving the needs of large numbers of people who are unable to pay market-rate fees but who are in great need of professional expertise. Architects have an important nonprofit effort, Public Architecture, doing heroic work in getting more architectural firms to donate 1 percent of their billable time to pro bono work.[8]

8 John Peterson, "Mobilizing Mainstream Professionals to Work for the Public Good," in this volume, 94–103.

But we need a career path, and possibly even a profession, of public-interest architecture, parallel to public health and public defense, that has its own educational requirements, practice models, financial support, and client base.

This career path could come into existence in a couple of different ways. A profession of public-interest architecture might emerge in partnership with public health. The latter arose out of medicine in the nineteenth century. Coincidentally, designer Frederick Law Olmsted was a major figure in the public-health movement's early history, through his leadership during the Civil War of the Sanitary Commission, which eventually became the American Red Cross. Today the lifestyle diseases arising from the sedentary habits of people in North America and the epidemic and pandemic diseases stemming from the sanitation problems of global slums have caused the public-health community to become newly interested in working with design professionals. That interest has, in turn, provided an opportunity for designers to connect with the funding sources and governmental and nonprofit organizations that have traditionally supported public health.

Because of that connection, the practice of public-interest architecture might end up having a much stronger body of research behind it, as well as a more diverse set of disciplines working with it. While the traditional design and engineering fields will continue to be a part of public-interest practice, professionals who do not normally work with architects—such as public-health physicians, social workers, sociologists, and anthropologists—might begin doing so. Public-interest architects might also have closer ties with the academy—not just with architecture programs but also with scientists and social scientists who can help study the impact of our efforts and bring their knowledge to bear on public-policy decisions that have a design component.

The recent transformation in the governmental perception of homelessness is a case in point. Once research showed that it is far more expensive for people to remain on the streets than to be housed, because of the number of police interventions and emergency room visits that the unhoused generate, local and state governments began providing the supportive housing needed to get people off the streets. A public-health model for design practice would be good not only for the many people served by it but also for the architectural profession itself, which has long suffered from a dearth of data to demonstrate the value of what we do.

Public-interest architecture might also emerge as a distinct field in the way that public defense has within law. While most public defenders have a traditional legal education, their practice differs substantially from that of private or other governmental lawyers. Public defenders are typically paid by the judicial branch of federal and state governments, either as full-time judicial employees or as members of private firms who work as assigned counsel or under contract with the public sector. This system arose from the public commitment to give every person a fair trial regardless of his or her ability to pay. Architects need to make the case—with the research to back it up—for a parallel public commitment to ensure that every person has affordable housing and access to essential services.

9 Amanda Hendler-Voss and Seth Hendler-Voss, "Designing with an Asset-Based Approach," in this volume, 124–31.

Those are the very goals that public housing strives to meet, although as we now know, such housing has served as a blunt instrument for handling a highly diverse set of needs. This is part of the reason that we have so many distressed public housing projects. Community design, like the public-defender system in law, has evolved a much more sophisticated set of methods to identify the needs—or more important, as Amanda Hendler-Voss and Seth Hendler-Voss argue, the assets—of people and communities, and consequently to develop a range of options for people to consider.[9] We need, in other words, a viable public process for securing housing and creating community, rather than a one-size-fits-all product like public housing.

While most law schools do not have a specific public-defender track, they do offer the essential civil and criminal courses needed by people going into this specialty. The same curricular components could easily be developed in architecture programs. In addition to the housing studios and the programming and environment-behavior courses that many schools offer, a track in public-interest architecture might guide students to specific courses elsewhere in the university related to working with diverse communities and dealing with issues of environmental health and safety. As with public defense, internship opportunities for students of public-interest architecture need to be established to facilitate their transition into this line of work.

10 Barbara B. Wilson, "The Architectural Bat-Signal," in this volume, 28–33.

The first signs of ideas like this already exist. The SEED (Social, Economic, and Environmental Design) Network has brought together individuals and organizations committed to public-interest architecture. I predict that, after a few more global storms come ashore, as they did with 9/11 and Katrina, SEED will become as central to social-justice efforts as the LEED (Leadership in Energy and Environmental Design) program has become for environmental issues.[10]

Meanwhile, we have much to learn to get ready for the winds heading our way, and this volume is full of examples of what many in the profession will someday be doing as the public looks to us, along with other professional fields, to help handle the flood of misery welling up from within our own borders and converging upon us from other parts of the world. No one looks forward to such a time, but the longer we fool ourselves into thinking we will always be in the eye of the storm, the more unprepared we will be when the typhoon hits land. See this book, then, both as a storm warning and as a guide for our future preparedness.

PREFACE

By expanding the
population we serve
and the services
we offer, designers
can play a significant
role in addressing
the most critical
issues we face in the
world today.

Expanding Design
Toward Greater Relevance

BRYAN BELL

Good design has the potential to benefit many more people than it currently does. Design can play a direct role in addressing critical social issues that we face. The process of creating the built environment can allow communities and individuals to improve and celebrate their lives. It can help solve their struggles by reshaping their existence.

But currently the opportunity to create a built environment is reserved only for the very few, the elite, the highest income bracket served to excess by market forces. Designers have let these market forces alone determine whom we serve, what issues we address, and the shape of all our design professions: architecture, landscape architecture, graphic design, industrial design, planning, and interior design.

How can we expand the practice of design to provide for the rest, the great number currently underserved, and to play an active role in responding to the social challenges we face in the world?

To make design more relevant is to reconsider what "design" issues are. Rejecting the limits we have defined for ourselves, we should instead assume that design can play a positive role in seeking answers to many different kinds of challenges. We have limited our potential by seeing most major human concerns as unrelated to our work.

Designers can also easily increase the number of clients that we serve. Right now there is a large contingent of potential clients that we are not reaching, and there is no competition for their projects. These clients have needs that represent the most exciting design challenges in existence. Yet the great majority of this public does not know what design is, or why they might want it, or how it could help them. It is our job to explain this, to define and communicate the value of architecture. If we do, we will all have enough work for many lifetimes.

We can use our training and talent to make much broader contributions to the world, but it will require that many of us change the way we practice architecture. In the first book I edited, *Good Deeds, Good Design: Community Service through Architecture*, Roberta M. Feldman defined *activist practice* as the act of architects leaving the office, engaging a community, and seeking a need for design in that community, rather than passively waiting for clients to come to them. In another essay from that collection, Jason Pearson defined *operative practice* as any intentional, creative action—formal, programmatic, fiscal, functional, physical, social, political, or aesthetic—that achieves lasting positive change. These two notions are examples of ways we can redefine practice so as to free ourselves from our traditional, limited role and to empower ourselves to make the contributions that we believe designers can and should make.

Over the last seven years I have been trying to find designers engaged in this type of proactive practice. Through my work on *Good Deeds, Good Design*, a series of conferences called "Structures for Inclusion," and the present book, I have had the opportunity to see the work of many who are bringing design of very high quality to bear on critical social, economic, and environmental issues. Some people have called this kind of work a movement, and I think there is enough of a critical mass to justify that claim. Ultimately, however, I prefer simply to think of it as the practice of architecture, just broader than before. Most of us doing this work do not need to decide whether we are in a movement or not. The crucial thing to remember is that these serious issues are not going away. I have been working with migrants to develop housing solutions for fifteen years now, and it is clear that there will be a need for this work for the rest of my life. That is all I need to know.

Though I may seem critical of the profession, I am actually extremely optimistic about the future of design. As society evolves let us strive for the improvement of the lives of all, not just the privileged few. Designers can play key roles as we give new forms to the diverse needs of this future.

INTRO-
DUCTION

Architecture
is political.
Architecture
is powerful.
The time is
right for an
ideological
architecture
that does good
by being good.

An Architecture of Change

JOSÉ L. S. GÁMEZ AND SUSAN ROGERS

Hope coincides with an increasingly critical perception of the concrete conditions of reality. Society reveals itself as something unfinished, not as something inexorably given; it becomes a challenge rather than a hopeless limitation.

PAULO FREIRE, *Education for Critical Consciousness*

Powerful voices are emerging to call for an architecture of change, an architecture that matters to everyone, and these voices are being nurtured and sustained by the activist practices of designers and citizens working close to the ground. As the voices grow louder, the message is becoming increasingly clear: architecture can both do good by societal standards and be good by professional standards, and design does not have to be compromised in the process of serving the needs of others. These voices have the potential to become an immense wall of sound and a primary force shaping the discourses that define the roles of the architectural academy and the profession of architecture. The voices of change collectively call for the activation of a politicized and spatialized project that will work to counteract the forces that typically control production of and access to space. They claim that the political work of architecture is not limited to the work of building. They assert that the political can be beautiful and that architecture can be socially engaged in ways that sidestep the conflicts of ethics versus aesthetics and finance versus virtue.

The emergence of new voices from the margins calling for and acting on an architecture of change, the continued presence of established voices, and the myriad voices in between illustrate the fluidity that characterizes contemporary architectural and intellectual landscapes. The forces that influence the ideas, knowledge bases, and practices of our discipline are in constant flux. If our political engagement is to move beyond "tiny empowerments" and toward systemic change, we must find a way to move out of the cacophony of a million voices and toward the harmony of a choir that obtains its power from collectivity.[1] What is needed is an architecture of change—an architecture that moves the field beyond the design of buildings and toward the design of new processes of engagement with the political forces that shape theories, practices, academies, policies, and communities.

Modernism: A Promise Unfulfilled

The call for an architecture of change is not new, but it has fallen out of favor. The early modern movement possessed a clear sense of political engagement, and it envisioned broad societal change as a crucial and fundamental part of its architectural practices. What Jürgen Habermas has termed the *project of modernity* emerged in the mid-nineteenth century, a transitional period of social unrest, armed revolutions, and rapid industrialization and urbanization, all occurring as logical outcomes of Enlightenment ideals.[2] The modern movement conceived of progress and technological advancement as tools to be employed in the service of social equality. Modernist architects strove to create "universal" spaces—rational, orderly, and accessible—that would give opportunity and freedom to everyone. While the utopian ideals represented by proposals such as Charles Fourier's *Le Nouveau Monde* were not to be realized, such projects are worth recalling, even as we question the universal truths and grand narratives they espoused.

1 Leonie Sandercock, "Insurgent Practices: 'A Thousand Tiny Empowerments,'" in Sandercock, *Towards Cosmopolis: Planning for Multicultural Cities* (Chichester and New York: John Wiley, 1998), 129–60.

2 Jürgen Habermas, "Modernity: An Incomplete Project," in Hal Foster, ed., *The Anti-Aesthetic: Essays on Postmodern Culture* (Port Townsend, Wash.: Bay Press, 1983), 3–15.

By the early 1900s many of the modernists' goals had been realized, aided in part by the professionalization of architecture and urban planning. In constructed form the flaws of a modernist architectural palette that is separated from utopian social ideals came clearly into view. Mainstream modernism as represented by the International Style was regarded as increasingly disconnected from the everyday social world. Modernist architecture reemerged powerfully during the 1960s as urban-renewal programs and public-housing projects remade landscapes in distinctly modernist idioms throughout the world; but by the end of the decade, the demise of the modern project was well within sight. Forces for social and political change were taking aim at modernism's evident limitations. Grand narratives were challenged by localized and unheard voices, universal truths were challenged in light of contextualized differences, and international formal styles were challenged by indigenous cultural expressions. Modernism as a movement was discarded not because of the ideals on which it was based but because of the conflicting principles by which it was realized—namely, the contradiction between the goal of social change and those of market capitalism and institutionalized power.[3] While most would agree that modernism's end has provided new opportunities, the loss of an ideological agenda has had a significant impact on the power of the profession to influence the production of space and the public realm at large.

The end of the modern movement also brought with it the end of the political project in architecture. As postmodernism stepped in with a series of variants to replace the modern paradigm, the political continued to disappear from mainstream architectural practice. This occurred despite the fact that many prominent critics of the modern project helped open discursive venues for previously unheard voices. Cultural theorists such as Jean Baudrillard, Jacques Derrida, Michel Foucault, and Jean-François Lyotard called attention to the totalization inherent in universal narratives, the falsity of external truth, and the impossibility of achieving the goals of overarching emancipatory projects. These theorists and many others pointed out the naiveté of the modern project's utopian musings, emphasizing that enlightened reasoning does not protect us from the whims of totalitarianism.

The fruits of modernity seemed to have rotted on the vine. Postmodernity opened up a space within which to question established thought, and that very questioning seemed to provide yet another new promise of emancipatory progress. A new utopianism began to emerge that questioned the construction and representation of the self and the other. Freed at last from the hegemony of modernity, society would rise up to show its intrinsic diversity. An implicit expectation of this *third space* was that it would not support universal frameworks.[4]

However, without the ability to address broad societal goals, architecture was left to focus inward. In this way the postmodern movement liberated critical thought from the confines of rationalism while continuing the liberation of architecture from politics. Postmodernism gave rise to severe contradictions between the emancipation of ideas that envisioned pluralistic power and the imprisonment of architecture within institutionalized power.

We are again in a period of rapid transition. Political, social, and economic changes have transformed the manner in which space is produced and accessed. Space has become the final frontier of capitalist expansion, and the political continues to be eviscerated from the architectural. Both modernity and postmodernity have failed to deliver on their respective emancipatory promises. Each in its own way promised to free the individual from repressive regimes, to improve our social standards, and equitably to distribute access to our social and physical landscapes.

Above
Women carry buckets of clean water back to Cité Soleil, a slum in Port-au-Prince, Haiti

3 Andy Merrifield, "David Harvey: The Geopolitics of Urbanization," in Merrifield, *Metromarxism: A Marxist Tale of the City* (New York: Routledge, 2002), 133–56.

4 Discussions of "third spaces" can be found in the work of Edward Soja, Homi Bhabha, Guillermo Gomez-Peña, and bell hooks, to name a few. We are using this term loosely here to refer to the possibility of a new form of spatiality that both breaks with modernity and promises to escape the confines of postmodern critique

5 George Baird,
"'Criticality' and Its
Discontents," *Harvard
Design Magazine*, fall
2004/winter 2005,
16–21.

The Postpolitical Turn

The postpolitical turn, which has been emerging for some time, has surveyed the current architectural and intellectual landscape and has pronounced that we have entered a *postcritical* age.[5] The implication is that architecture's recent infatuation with critical theory has now run its course, leaving us with a pragmatist's agenda for the foreseeable future. This is a pragmatism of expedience, not the pragmatism of the philosophers, which was founded upon a critical stance toward the autonomy of theory. Philosophical pragmatism reminds us that theory is not an end in itself, and it seeks to test ideas and measure their ultimate impacts for a collective social good. This uniquely American contribution to philosophical investigation has held promise, but a postcritical orientation cuts off the one good leg of a pragmatic stance: without a critical engagement with the world around us, we are left with just another way of doing things, and little or no formal, ethical, or intellectual guidance to help us choose a path.

The postcritical is not pragmatic; it is symptomatic. It is symptomatic of a profession that has benefited from an economy that limps ever forward. It is symptomatic of an academy that has been seduced by fashionable theoretical projects, only to reproduce them in bastardized form. Not only have American architectural efforts in the last fifty years been largely aesthetic exercises, but they also have flirted only briefly with the political—and then only in symbolic form. If modernism's political project failed to journey across the Atlantic as a part of the Museum of Modern Art's famed exhibition in which Henry-Russell Hitchcock and Philip Johnson first exposed the North American project to European modernism, then critical theory and its potential for radical reforms have now been sent back overseas to their Continental homeland as the summer of '68 continues to fade in our collective memory.

Political blindness is not new to architecture, nor is it rare in society. To stake a political claim is to run the risk of clashing with a divergent set of cultural values and alienating potential clients, prospects that few find enjoyable. Discussions concerning the political and issues such as equitable representation in real and imagined spaces are potentially painful and are therefore frequently avoided. The political thus remains an invisible and often unspoken subtext to otherwise well-grounded discourses and practices. The

disciplinary vacuum within which architectural ideologies are often investigated further fosters a social and political blindness that a postcritical stance can only reinforce. If we adopt a position that ignores the advancements that postmodern thought and critical theory provided us—a utopian goal of equity, fruitful diversity, and a critically engaged process of cultural production—we may find ourselves indulging in a naiveté similar to that of early modernism, which promised societal change almost solely through architectural practices and failed to recognize that space and its production are controlled by the dictates of capitalism and politics.

It is important to reclaim the critical utopianism of the postmodern project and critical theory. Critical social and cultural theories can form the backbone of a revived political agenda. They can challenge both the unevenness of social landscapes and the forces that produce such landscapes by looking at the way things are in terms of the way they could or should be.[6]

We must find a way to be both unified and diverse. This is not a renewed call for all of us to just get along; this is a call that requires a fundamental rethinking of the political in a changing society. To question the political in this era is to challenge societal conditions in an age of multicultural values, identity politics, and liberal agendas largely in retreat in a post-9/11 world. Contemporary American liberalism is dominated by a notion of multiculturalism that is essentially apolitical. For this reason mainstream multiculturalism is an ideology that downplays the potential clashes within a radical cultural pluralism in favor of established models of cultural integration. Mainstream liberalism and multiculturalism seek to eliminate discussions of uneven political, social, and economic empowerment in favor of a reformulated cultural melting pot, in which everyone has ostensibly had an equal opportunity. Mainstream liberalism and multiculturalism are fundamentally antipluralist ideologies in three primary ways: they advocate an adherence to a set of core values; they reject political consciousness; and they overlook questions of political and social parity, asking us instead to turn our backs on the question of power.[7]

6 Steve Best and Douglas Kellner, The Postmodern Turn: Paradigm Shifts in Theory, Culture and Science (New York: Guilford Press, 1997).

7 Avery F. Gordon and Christopher Newfield, "Multiculturalism's Unfinished Business," in Gordon and Newfield, eds., Mapping Multiculturalism (Minneapolis: University of Minnesota Press, 1994), 76–115.

8 Edward Soja and Barbara Hooper, "The Spaces that Difference Makes," in Michael Keith and Steve Pile, eds., *Place and the Politics of Identity* (London: Routledge, 1993), 183–205.

Left
Sunhouse built through a university-community partnership. See Steve Badanes, "Building Consensus in Design/Build Studios," in this volume, 248–55.

How to Expand Architecture

Architectural discourses and practices are now almost entirely apolitical due to the loss of a unifying agenda. For many this trend comes as no surprise, nor is it alarming; but for those who are seeking a new paradigm with the potential to create systemic change, the postcritical move in theory and practice is a phenomenon that must be countered. We need an architecture of change that will promote progressive and inclusive strategies in practice and education, strategies that have the potential to transform the production of space and to be more than a disparate set of points of action without an organized plan of attack. What is needed is an actively critical agenda that can inform the practices that lead to good design.

In order to rekindle architecture's political engagement, we must look at the forces that not only produce marginalization but also replicate it as an ongoing system of inequity.[8] Civil society is produced and reproduced through its civic, academic, and professional institutions. The academy plays a particularly important role as a filter for ideas and practices, and architectural education is no exception. Furthermore, education does not exist outside the practices and theories that form the background against which actions, ideas, and knowledge are produced. Therefore, in the task of transforming the architectural profession into a socially and politically relevant field, the academy must be considered a front-line combatant, strategizing the attack in collusion with the people on the ground who at this moment are leading the insurrection.

Experiments in architectural education have the potential to expand the field of engagement and to initiate students and faculty into the political aspects of architecture. If we begin with the foundation laid by the programs and projects featured in this book, we can create a framework for an architecture of change that returns the political to design, not selectively but completely. When we pull our collective head out of the sand, we can no longer deny the undeniable: space and its making are *political*. The return of the political to architecture does not involve designing a building but designing a process of political engagement—one by which architectural ideas, strategies, practices, and values are developed and disseminated in collaboration and contestation with greater society. This is a vision in which the only avenue through the architectural academy involves engagement with real issues affecting citizens and communities. Without such a requirement, the projects presented here will simply comprise one route available to activist students and faculty, and be vulnerable to the fluidity of currents and movements. In addition, other extant avenues will abide by and reinforce the status quo, reproducing elitism and continuing to formulate ideas and designs that serve no more than 2 percent of the population.

To support an architecture of change, a foundational theory that is based on action and provides a counterpoint to the current postcritical turn is necessary. We need a theory that is practicable and asks citizens to participate, architects to reinvent, academic administrators to rethink, and politicians to again become accountable. We need a theory that encourages designers to infiltrate city halls, statehouses, national offices, city streets, community meetings, and back rooms, as well as the offices of chancellors, developers, policy makers, and bank executives. Such a theory would examine the fragmentation in the current system of architectural education and practice—the rift where the political has been separated from the profession's aesthetic, cultural, and economic dimensions—and it would attempt to reconnect these domains. To achieve this goal such a theory would collapse the layers of politics, culture, and economics presently strewn about the landscape of architectural education in an attempt to build a unifying framework within which to capture the trajectories of change. In collapsing these layers it is imperative that we examine their impacts both independently and jointly on architectural curriculums and pedagogy. This project therefore entails a complete reconstruction of the current system of education and practice.

Such a reconstruction would require three points of action. First, an understanding of the role of the market in realizing design should be integral to the education of an architect. We must know how to calculate and evaluate the effects of our proposals, both in terms of dollars and relative to their contributions to the spaces of our cities. Architecture should not be manifested at the expense of our communities. At the same time we also must question the tendency to blindly accept the market as a guiding principle. This uncritical acceptance is disempowering and undermines our capacity to conceive of alternatives or to define architecture differently. Instead of trying to move entirely outside of the influence of capitalism (a task nearly impossible in the twenty-first century), we need to challenge capitalism from within. We can refuse to play unquestioningly by market rules that insist on the profitability of design; we can investigate the market's spatial impact and look for ways to circumvent its negative influences. This can be accomplished through actively engaging citizens and communities in democratic design strategies and participatory architecture. Such practices refuse to conceive of architecture as a product that is designed and then turned over to the market for realization. Instead architecture should empower architects, designers, and, more important, citizens to build their own future. This requires that designers ground themselves in our diverse communities and be prepared to collaborate. The goal is to transform design from a reactive process to a proactive one, working through collaborative and dialectical relationships with citizens to imagine new possibilities, processes, and implementation strategies that challenge traditional methods and market norms.

Second, we must reconsider the power of utopian thinking as a way to form a unified front. Utopian thinking can help consolidate a movement behind a set of ideals, goals, and principles that redefine design as a mode of political and social action. This is not a nostalgic act but instead an attempt to redefine utopianism as a process and to view social and political organization as tools to help us articulate new emancipated spaces, not universal spaces. Modernist utopias failed in part because of their dependence on the state and capital for their realization. The system that utopian practices were intended to transform was in fact the same one required for their construction. As a result these spatial utopias were stripped of their broader social agendas when they became real spaces or architectural objects. We have to reconceive utopianism not so much as a practice but as a process, one that has the potential to transform both the production of space and the distribution of social and political power. This concept moves architecture beyond a solely physical practice and redefines academic and professional architecture as fields that envision alternative futures and have the means to help realize them.

Finally, as a liberated process, architecture should illustrate the value of alternative spatial practices with a plurality of aesthetic and spatial modes of civic expression that facilitate a diverse set of public realms. This requires both discourse and action. Discourse is called for to address the production of place as tied to specific positions within a social matrix of power, culture, identity, and politics. Such a discourse asks that architecture become a participatory practice, one that engages diversity of thought, action, and collectivity from both within and without. It suggests that projects in the academic studio and in practice should not be removed from the influences that shape their realization, but should instead be grounded in the processes and practices that mold our built environment and our forms of social and political organization. This is a call to act, to apply liberating spatial practices that work toward a realization of unity and diversity in our communities.

Ultimately, we have to recognize that acting in the world means taking responsibility for the consequences of those actions. By acting, we have chosen one route over an infinite number of others. The alternative is to not take any action and to accept conditions as they stand—and that is unacceptable.

Who Has Access to the Idea of Architecture?

Power is increasingly an asymmetrical component of the production of space. Developers, financial sectors, and public policy have served the purposes of powerful interests, and the architecture profession has followed behind blindly. In addition, the economic landscape has constrained the possibilities of design, particularly for those who have little access to the lending, banking, and investment industries. Prestige must be achieved through making design relevant to community practices and issues, instead of through costly work for the elite. The percentage of those able to afford architectural services must be increased, and that goal entails a growth in the number of those who have access to the *idea* of architecture.

If the relevance of architecture can be transformed through a critical engagement with the practices that shape the production of space, then the culture of architectural education (followed by practice) can also be transformed to create an economically and culturally diverse set of actors and audiences that perceive the profession as an active participant in the transformation of society. Along with the family doctor, dentist, local shopkeeper, and mail carrier, everyone would know a local architect, and they would know how she or he contributes to the greater good. Until then, the doors of the academy must be thrown open and its ivory towers infiltrated and transformed by the real issues facing our society. The academy has been far too limited in its ability to meet the needs of diverse students, citizens, and communities, and this condition will likely worsen as the resources available for higher education are reduced and the cost of a university education rises. We need a radical transformation in education if the academy is to become an accessible and effective agent of change.

Charles Moore is rumored to have said that there was nowhere in Los Angeles to have a revolution. The same is true of the contemporary university. We need a new school for a new school of thought, and this necessitates a liberated intellectual venue. The theory behind an architecture of change would free education by infiltrating and dismantling academies, informing policies, transforming architectural practices, and dispersing knowledge to and from communities and citizens: an architecture of the streets. This theory would suggest that architectural education will be elevated by being grounded in the needs and agendas of a diverse and engaged audience with the capacity to influence the production of space and build places to have a revolution—and in fact to build the revolution itself.

The foundation of architectural thought is constantly shifting. Theories are offered, accepted, disproved, and abandoned in rapid succession. Each movement reflects the political, economic, and cultural issues of the time, representing a different amalgamation of good deeds and good design, and profoundly influencing the practice and education of architecture. If we do not act now to begin a spatialized political effort and to implement an architecture of change, the polarization emerging around the globe will continue; the twenty-first century will be defined by a paradigm of access to space through division; and the tools for transforming space will become increasingly concentrated in the hands of the few.

SOCIAL, ECONOMIC, AND ENVIRON- MENTAL DESIGN

The Architectural Bat-Signal:
Exploring the Relationship
between Justice and Design

BARBARA B. WILSON

A new group
has emerged to
facilitate design
in the service
of social, economic,
and environmental
justice. The SEED
Network taps
the wisdom of
communities and
designers to create
positive change.

1 Herbert Simon,
The Sciences of the
Artificial (Cambridge,
Mass.: MIT Press,
1972), 55.

2 Structures for
Inclusion Roundtable
Dialogue, "How to
Grow a Movement?,"
Loeb Fellowship
presentation, Harvard
Graduate School of
Design, Cambridge,
Mass., Oct. 28, 2005.

The political scientist Herbert Simon once wrote that design is "changing existing situations into preferred ones," and many architects pride themselves on doing just that—making places, communities, cities, and thus our world, better.[1] But only a small, elite percentage of the population typically benefits from architectural services. This inequity, augmented by other injustices like pollution, racial discrimination, and the high costs of housing, creates many places that are not "preferred." With most of the population lacking a voice in design processes, our communities lose the character, diversity, affordability, and integrity that make them thrive. How do we stop this pattern of injustice?

The community design (or public-interest architecture) movement has developed in response to this issue. These practitioners argue that their work *does* give the community a voice, that they are serving the underserved. But how can they prove that they actually help communities in the ways they say they do? How can we quantify "justice" in terms of design? These are a few of the questions that must be answered if community-based design is ever to grow as a movement. These answers are the start of better communication between committed designers and the public, beginning the conversation about the positive impact that design can have.

Building a Movement in Social Architecture

In search of answers to these questions, a group of thirty architects, designers, and other experts in this public-interest design movement gathered in the fall of 2005 for a roundtable at the Harvard Graduate School of Design. The goal of the meeting was to discuss how the design professions could more relevantly address the social, economic, and environmental issues faced by communities and strengthen their roles in communities where they are needed most. The group represented more than one hundred organizations, institutions, artists, practitioners, and activists, including the Association for Community Design, six major universities, and the U.S. General Services Administration. At the meeting the dean of University of Virginia's School of Architecture, Karen Van Lengen, asked a significant question: How

could the community design movement become integrated into popular discourse—how could the creation of inclusive, culturally appropriate, and just environments become a consideration to all designers, practitioners, and policy makers working with the built environment? Her question articulated the need that everyone felt required attention and helped the group move forward.

Maurice Cox, an associate professor at the University of Virginia School of Architecture, also challenged the group to redefine the parameters of architectural practice: "While health, safety, and welfare may be promoted as the standards for professional licensure, they should not be the limit of architects' professional roles....We know from experience that people can shape their own world. What results is far superior to anything an outside 'expert' could arbitrarily come up with."[2] Meeting members hypothesized that incentivizing and popularizing socially oriented design in the architectural realm might be satisfied through two complementary activities: 1) creating an evaluation system for socially responsible design like the Leadership in Energy and Environmental Design (LEED) certification system, which provides incentives for green design through tax breaks and marketing schemes, and 2) encouraging architecture critics to acknowledge the importance of community-invested design in the built works they evaluate.

From this discussion emerged the Social, Economic, and Environmental Design (SEED) Network, created to fulfill the movement's need for a web of support and communication. Reed Kroloff, then dean of the Tulane School of Architecture, offered to host a follow-up meeting a few months later on Tulane's campus, with the hope that the group could further refine the SEED Network vision while also finding ways to use the collective will of the group to assist in hurricane-relief efforts on the Gulf Coast.

The SEED Network's mission is to advance the right of every person to live in a socially, economically, and environmentally healthy community. The network hopes to integrate itself into the larger social-architecture movement, supporting those who believe in design's potential to empower, invigorate, and unify communities. Professionals with experience in design or development work alongside residents, allowing the design to benefit from both expert and local knowledge. Often referred to as community-based design, this practice of "trusting the local" is increasingly recognized as the most effective way to sustain the health and longevity of a place. Encouraging what SEED member Stephen Goldsmith refers to as a "more holistic ethic for building," the group acknowledges the value of involving community members in the shaping of their built environment, while still honoring other aspects of thoughtful design.

Six defining principles were selected by the network using an Internet participatory survey. They received a majority of votes out of over forty proposed:

1. Every person has the right to live in a socially, economically, and environmentally healthy community.

2. Advocate with those who have a limited voice in public life.

3. Build structures for inclusion that engage stakeholders and allow communities to make decisions.

4. Promote social equality through discourse that reflects a range of values and social identities.

5. Generate ideas that grow from place and build local capacity.

6. A community's design should help conserve resources and minimize waste.

The Irrelevance of Design

The practice of architecture is inherently social, weaving together the needs of patrons, users, and the greater community to create usable, beautiful spaces in the built environment. In turn the built environment has profound effects on its surroundings and its citizenry. Yet while operating on the assumption that buildings will solve human problems, architecture is rarely considered in terms of its relationship to its users or its larger community. It has been claimed that private architecture firms only serve as little as 2 percent of the population—a problematic proportion for such a social profession.

Not surprisingly, the loss of place and the need for "social architecture" are common narratives in the contemporary discourse. In addition there are those who speak of the need for community participation and a deeper civic awareness of the ecological perspective, asserting that the more defined our sense of place and community are, the better we will treat our environments and our neighbors.[3] In myriad different contexts, alienation from our physical communities is cited as a major problem currently facing the United States.

Historically, architects have been deeply aware of their intimate relationship with societal and ecological concerns. However, as the historian Richard Ingersoll points out, the ecology question and the social question have always been at odds in the architectural realm.[4] Affordable-housing advocates often find themselves arguing with environmental advocates instead of joining forces to promote justice for both humanity and the environment. Their mutual exclusivity is due in part to the nature of our regulatory systems. As issues in society arise and enter the public awareness, regulations emerge to address them. Thus, recently popularized topics such as global warming and dwindling nonrenewable resources currently drive the architectural field to concentrate on ecologically based issues. Similarly, coding and certification systems in the U.S. only apply to the protection of the "public good" through the protection of safety and health concerns.[5] This focus on public health relieves those creating the built environment of the burden of considering the implications their creations will have for other forms of societal justice,

3 Tim Beatley, *Native to Nowhere* (Washington, D.C.: Island Press, 2004

4 Richard Ingersoll "Second Nature: On the Social Bone of Ecology and Architecture," in Tom Dutton and Lian Hurst Mann, eds., *Reconstructir Architecture: Critical Discourses and Social Practice* (Minneapolis: University of Minnesota Press, 1996), 144.

5 Steven Moore, "Building Codes," in Carl Mitcham, ed., *Encyclopedia (Science, Technolo(and Ethics* (Detroit: Macmillan Reference USA, 2005), 5.

cultural preservation, and placemaking, which in turn allows architecture to disengage further from its community. Public health and environmental protection are vital and noble ethics for the built environment, but they are not enough to ensure that our communities are socially responsible to their citizenry.

Redefining Design

Ludwig Mies van der Rohe observed, "Not yesterday, not tomorrow, only today can be given form. Only this architecture creates."[6] Architecture as it is practiced today lends itself to SEED's definition of design as a collaborative, transdisciplinary process with the desired outcome of improving human circumstances. However, more traditional notions of architectural design differ dramatically from this practical definition, stemming from an effort to promote the profession's relevancy that began in the Gilded Age. The age of professionalism, which originated after the Civil War and ended around 1920, established "a primary link...between a standardized expertise and a market for services."[7] When the American Institute of Architects was formed in 1857, it was already responding in part to a perceived need to standardize and regulate the rapidly developing cores of American cities. Engineers exerted dominion over the technical aspects of design, but architects could claim sole ownership of the "design-as-art" expertise that had descended from the École des Beaux-Arts in Paris.[8] In 1923 Mies further elevated the status of the profession, defining architecture as "the living will of the age conceived of in spatial terms. Living. Changing. New."[9] Mies and others who shared his position saw architecture as the design of built works of art, but not of buildings.

In some spheres the profession is still conceived as a technical and creative process that is generated and executed in a vacuum by the artist-architect. If, as the critical theorist Theodor Adorno claims, "art works are a constant indictment of the system of practical activities and practical human beings," then architecture as it is traditionally defined must be a paradox, artistic and practical at the same time.[10] Thus, the conundrum of how best to perpetuate this profession while maintaining both its

detachment from and its relevance to society becomes almost impossible to resolve.

Reflective Practice

Community-based design brings practitioners, artists, neighbors, students, teachers, and social and ecological activists together to address urgent needs in communities around the world. The urban planner and sociologist Donald Schön calls this method of inquiry *reflective practice*.[11] In this model the client and the practitioner work collaboratively to create something usable, sustainable, and profound.

This attention to the community's local knowledge is seen as a valuable commodity for designers, as it helps bridge the ever-widening gap between architects as experts and the societies they serve. As the architectural educator Howard Davis acknowledges: "Many communities and organizations maintain the view that professional expertise of any kind is unhelpful. They see professionalism as akin to colonialism, and in some ways they are right, and can point to experiences where professionals attempted to exert their own will on situations in which such an attitude was inappropriate."[12] In the context of social architecture, practitioners work with community members to build their neighborhood's political and social capacity, empowering participants with the design tools needed to shape their surroundings. Designers in these settings benefit from a culturally significant palette they can use in searching for innovative ways to make the built environment truly conducive to positive transformation at the local level.

The Architectural Bat-Signal: Connecting People, Catalyzing Change

Advocating for design as a mode of community support and empowerment, SEED participants hope to facilitate culturally and ecologically sensitive community-based design efforts through the supportive web of its membership. A more reflective form of professional practice allows citizens and experts to fuse their knowledge, blending the residents' richer understanding of the community with the practitioner's expertise in the field of design. By meshing local and professional resources together, the SEED

6 From Ludwig Mies van der Rohe, "Working Theses," in Ulrich Conrads, *Programs and Manifestoes on 20th-Century Architecture* (Cambridge, Mass.: MIT Press, 1971), 74.

7 Dana Cuff, *Architecture: The Story of Practice* (Cambridge, Mass.: MIT Press, 1991), 23.

8 Ibid., 31.

9 Mies in Conrads, *Programs and Manifestoes*, 74.

10 Theodor Adorno, *Aesthetic Theory* (London: Routledge and Kegan Paul, 1984), 343.

11 See Donald A. Schön, *The Reflective Practitioner* (New York: Basic Books, 1983).

12 Howard Davis, "Architectural Education for the Emerging Vernacular City: Seven Assumptions That Need to Be Challenged" (speech, annual meeting of the International Union of Architects, Istanbul, July 3–7, 2005).

Network hopes that communities will obtain both the most appropriate means and the best approaches to their own challenges. The vision for the network is that communities in need could contact SEED for help, "shining the Bat-Signal into the night sky," as one SEED participant eloquently said. A consortium of SEED members would then meet with community members, with the local community defining the focus of the gathering. Ideally, a solution to address each challenge would emerge from the collective dialogue.

For instance, when the SEED Network accepted Reed Kroloff's invitation to hold its first official meeting in New Orleans in February 2006, SEED members began exploring ways to contribute to and learn from the city's recovery effort. More than sixty architects, planners, developers, academics, advocates, and artists convened in New

Orleans to explore the process of "reinhabiting," as some of the local residents call it. "We recognize that professionals across the United States want to help, but we need to make sure our solutions are developed here," said Clifton James, the head of the Urban Design Research Center in New Orleans.[13] A poster for the People's Hurricane Relief Fund that quoted a South African slogan, "Nothing about us without us is for us," sent the message loud and clear.

After discussing the needs, hopes, and plans of New Orleans with local activists, designers, and professors on a bus tour around the city, SEED members identified three priorities: removing debris, rebuilding homes, and creating jobs. Because the SEED Network could synthesize the varying perspectives of residents and visiting experts, new solutions for old problems developed. The idea of the Katrina Furniture Project

13 Speech given by Clifton James, New Orleans, La., Feb. 3, 2006.

emerged almost immediately in response to these needs. The project was created to help reemploy New Orleans residents, who would create furniture and other useful objects out of material salvaged from the storm's debris. "We want to support local efforts that bring the resilient, creative spirit of local artists and others together as they unite to rebuild their homes," said Stephen Goldsmith, one of the generators of the idea. "The furniture project expresses our commitment to bringing SEED principles to community-development processes at every scale." Initially, with very little local infrastructure, the project focused mostly on the technical aspects of the proposed system—recycling debris with other organizations and working with students to design beautiful furniture from the refuse. Three elegant designs were developed in this early stage through the efforts of Sergio Palleroni's BaSiC Initiative and his work with students at the University of Texas, Austin, and disseminated widely through the media. These designs caught the attention of *Time* magazine, the Cooper-Hewitt Museum, and the National Council of Churches, which found the pew design especially appealing when faced with the rebuilding of the thousands of churches destroyed in the hurricane

Locally, the project did not take flight as easily and, Goldsmith admits, there were "a few missed steps in the community involvement portion of the project" in the first two years after the storm. But the organization is now incorporated as a nonprofit in the state of Louisiana and has a local acting director, Gilda Lewis, as well as a system to provide referrals for furniture commissions to New Orleans residents through the Craft Emergency Relief Fund. This project is an example of the SEED Network's connective, integrative power, the capacity of thoughtful, socially responsible design, and the incredible collaborative effort required to successfully empower and engage a design idea and a community.

Hopes for the Future

After meeting again in Baltimore and Cambridge, the SEED Network has a mission, guiding principles, a national coordinator, and goals for the future. First, SEED has been working to develop a supplementary system to "green" certification systems like LEED. In January of 2008 a workshop was held in Dallas with scholars, activists, and designers outside of the original SEED web, which produced a "tool kit" to be used to measure community-based projects. The SEED Network Policy Forum will convene in 2009 to share this system with a wider audience and broaden the conversation to include those who can most effectively make political change. The forum and resulting publication will give policy makers and elected officials the tools they need to enhance their work by advancing the right of every person to live in a socially, economically, and environmentally healthy community. Slowly, as the number of people participating in this conversation about socially responsible design grows, so will the movement.

Right
The idea of using salvage material in the Katrina Furniture Project has been expanded in scale by SEED members to create extra rooms for families living in FEMA trailers on the Gulf Coast.

Toward a Humane Environment: Sustainable Design and Social Justice

LANCE HOSEY

A thoughtful consideration of sustainability reveals new principles for the design of a built environment predicated on social justice.

Left
Hans and
Pieter Hendrikse
Q-drum
Manufactured by
Kaymac Rotomoulders
and Pioneer Plastics

1 "Green Building
Rating System for
New Construction and
Major Renovations,"
v. 2.2 (United States
Green Building
Council, Oct. 2005),
www.usgbc.org/
ShowFile.aspx?
DocumentID=1095.

2 World Commission
on Environment and
Development, Our
Common Future (New
York: Oxford University
Press, 1987), www.
un-documents.net/
wced-ocf.htm.

3 One of several
versions of the famous
definition: "Humanity
has the ability to
make development
sustainable to ensure
that it meets the
needs of the present
without compromising
the ability of future
generations to meet
their own needs." Our
Common Future, 24.

4 Haudenosaunee
Faithkeeper, Chief
Oren Lyons, address
to the United Nations
General Assembly,
Dec. 10, 1992, www.
indians.org/welker/
onondaga.htm.

5 "The State of the
World's Children:
Childhood Under
Threat," UNICEF press
release, Dec. 9, 2004,
www.unicef.org/media/
media_24469.html.

6 John Elkington,
Cannibals with Forks:
The Triple Bottom
Line of 21st Century
Business (Stony Creek,
Conn.: New Society
Publishers, 1994).

7 Our Common
Future, 54.

Sustainable design is changing every area of human enterprise, but as it becomes more popular, its definition and goals become less clear. As it is typically used, the word "sustainable" implies environmentally responsible development, but only vaguely. What "environmentally responsible" means is subject to debate, and any attempt at clarification inevitably leads to disagreement, especially among designers. Architects often use "sustainable design" interchangeably with "high-performance building," as if the term refers only to the construction industry and includes only the efficient use of resources. But the foundation and future of sustainability are much broader.

American architects' familiarity with sustainability over the last several years has come in large part from the U.S. Green Building Council's (USGBC) Leadership in Energy and Environmental Design (LEED) rating system, a popular method of measuring the environmental impact of buildings. For many, LEED has become synonymous with sustainable design, an impression strengthened by the USGBC itself. In 2004 at "Greenbuild," the organization's annual conference, its president declared, "If it's not LEED, it's not green." Yet, in the eighty-one-page document outlining the LEED rating system for new construction, the word "sustainable" appears only a few times, and it is never defined. The manual claims that a "green building...helps create a sustainable community," but it neglects to describe what such a community entails.[1] Architects equate LEED with sustainable design, but LEED itself does not clarify what sustainable design is.

Undoubtedly the most frequently quoted definition of sustainable development comes from Our Common Future, the United Nations study commonly called the Brundtland Report, after the former chairperson of the World Commission on Environment and Development, Gro Harlem Brundtland.[2] The year 2007 marked the report's twentieth anniversary, and over the last two decades a variation on a single passage has become a mantra for many environmentalists and designers alike: "meeting the needs of the present without compromising the ability of future generations to meet their needs."[3] Many interpret this to mean that we cannot squander current resources and leave nothing for our heirs. In his oft-cited 1992 address to the UN, Native American leader Oren Lyons urged societies "to make every decision on behalf of the seventh generation to come; to have compassion and love for those generations yet unborn."[4] Our legacy should be one of hope, not destruction.

Yet the syntax of the Brundtland statement suggests a focus on the present, not the future: meet current needs, but do so gracefully, thoughtfully, with foresight. This raises a simple question: How well we are meeting our current needs? Although industrialized nations now are wealthier than any society in human history, globally there are also more poor people than ever before. More than 1 billion live in extreme poverty; one-sixth of humanity is literally starving to death. More than twenty thousand people die every day for lack of food, water, and sanitation, and most are children. The seventh-generation view protects tomorrow's children, but what about today's? Even in wealthy nations, the proportion of children living in low-income households has increased over the last decade. UNICEF's Carol Bellamy has put it this way: "When half the world's children are growing up hungry and unhealthy, when schools have become targets and whole villages are being emptied by AIDS, we've failed to deliver on the promise of childhood."[5] The needs of the present are far from being met.

For many, poverty may not seem the focus of sustainability, but in fact the very concept was founded on this concern. The "triple bottom line" (a phrase coined by John Elkington in 1994) recognizes the links between ecological, economic, and social conditions.[6] The popular Brundtland definition is invariably cited out of context and is rarely, if ever, discussed in terms of economic and social equity, though the report itself focused on global community and poverty eradication: "Sustainable development requires meeting the basic needs of all and extending to all the opportunity to fulfill their aspirations for a better life. A world in which poverty is endemic will always be prone to ecological and other catastrophes."[7] The basic needs of all: the very idea of sustainability stemmed from the recognition that poverty is the most significant problem of our time.

Sustainability's original focus has been forgotten. The word "green" brings to mind trees and streams, not the plight of the poor. We have overlooked this crisis because most of us are not in direct contact with the poor, and empathy often depends on proximity. The UN and other organizations identify three types of poverty: relative, moderate, and extreme. Relative poverty means living below a regional standard. The U.S. Census Bureau defines the national poverty line for an individual as an annual income below $10,500, approximately $30 per day.[8] With moderate poverty, a person has enough to survive, but just barely. And extreme poverty is poverty that kills. A large majority of the world's poorest countries live on less than the equivalent of $1 per day, and many have far less than that. Extreme poverty does not exist in developed nations. We do not live with it, and most of us have never witnessed it. As a culture, we are blind to it.

In an effort to correct course, all 191 members of the UN have signed the Millennium Declaration, which includes eight key goals for the year 2015:

1. Eradicate extreme poverty and hunger.

2. Achieve universal primary education.

3. Promote gender equality and empower women.

4. Reduce child mortality.

5. Improve maternal health.

6. Combat HIV/AIDS, malaria, and other diseases.

7. Ensure environmental sustainability.

8. Develop a Global Partnership for Development.[9]

The Millennium Development Goals constitute a common set of values for all of humanity. While the goals are connected, some are considered more urgent than others, and the primary concerns are universal equity and health. Eradicating extreme poverty and hunger is the first priority, and "environmental sustainability" does not appear until late in the list (goal 7 of 8). In other words, socioeconomic concerns precede ecological ones.

Design can make a difference in pursuing these aims. To date, sustainable design has focused on technical solutions, an important step in increasing our efficient use of resources. Yet, as the Brundtland Report pointed out twenty years ago, "Human progress has always depended on our technical ingenuity …but this is not enough."[10] What we need is a new mindset, a new culture of design. Designers can benefit the global community by reconsidering the purpose, process, and products of design all at once.

Think about plastic bottles. Approximately three quarters of all plastic containers, about 40 million of them, end up as litter or landfill every day. Because the material basically never breaks down and gets absorbed into the earth safely, environmentalists dream of a better bottle. But instead of dealing solely with the container, consider the contents. Clean water is an extremely scarce commodity in impoverished regions, and dehydration and poor sanitation are primary causes of death. To get clean water, many women and children in sub-Saharan Africa spend up to eight hours a day doing what we in the West do each time we turn on a tap. Trips to the closest potable source can take more than an hour each way, and because people only transport what they can carry on foot, they must make this trip at least three times daily. The vessels they use are often heavy ceramic urns supported on their heads or shoulders, so bodily injury is common.

When smart designers turn their attention to this problem, they can save lives. In 1993 South African architects Hans and Pieter Hendrikse invented the Q-drum, a double polyethylene cylinder that even small children can easily tug across sandy terrain. Lighter than typical jars and pulled rather than carried, the drum reduces physical strain and travel time, and a hygienic seal prevents

8 U.S. Census Bureau, Housing and Household Economic Statistic Division, "Poverty Thresholds 2006," www.census.gov/ hhes/www/ poverty/threshld/ thresh06.html.

9 www.un.org/ millenniumgoals.

10 *Our Common Future*, 48.

contamination. With a little ingenuity, the Hendrikses created a simple device that can radically alter the lives of thousands of people.

Another simple innovation eliminates the hauling of water altogether. The LifeStraw, invented by Torben Vestergaard Frandsen and named the best invention of 2005 by *Time* magazine, cleans dirty water right at the source. The thick polystyrene tube has a patented inner coating that kills virtually all bacteria and viruses and removes particles down to fifteen microns. Used in several poverty-stricken regions in Africa and Asia, it has proven effective against waterborne diseases such as typhoid, cholera, and dysentery. With no moving parts, it is not likely to break, and it can last up to a year without being cleaned. Like a sanitation plant in a straw, LifeStraw requires no energy other than the user's ability to draw water up through it.

Perishable foods are another persistent challenge. Many of the poorest regions lie along the equator, where extreme heat makes storing food difficult. Refrigeration often is unavailable, so fruits and vegetables spoil quickly. Mohammed Bah Abba, a Nigerian teacher, solves this problem with a simple solution: the Pot-in-Pot Preservation Cooling System. The Pot-in-Pot is exactly what the name suggests: an earthenware vessel nestled inside another like a Russian doll. Between the two is a layer of moist sand acting as an insulator. As the water in the sand evaporates, it conveys heat outward, away from the food stored in the center. Vegetables last up to a month, instead of three days, expanding the life of the food tenfold.

These examples apply design directly to the problem, as when architects create better temporary shelters for disaster-recovery areas. In such cases, the *product* of design serves people, but the *process* of design and construction can also benefit people by proposing commerce as a form of service. Every year, U.S. foreign aid falls far short of UN commitments and ranks last among developed nations as a percentage of gross domestic product. Industry can help meet these commitments by shifting the focus to trade instead of aid. The annual value of the U.S. construction industry is nearly a trillion

dollars. Imagine the buying power if some of this money were used to combat poverty in developing countries. If only 2 percent of the construction industry traded with emerging markets, the resulting flow of money into developing countries would equal the total of U.S. foreign aid. More than half the population of Mauritania, whose chief export is iron ore for steel, falls below the extreme poverty line. Strategic trade can benefit every stratum of the global economy and alleviate a dire problem at the same time.[11]

The U.S. already imports much of its construction material and products, including a quarter of all steel and cement, and these numbers will rise. Statistics show that the population of wealthy nations continues to age and dwindle, while poor regions are growing more crowded with younger people. As a result, we inevitably will outsource more services and import more goods. Yet at the moment we have no way to observe or control the conditions under which most of these products are made. Who is making them, and what is their standard of living? Fair trade ensures equitable wages for economically disadvantaged workers worldwide, and the fair-trade coffee movement has helped alleviate extreme poverty in many areas. But of the many trillions of dollars in goods exchanged globally every year, fair trade accounts for only one one-hundredth of a percent, and no construction-related companies currently belong to the Fair Trade Federation.

To address these issues, concerned designers have started the Just Building Alliance (JBA), an organization dedicated to reconsidering how building can serve the global community.[12] The JBA promotes emerging markets in developing regions and explores ways to ensure safe working conditions and living wages. The design and construction industries need new standards to judge not just whether a building is good, but whether it *does* good.

Design can
make a difference.
Designers,
make a difference.

11 For a more specific discussion of this idea, see Lance Hosey, "The Ethics of Bric *Metropolis* (June 2005), 128, 130–3

12 www.justbuilding

13 Martin Luther King, Jr., "Letter from Birmingham City Jail," Apr. 16, 1963, first published in *The Christian Century*, June 12, 1963; Mahatma Ghandi, quoted in Louis Fischer, ed., *The Essential Ghandi* (New York: Random House, 1962), 229.

14 John F. Kennedy inaugural address, Jan. 20, 1961, www.bartleby.com/124/pres56.html.

15 Aldo Leopold, *A Sand County Almanac* (New York Ballantine Books, 1966), 239.

Five Principles Toward a Humane Environment

Sustainable design and development can honor their origins by following five simple principles to embrace people and planet together:

1. People come first.

The problem of the planet is first and foremost a human problem. To reverse the devastation of nature, we need to reverse the devastation of culture. We can better the environment by bettering ourselves. The UN has set poverty eradication and universal health as the world community's first priorities. Every industry has a responsibility and an opportunity to promote this goal.

2. Now comes before later.

Definitions of sustainability focus on the future. While we cannot squander our resources today and leave little for tomorrow, we also should not forget our responsibility to the generations currently occupying the earth. If the living do not survive, their heirs will never exist. The present cannot be sacrificed for the future.

3. More for more.

Prosperity must be measured with all of humanity together. No one is completely settled if anyone is truly suffering. As Martin Luther King, Jr., put it, "We are all caught in an inescapable network of mutuality, tied to a single garment of destiny. Whatever affects one directly affects all indirectly." Or in the words of Mahatma Gandhi, "Though we are many bodies, we are but one soul."[13]

4. The triple bottom line is bottom up.

Social justice may be defined as first helping those most in need. Social, economic, and ecological value must be built from the ground up, beginning with the most disadvantaged among us. "If a free society cannot help the many who are poor," said John F. Kennedy, "it cannot save the few who are rich."[14]

5. Nature knows no borders.

In the age of global warming, national boundaries have little bearing on the most pressing problems. Natural and human communities transcend politics. American environmentalist Aldo Leopold wrote, "All ethics...rest upon a single premise: that the individual is a member of a community of interdependent parts."[15] We share one world.

Left and right
LifeStraws in
use in Africa

El Programa de Vivienda Ecológica: Building the Capacity of Yaqui Women to Help Themselves

SERGIO PALLERONI AND
MÓNICA ESCOBEDO FUENTES

A low-income self-help housing program addresses issues of development and cultural identity as well as helping the new homeowners assimilate into the capital and credit markets of Mexico.

How can a community help its poorest members provide for their own housing and economic well-being?

El Programa de Vivienda Ecológica, a private/public community-housing initiative in northwestern Mexico, has been tackling this issue by offering marginalized Yaqui Indians the opportunity to participate in a low-income self-help housing program.

The Social/Political Situation of the Yaqui

Two cultures have coexisted in Sonora, Mexico, since Spanish colonization of the region in the late sixteenth century: a Spanish-mestizo culture in the region's few urban centers, and a native population of hunter/gatherers and subsistence farmers living as extended families in rural hamlets. After colonization, the Yaqui lacked the cultural mechanisms to participate in the region's formal economy, so they maintained their traditional way of life the best they could. The Yaqui's lack of participation in the larger culture caused economic and social disparities that have persisted and become more accentuated in the twenty-first century. The recent rapid growth of large-scale export farming has deprived the Yaqui of their traditional hunter/gatherer migratory patterns, and an increasing number of Yaqui men are immigrating across the border for jobs without returning, giving rise to a new phenomenon: the single-mother household, which today numbers in the thousands among the Yaqui.[1] The Yaqui standard of living—and their social fabric—has deteriorated dramatically.

In response, a Sonora-based initiative has emerged to provide housing to the Yaqui while addressing their social, economic, and ecological needs. PROVAY, a Sonoran nongovernmental organization, promoted the creation of a populist, community-based, microcredit ecological housing campaign for the Yaqui: the Programa de Vivienda Ecológica (PVE). Under the technical leadership of PROVAY, the Fundación de Apoyo Infantil Sonora (FAI), and the Center for Sustainable

Development at the School of Architecture at the University of Texas at Austin, the PVE has been working to provide ecological housing for the region's growing population of families at risk. At its core, this is a local community project to protect the physical and cultural survival of the community's poorest citizens.

Financing a Home in Mexico

Public-housing financing in Mexico is dominated by three government agencies—INFONAVIT, FOVI, and FOVISSSTE—which account for close to 87 percent of the financing of social and public housing, with private banks accounting for only 1 percent of the market.[2] Most of this financing is directed at the Mexican middle class, creating a financing gap for the most needy. In Mexico today, 65 percent of the population earns less than the minimum wage needed to qualify for one these financing programs.[3] The financing problem is further aggravated for Mexico's rural native populations by their cultural practices and modes of survival. In a country of 100 million, 11 million inhabitants like the Yaqui are isolated by their continued adherence to their traditional ways of life (with another 30 million living as urban poor).[4]

The PROVAY Response

In 2000, the PVE was founded in the municipality of Cajeme, Sonora, to address the housing problems faced by the Yaqui. Cajeme is the site of several of the larger Yaqui settlements in Sonora, all of which are among the poorest communities in Mexico. The PVE approaches the Yaqui housing problem as a social issue of the entire Cajeme community, a strategy that has allowed PROVAY to engage a broader segment of the society than in previous efforts to house the Yaqui. Depoliticizing the issue has also allowed PROVAY to engage segments of society (principally the business sector) that would not normally be involved with grassroots organizations. Although PROVAY and FAI were the main instigators of the PVE alliance, the active involvement of civic, governmental, and private organizations has made it possible for this program to overcome many of the financial, social, and political obstacles that undermined earlier programs. This multisectoral participation has also

1 PROVAY, "Problemas de a Vivienda en Cajeme," 2002 report published by PROVAY).

2 L. Rojas, O. Fernando, and S. Topelson de Grinberg, *Financiamiento de la Vivienda en México* Mexico City: Cuadernos FICA, 2001).

3 INEGI, "Fuente XII Censo de Población y Vivienda," 2000 report published by INEGI).

4 INFONAVIT, Población y Vivienda en México," 2003 report published by INFONAVIT).

allowed the PVE to gain widespread support and active involvement from both rural and urban communities. PROVAY and FAI's use of a community-asset-based approach to solicit contributions and participation has also strengthened the housing alliance by allowing each member of the alliance to make significant contributions within its capacity and means.

The PVE's central strategy is to base Yaqui access to dignified housing on their capacity to form, with the help of FAI, small credit-support groups from the Yaqui women who are in need of a housing credit. Based on the theories and principles of microcredit lending and social-capital formation developed on the Indian subcontinent, the PVE requires clients to have active membership in good standing with a credit-support group for at least six months before being considered for housing credit.[5] After the six months have elapsed, credit is granted, but clients must remain members of the credit-support group for five years thereafter. These groups typically are composed of twenty to twenty-five women who belong to the same community and have demonstrated the need and the capacity to participate in the program.

Through workshops and seminars on economic and social organization and development conducted by FAI in Cajeme, each new credit group eventually gains autonomy and becomes financially and socially self-regulating, with the assistance of FAI social workers who act as facilitators and consultants for the life of the group. As each member demonstrates her good standing in the credit-support group through active and responsible participation and regular monetary contributions to the savings program, she is admitted into the housing program and is offered a place in the housing rolls.

In the first five years of the program, PVE has experienced lower rates of default on its homeowner loans than INFONAVIT, the largest housing-finance provider in Mexico.[6] The PVE experience has demonstrated in Mexico what has already been proven worldwide: community-based microcredit loan programs create a more credit-worthy community. The women who enter the credit-support group find that they are able to self-regulate better than their peers who lack such support. Also, group members reinforce each other's efforts through other forms of capital exchange and generation, such as babysitting, helping with the construction of one another's houses, and joint fundraising efforts.

The PVE encourages and supports the formation of these other types of capital by giving women in the group the opportunity to build equity in their homes through other forms of capital exchange, such as making their own adobe blocks and insulating panels. This lowers the cost of the house, and the members learn that through the strength of the collective, a positive financial outcome can be achieved—often the first successful economic experience many of the women have had. The PVE's capital-exchange features also cultivate the group's growing awareness of its potential to act on its own behalf.

The use of a social-capital strategy to remedy housing issues has had a collateral benefit that has been at least as important to the long-term welfare of Yaqui society as any housing reform: the creation of citizen groups that have reestablished the presence and voice of the Yaqui community, consequently strengthening the social fabric of Cajeme.

Moving Toward a Healthier Home

The PVE is addressing another issue of importance to the Yaqui: the declining health of its communities. Nearly fifty years of large-scale "green revolution" farming in the area has given this part of the Sonora Desert one of the highest cancer rates in the Americas. Furthermore, Yaqui women in this region have one of the highest rates of reproductive-organ cancer in the world. The PVE addresses these issues by promoting ecological housing and home sites. In the PVE model, sustainable housing design includes long-term resident health as a design parameter.

Another benefit of ecological housing is that it can create a design/build process that is culturally appropriate to the Yaqui and their traditions by embracing the sustainable practices already present in Yaqui culture. For example, adobe is the Yaquis' main wall and roofing material, for both thermal reasons and cultural reasons. The Yaqui have a long tradition of wattle-and-daub earthen construction that makes use of the scant building materials available in

Right
Like the locally produced adobe blocks, rooftop insulation panels are made from recycled cardboard beer boxes and straw, lightweight materials that are inexpensive and perform well in the desert climate.

5 These strategies are based on the capacity of individuals to work together in groups and organizations that determine their level of productivity in search of common objectives

6 The home loan default rate is usually around 2 to 3 percent. PROVAY, "Construcción de Vivienda y Construcción de Comunidad en Cajeme," 2004 (report published by PROVAY).

7 Sergio A. Palleroni and Christina Merkelbach, *Studio at Large: Architecture in Service of Global Communities* (Seattle: University of Washington Press, 2004).

the Sonoran Desert. The PVE has used the Yaqui familiarity with desert materials as the basis for the development of a more thermally insulated wall system that can be standardized so that credit-support groups can produce the adobe blocks en masse to build equity in their future homes, and so that the construction system can be repeated at the scale of a housing program.

8 The member universities of the BaSiC Initiative are the University of Texas, Austin, the University of Washington, Penn State University, Universidad de los Andes (Bogotá, Colombia), and Universidad Católica de Chile (Antofagasta).

9 Palleroni and Merkelbach, *Studio at Large*.

The new adobe block developed through this process also has a higher bearing capacity than the traditional blocks. This advance was achieved through research conducted in partnership with civil engineers at the Universidad Tecnológica del Sur de Sonora. The engineers weighed the need for improvements in the adobes' insulating and weight-bearing capacities against the need to develop a block that the women could produce themselves economically. The result was a culturally sensitive reformulation of the adobe that takes into account the fact that Yaqui women's social practices are different from those of Yaqui men. Rather than producing the adobe mixture on the ground with their feet, as men traditionally do, the adobes are now produced in upright tubs made from split oil barrels, a plentiful waste product in an oil-producing country like Mexico. This allows the women to engage

socially with other women and their children during their work parties.

The active participation of the Universidad Tecnológica del Sur de Sonora in this process has also helped revive what was once a pedagogical cornerstone of Mexican public universities, and particularly of their schools of architecture: an involvement in the country's social agenda. Ironically, the University of Texas's BaSiC Initiative, a program founded at least partially on the social theories and practices of these earlier Mexican programs, has come to play a crucial role in reestablishing this critical, reflective housing practice in Cajeme.[7]

The BaSiC Initiative is a collaborative, multidisciplinary educational outreach program that was created to promote social and material sustainability in marginalized communities throughout the world. The program has faculty in five institutions in the United States and internationally; for almost two decades it has focused on many areas around the world, including native villages in the central highlands of Mexico.[8] The initiative is based on the belief that all communities have the potential to implement long-term sustainable practices that develop identity, dignity, and stability. The programs of the BaSiC Initiative provide assistance to communities that are economically, socially, or physically separated from the services and resources they need to sustain their cultures. As an education program, the BaSiC Initiative's mission is to use active collaboration and partnership with communities in need to teach students to meet the challenges created by current human conditions and practices. The result is a set of participatory ecological and epistemological approaches and protocols that teach both the client communities and the students and faculty about the potential for positive ecological change.[9]

Despite the success of the collaboration with the Universidad Tecnológica del Sur de Sonora, two areas of concern led the PVE to ask the BaSiC Initiative for help. First, the Universidad Tecnológica del Sur de Sonora and other local universities lacked knowledge in the field of water catchment management and treatment of human wastes—a critical issue in the physically isolated Yaqui settlements, and a knowledge the BaSiC Initiative had developed over the years in its work in the field. In addition, PROVAY wanted to promote locally the BaSiC Initiative's model of engaged student activism. Although several important universities in the region constituted an important segment of society, the local students were being left out of the PVE's community-housing project. The hope was that if the BaSiC Initiative's service learning model was implemented in Sonora's universities, local students would emerge from the experience more engaged and capable as citizens of making the changes necessary to create a more equitable and ecologically minded society for the municipality of Cajeme and the state of Sonora.

In 2004 and 2005 the BaSiC Initiative introduced composting toilets and other water-saving technologies to make the PVE's housing more appropriate to Sonora's desert climate. These ideas were drawn directly from the BaSiC Initiative's previous experience with water conservation (including limiting contamination, using cisterns and water-conservation technologies, and employing relevant cultural practices), and the utilization of locally available water resources (for example, rainwater catchment and ecologically sustainable treatment and reuse), both of which have been program priorities since the 1980s. The challenge has been to arrive at solutions appropriate to the ecological conditions and cultural practices of the Yaqui, in particular to their single-mother households, which often include cottage industries as a way to supplement incomes.

In 2005, when the first households attempted to use the technologies proposed by the BaSiC Initiative, the most apparent obstacle was a lack of knowledge on the part of both the builders and the community. In central Mexico, where the BaSiC Initiative developed its Mexican version of these technologies, the indigenous communities have led a settled, agricultural way of life for thousands of years. Over this length of time, they have learned to deal with human waste by turning it into compost and using it in agriculture, and they have developed a rich variety of building skills. The BaSiC Initiative's central Mexico program reincorporated the bathroom into the building rather than removing it as an outhouse, as is the traditional practice, and treated the waste so it could be more safely incorporated into agriculture.

These initiatives represented modifications of existing practices; among the Yaqui, whose practices are still based on their traditions as hunter-gatherers surviving by continuously moving their camps, no such tradition existed to form the basis of either a composting-toilet program or a sustainable modern-construction tradition, which would be needed to create permanent housing.

Another problem is that the BaSiC Initiative limits the use of cement, a contaminant whose production and utilization is one of Mexico's most significant sources of pollution. The BaSiC Initiative promotes the use of ferro-cement construction instead, and while this technology has had a significant impact on the material efficiency of composting toilets and cisterns, it is an almost nonexistent practice among local builders. Both problems show that teaching the homeowners and the builders about these appropriate technologies is going to be a concern if the PVE is to meet its goals.

The BaSiC Initiative/PROVAY partnership is currently experimenting with two methods of education. The first is a series of seminars, to be conducted within the context of the credit-support groups, which will improve homeowners' capacity to engage these ecological solutions. The other source of dissemination will be the work site, where, using a pedagogical idea that has been central to the BaSiC Initiative's projects, the site is redefined as a place of learning.[10] Instead of the exclusive domain of builders and craftsmen, the site becomes an inclusive place where homeowners, community members, students, and the builders conduct an open exchange and learn from each other. This has been one of the BaSiC Initiative's most successful strategies for introducing new design ideas and appropriate technologies. The change toward making the construction site a design forum was implemented prior to the construction of the first two prototype homes as a condition of the BaSiC Initiative's collaboration with PROVAY.

One of these new prototypes—a double-volume home that incorporates the Yaqui use of outdoor space to open the house and enhance natural ventilation—emerged from exactly these kinds of "site-of-learning exchanges"; it also allowed the new adobes,

Top
Model of one of the first two house realized under the BaSiC Initiative/ PROVAY partnersh

Bottom
The two volumes of this prototype house completed i 2005 by the BaSiC Initiative create a shaded outdoor living room, which helps mediate the heat in Estación Corral, a Yaqui community outside Ciudad Obregón, i the Sonoran Dese

10 For a full discussion of the "sites of learning" pedagogical methodology and its outcomes, see Palleroni and Merkelbach, introduction, Studio at Large.

which are easier for the women to make but limited in bearing capacity, to be used more effectively. On-site information sharing, which can make the sometimes-abstract ideas of sustainability more tangible, also led the women to consider composting toilets and rainwater catchment. This approach will be used more fully in future PVE projects to increase the community's capacity to engage new technologies.

Moving Forward

The PVE housing program has demonstrated the potential of community-based nongovernmental housing programs in Mexico to address the needs of the most marginalized segments of society. Though a relatively new phenomenon in Mexico, private-public housing alliances such as the PVE's are showing that indigenous communities like the Yaqui can be active, credit-worthy participants in self-help housing programs.

Credit-support groups that serve as agents in the development of each member's capacity to finance a home and to actively participate

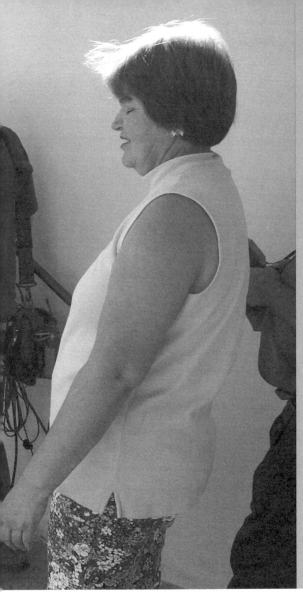

The PVE's emphasis on ecological housing that allows the Yaqui to maintain their relationship with the land is proof of the women's growing political capacity to express their opinions and act on them.

in the home's creation are having a longer-term sociopolitical impact worldwide. For Yaqui women, these groups have become the foundation of their emerging power as a constituency. Through their emphasis on communication, they encourage their members to become active citizens of societies that historically have excluded them. The PVE's emphasis on ecological housing that allows the Yaqui to maintain their relationship with the land is proof of the women's growing political capacity to express their opinions and act on them. In turn, a renewed apprecia-tion of the Yaqui conception of home and its

fundamental relationship to its habitat, the Sonoran Desert, is helping inform the current debate in the municipality of Cajeme on how to remedy the impact of fifty years of green revolution. As the inauguration of each PVE house proves in the changes it makes possible in the life of each of its owners, the inclusion of a minority whose experiences have been a subtext to the dominant history of Sonoran society since Spanish colonization may, in the end, help the society of Cajeme as a whole to survive.

Unbearable Lightness

DEBORAH GANS

**Seeking to expand
architecture to
address humanitarian
crises, a design
studio confronts
the heaviness and
lightness, permanence
and instability in
the world today.**

Left
A UNHCR-issued
ent set up in front
of a damaged and
uninhabitable house
in Bosnia. 2002

Below
Deborah Gans and
Matthew Jelacic
Entry for Transitional
Housing Competition
or Refugees
Returning from
Kosovo, sponsored
by Architecture for
Humanity. 1999

Our current fascination with light, portable, prefabricated structures satisfies a number of conflicting cultural impulses. We desire lightness for ourselves as a kind of antidote to our consumption of the heavy: SUVs, many-carat bling, fried food. In contrast, we propose lightness for others as an antidote to deprivation, in the form of disaster-relief housing for the refugee and the displaced. I recently saw a coffee mug in a Hallmark store (the kind usually inscribed with "Best Dad") that read "urban nomad," proof of the pervasiveness of this new ideal of lightness, embodied in a free-floating world citizen.

There are certain wisdoms in the conceit of lightness and its designer tents. The conceit of lightness turns our technological imagination toward a social problem where it can actually be of use. It overcomes our tendency to impose dwellings of lesser aesthetic merit upon those who are impoverished. Lightness is certainly paramount in transporting a structure to a disaster situation, where roads are often impassable by large vehicles; in distributing those structures upon arrival with a minimum of fuss; and in assembling them

without the need for complicated equipment. The ubiquitous tarp of UN camps is the product refined by these tests: simply a square of material, without seams that might come undone.

The ideal of lightness also contains flaws that become clear with an understanding of the environments to which it is tethered. Most disturbing is the tent's presence in refugee settlements of long duration (some of which have been in place for decades). In these cases the tent dwelling is a political ploy on the part of hosts who fear that more suitable solutions would indicate their acceptance of the refugees as residents. Meanwhile, the tents collapse in snow and wash away in heavy rains, trapping the refugee in an unending series of Sisyphean tasks.

The disaster-relief housing our studio designed for a competition sited in Kosovo argued against the long-term camp per se. The housing consisted of a transportable domestic core for water and waste housed in two hollow structural columns that were strong enough to support a roof or even a second floor. The design sought to enable

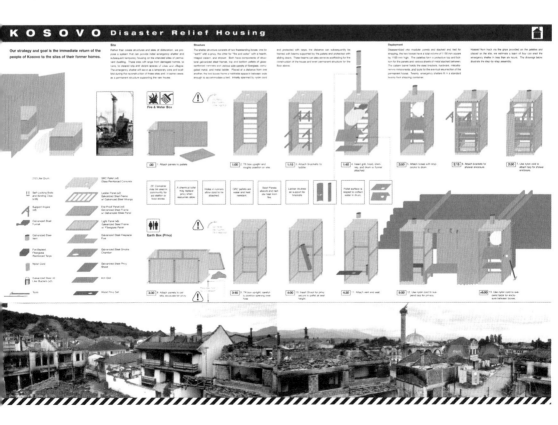

refugees to return home and stake their claim to their property before civic systems could be replaced, reseeding the city with small, light infrastructures.

After our office obtained a grant to further pursue our designs for disaster-relief housing, my partner in the project, Matthew Jelacic, visited Bosnia, where he saw our imagined scenario in action. Families were camped in front of their burned-out houses, but they were living in tents issued by the UN High Commission on Refugees (UNHCR) without heat, water, or sewers. Meanwhile, I attended a seminar on refugee issues for human-rights lawyers and nongovernmental organization (NGO) field professionals at the Refugee Studies Center at Oxford University, where I came to better understand the long-term camp and how tents adapt in beneficial ways to become "heavy."

My colleagues at Oxford were completely puzzled as to why I was there. Their skepticism regarding architecture's relevance to refugee issues did not arise from some feature of international law; as I learned while I was there, refugee law explicitly values housing. Instead they were simply prioritizing the needs of refugees and relying on established protocols. The lawyers were understandably most concerned with issues surrounding "non-refoulement," the term for the nonextradition of refugees back to their abandoned states, while the field workers were most concerned with preventing cholera outbreaks and internecine violence. Given these priorities, who would question the tried-and-true procedures for setting up basic tents in military fashion?

International refugee law acknowledges the importance of architecture and urbanism in the wording of its mission, which is to establish "permanent solutions" to displacement and to stabilize the condition of displacement of any duration.

The Status of Refugees of 1951 gives refugees the right to housing, protection of movable and immovable property (article 13), and legitimacy of the continuity of residence, while protecting the right to freedom of movement (article 10). These articles are extensions of the Universal Declaration of Human Rights of 1948, which lacks the enactive force of refugee law but provides the conceptual framework upon which those laws are based. The declaration guarantees the individual's "right to a standard of living adequate for the health and well-being of himself and his family including food, clothing, housing, and medical care and necessary social services." It broadens the theater of the individual from the house to the spaces of community, which are presented as fundamental to civil society. The declaration affirms the right of individuals to freely associate (article 7), the right to leisure (article 20), and the right to peaceful assembly (article 13),[1] all of which imply an urban "collective space of appearance," to use Hannah Arendt's terminology.

The particular issue facing refugees is that while the individual is the entity of right, the individual depends on the state to defend the exercise of that right. Thus, the problem of disaster relief or refugee housing is, in its most fundamental sense, the problem of securing the rights of the individual who lacks a state to do so. Camp residents are protected from extradition to the states they have fled, but the states that accept them are reciprocally protected from undue burden in hosting them and from the responsibility of granting them permanent asylum. Refugees are stateless, and a refugee camp is a "city without citizens."

Finding a place in human-rights discourse for architecture and planning turned out to be a matter of simply restating the problem of the house beyond the terms of its production cost and within the terms of well-trodden architectural discourse, such as the Albertian construct of many-layered public and private space, and the Corbuisan/Giedionesque instrumentalization of the house as kitchen and bathroom. The lawyers and field-aid workers could thus understand the house as a tool that could participate in the larger life of the camp. I offered our proposal for Kosovo, with its instrumental cores and fluid layering

1 Universal Declaration of Human Rights, General Assembly of The United Nations, 1948, www.un.org.

Right
Deborah Gans
Material renditions of
infrastructural cores.
2004. From left:
lightweight ceramic,
bamboo, paper

of private and public spaces, as the submission for my colleagues to critique in light of the specific needs and culture of the camp.

Statistically speaking, the typical refugee-camp client is a woman of childbearing age. These women usually must maintain the household and care for children and elders by themselves, which includes gathering fuel and water for cooking. If they are lucky and the camp has some sort of internal economy beyond the dole, they need to figure out how to earn some money or goods while simultaneously caring for the family. The UN and related agencies are increasingly sensitive to the difficulties of women in this position, such as their vulnerability to rape while foraging for fuel or requesting assistance with physical tasks, the social tensions produced by their assumption of nontraditional roles, and the corresponding pressures to sustain certain traditions and rituals for the good of the family and the community.

The lawyers turn to existing human-rights law to define the rights of these clients. A body of international law has evolved to protect women from abuse, to guarantee equality of gender, to designate the family and mothers as subjects of special interest, and to require the schooling of young children. Field workers have developed strategies for conflict resolution within the structure of the camp and mechanisms for the establishment of small lending institutions to foster the development of women-owned businesses. Given the issues facing this population, the lawyers and field workers had always regarded the question of housing as peripheral, a matter of shelter against the storm.

Reviewing our proposal, my colleagues discerned features that could benefit women specifically and the camp population in general, but they questioned the complexity of the assembly. They appreciated how the

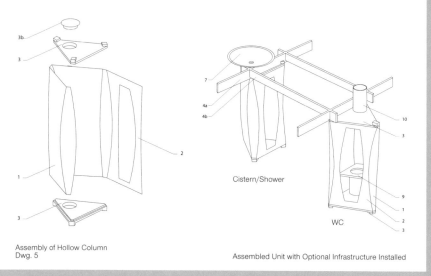

3b
3

1

2

3

Assembly of Hollow Column
Dwg. 5

7

4a
4b

Cistern/Shower

10
3

9
1
2
3

WC

Assembled Unit with Optional Infrastructure Installed

core columns could reduce a woman's need to search for water and fuel, thus obviating the vulnerabilities accompanying that search and increasing time at home or in the workplace. By eliminating exposure to the larger camp population, the individualized infrastructure could mitigate the spread of disease.

The columnar system could provide flexible floor plans and the ability to create clusters of shared space such as private courtyards where children could play safely, public thresholds for cottage industry, and collective places for leisure and assembly. Because the "order of the column" would eventually be subsumed within the exterior walls, the appearance and materiality of the house could vary according to available material and custom. My colleagues' critique of the assembly process led us away from our initial stick system to a folded one that could be erected with something like a car jack (the idea being that every able-bodied woman can change a tire), while their description of various cultural norms led us away from a universal column to a palette of materials and geometries.

I count as my largest accomplishment not our particular shelter design but the UN/Oxford community's acknowledgment of the house as a site of integration of camp life, where issues of work and water, fuel and community connect, much as they do in the experience of the refugee. Without this reevaluation of the role of the house in the settlement, there will be no incentive strong enough to replace the tarp/tent, with its unassailable price point. Only by amortizing the cost of the structure over its true duration and according to all its cost benefits in areas such as sanitation, health, economic productivity, social well-being, and dignity can any alternative become a salable product. As a representative from the organization War Child told me, "We thought we were in the business of caring for children; but it has become increasingly apparent that we are then in the business of housing."

Despite this shift in mindset among UN/NGO officials, replacing the tarp is a hard sell, made more difficult because of catch-22 procurement procedures that demand a product be approved for deployment without having ever been deployed; because of the need for tested protocols in the midst of disaster; and because of the political resistance to any whiff of permanence. There are some venture capitalists interested in producing our latest folding design, but their attraction to the unit and their vision of it as a commodity is based on its ever-increasing lightness, rather than on its integrated infrastructure, which they have not figured into their marketing or cost analyses.

The heaviness of refugee housing in the long-term camp is not the weight of the original structure, but the weight gain of permanent cladding, collected water, additional rooms, expanded enclaves and functions, and the connection to networks of economy, sociability, and the routines of daily life. Our notion of a light house that puts down a rooted physical and social structure sounds new, but long-term camps left to their own devices tend to develop this heaviness naturally. Though at first the logic of a refugee camp resembles that of a military operation, especially immediately following disaster, this framework slackens as prospects of speedy return fade. In Dadaab, Kenya, after more than a decade, the military rows of tents have given way to clusters of thatched houses that bespeak the settlement patterns of tribal origins. Plumbing has been run to each block, causing the block to become the social unit. The camp markets capture trading routes traversing Kenya and Somalia. One of the camps has been razed several times by the government, but the permanence of its informal economy and networked community was so strong that a settlement persisted and grew around the voided center, like a suburb around a declining city.

The heaviness of a refugee settlement can be destructive: forests decimated through a search for fuel, soils eroded by being staked but not planted, ecosystems degraded through intensive hunting and gathering. The organizational framework of a short-term camp may leave its traces long after its reasons for being have faded, dominating the structure of the virtual city for decades. Paradoxically, the camp with the lightest imprint is one planned with more permanence. For instance, flooding in refugee camps in Indonesia spurred the UN to cultivate rice paddies in the camps to halt erosion, as well as to provide rice. Eventually, the refugees were able to join with neighboring residents in planning an expanded geography of cultivation that does not recognize the borders of the camp. We have come to believe that

the real arena for the betterment of refugee conditions is the planning of the settlement, in which the conception of the shelter as atomized infrastructure plays one part.

Refugee camps are conceptually as light as the tent itself—sites of flash inhabitation that are intended to disappear soon. In practice, they exist for decades, and their sites are marked in ways that persist even if their original populations disband. Given the history of colonial outposts like Madras and Bombay, which grew unplanned and unintended into metropolises, it is quite possible that the camps of today could be the cities of tomorrow. In their heavy state, these camps can contain marks of spontaneous and organic civility—agoras, caravanserai, plantations, trade routes—that are spaces of work, leisure, movement, and assembly as outlined by the Universal Declaration of Human Rights and by that parallel document, the Athens Charter.

Conceived in 1933 by the Congrès International d'Architecture Moderne but penned and published by Le Corbusier in 1942, the Athens Charter states that the good city (in the Athenian sense) encompasses the "four essential functions of dwelling, work, leisure, and movement/circulation."[2] This grand formulation gives a physical shape to the "permanent solution" promised by the Universal Declaration of Human Rights.

When I compare the two documents, I cannot help but hear the resonance between the Charter's spaces or zones and the Declaration's rights, and I imagine how the refugee camp—that most extreme of heterotopias—might, in effecting the physical manifestations of the Declaration, become a site of hope, and eventually of urbanity.

2 Le Corbusier, *The Athens Charter*, trans., Anthony Eardley (1943; reprint, New York: Grossman Publishers, 1973).

PARTICI-PATORY DESIGN

The Creek That Connects It All: Participatory Planning in a Taiwanese Mountain Village

CHIA-NING YANG AND
HSU-JEN KAO

Community activation
and empowerment
can be sparked by
participatory design.
An abandoned creek
forms the centerpiece
of a village's new
vision of its own future.

Left
One of the swimming
ponds built in
Chu-Keng Creek by
residents of Kuo-Hsin

Many little waterways in Taiwan do not have names. Called "anonymous creeks" or "wild creeks," such waterways often provide enjoyment for many generations of nearby residents, but many of these anonymous creeks are now getting piped or channeled as part of the feverish development overtaking the landscape of rural Taiwan. Given this situation the creek that flows through the village of Kuo-Hsin is fortunate for a number of reasons: it has a name, although almost no one outside the village knows it; it is too remote to be a good candidate for large-scale "channel enhancement"; and although it was polluted and neglected, it was never completely forgotten by its people.

Because of these factors and a unique twist of fate, Chu-Keng Creek has now become the core of the Kuo-Hsin Village Master Plan, an unprecedented attempt to establish a comprehensive master plan at the village level in Taiwan. Chu-Keng Creek has also become the site of the first genuinely nature-friendly stream construction work in rural Taiwan. The story of this little creek illustrates the struggle we continue to face in attempting participatory planning in rural communities in Taiwan.

A Search for a Community's True Needs

Hsu-Jen Kao and his colleagues from the Building and Planning Research Foundation (BPRF) at National Taiwan University were first introduced to Kuo-Hsin during the aftermath of the devastating earthquake that hit central Taiwan on September 21, 1999. Kuo-Hsin is a mountain village of about two hundred households near Nantou, Taiwan. Long before the catastrophe, Kuo-Hsin was experiencing serious problems: a pronounced outflow of youth, a dwindling agricultural sector, and significant environmental degradation due to severe deforestation caused by large recreational developments. The damage and casualties caused by the earthquake put a number of small mountain villages in the national spotlight, attracting intellectual and financial resources while rekindling a desire to address the villages' ongoing problems.

Searching for effective ways to improve the compromised local environment at Kuo-Hsin, the BPRF team first considered simply rebuilding the village's damaged residential units. However, they soon realized that a large-scale rebuilding effort would involve renewal ordinances that are far too complicated to implement at the village level. BPRF planners had ample experience in participatory planning and design for larger administrative units, such as cities and counties; the mountain village was a different world to the planners.

Fortunately, they found a valuable local contact in village coordinator Kun-Ming Chuang, the only government agent in Kuo-Hsin. The village coordinator is the lowest-level official in the bureaucratic system of rural Taiwan. He is also the only government official who has a true understanding of village life and of the fiscal and administrative difficulties with which the village must cope. After lengthy discussions with Chuang, BPRF planners realized that their initial plans, such as providing housing for the elderly or enhancing prefabricated temporary housing, were either not feasible or unnecessary. Instead, what the village really needed was a master plan.

There are no official plans or fiscal mechanisms at the village level in Taiwan. Higher-level governments execute construction or capital improvement projects in villages as parts of larger projects. Village-level fiscal items typically are budgeted as a way of balancing distributions among different interest groups, rather than as the consequence of thoughtful planning. Villages exist at the tail end of the distribution process, so they seldom refuse such allocations, even though the budgeted project may not be needed or may be improperly designed or constructed. From the residents' point of view, if there were a master plan at hand, it would greatly improve the quality of the public works carried out within the confines of the village. For example, if the community were asked for its opinion about a last-minute incidental budget item, it could respond immediately based on the needs and specifications laid out in its master plan. A master plan would allow the villagers to take some degree of initiative in public works projects.

It also became clear that Kuo-Hsin needed to establish an economic alternative to agriculture, which was on the wane. The BPRF and Chuang reached a consensus that the comparatively intact environment around Chu-Keng Creek had the potential to be the

village's chief economic resource. Therefore, the centerpiece of the master plan would be a tourism development plan focusing on how to transform the abandoned creek into a valuable asset for the villagers and make it the central icon of the village.

Strategizing for Chu-Keng Creek's Future

Chu-Keng means "bamboo pit." Bamboo groves adorn the creek's banks and reflect the valley creek's geographical feature—every turn of the meandering creek forms a small, enclosed landscape corresponding to the human scale. In subsequent field investigations the BPRF discovered the rich tourism potential of the 1.7-mile-long creek channel—historic stone arch bridges, rockwork banks, earth-god shrines, and the legendary Pearl Hill, the site of one of the seven sacred dragon balls believed to be buried in the region. However, signs of neglect were hard to miss. Mattresses and discarded furniture were strewn on the flood plain, and in a few spots the odor of rotting kitchen refuse was suffocating.

In planning the future of Chu-Keng Creek, Kao of the BPRF had two goals: extend participation to diverse community groups, and base any physical transformation of the creek on scientific grounds. Neither goal would be easy to achieve.

In Kuo-Hsin, patriarchal traditions constrain the breadth of citizen participation.

Males dominate public affairs, while females tend to be silent and to confine themselves to roles of servitude. Consequently, Kao invited housewives' groups—the Mama's Classroom and the Folk Dance Club—to all events organized by the BPRF. As for ecological planning, there were two challenges: no hydrological or ecological data about the creek were available, and the creek is officially under the jurisdiction of the Water and Soil Preservation Bureau, an agency known for its vast concrete grade-control dams that destroy rural landscapes and local ecosystems. Kao decided to sidestep the bureau and resort to his personal connection with planner and landscape architect Chia-Ning Yang.

In an environmental assessment Yang concluded that the creek's primary ecological problem was its dispersed flow patterns. The massive disturbance created by the earthquake had caused the creek bed to be covered in coarse sediment, destroying the creek's step-pool formations. The creek would eventually form a new balanced low-flow channel, but this could take a decade or more. In addition, during the creek's self-adjustment process, unexpected downcutting and bank erosion could be hazardous to neighboring residents. Yang thus suggested constructing a series of small rock weirs or spur dikes at strategic positions to facilitate the natural process of

left
Chia-Ning Yang
Conceptual
drawing illustrating
the proposed
reorganization of
flow patterns of
Chu-Keng Creek

channel stabilization and to protect neighboring properties. However, the concept
of nature-friendly stream construction was
largely unknown in Taiwan, and it was
doubtful that any engineering consultant
or contractor possessed sufficient skill to
execute this plan. Moreover, any work carried
out on behalf of Kuo-Hsin was done on a
volunteer basis; no funding was appropriated
for this project.

Coincidentally, Shubun Fukudome, a
pioneer and top practitioner of nature-friendly
stream construction in Japan, was scheduled
to visit Taiwan later that year to instruct
government agents on nature-friendly
stream-construction techniques. Yang had
worked under Fukudome a few years earlier,
so she invited him to use Chu-Keng Creek
as a demonstration site where he would
construct nature-friendly grade-control work
in concert with local residents. Fukudome
enthusiastically accepted the proposal.

Cultivating Community Awareness

Meanwhile, the BPRF was actively exploring
participatory strategies with Kuo-Hsin
residents. To help the villagers recognize
the value of their local treasure, and
to counteract the image of large-scale
commercial facilities commonly associated
with tourism development in Taiwan, Kao
promoted a slogan that struck a chord with
the community: "Just restore our place
as it used to be." The BPRF held community
seminars to explain the results of the environmental assessment to discuss the idea
of making bed-and-breakfasts available for
small groups of tourists, and to help the village
combine several smaller government projects
into the $60,000 Pearl Hill Trail Project, the first
construction project that would comply with
the new village master plan.

During the process the planners saw the
villagers' attitudes shift from indifference
to investment. The BPRF first held an on-site
meeting with the villagers and a landscape
architect to determine the plan. It then helped
the villagers examine the schematic design
and add a proviso to the contract requiring
community approval of the final product.
When construction started, some residents
became volunteer foremen who stopped by
frequently in their daily routines.

Pages 62–63
The construction
of the grade-
control work at
Chu-Keng Creek

However, the contractor was underquali-
fied, a common problem in these areas,
and the landscape architect did not want
to take the trouble of supervising the small,
remote project, as the contract specified.
When the residents found that the fully constructed plank path and low retaining wall
were nothing like what was promised in
the drawings, they became furious. Under
pressure from the residents, the contractor
tore down what he considered to be
completed work and rebuilt the wall twice.
In the end the trail's construction was a
point of pride for the community—the project
achieved a level of quality unseen before in
Kuo-Hsin. This experience encouraged the
villagers to believe that their intentions could
make a positive difference for their village.

When Kao conveyed the news of
Fukudome's visit and of the demonstration
of state-of-the-art construction techniques,
the villagers got excited. Someone mentioned
that they all knew who was dumping garbage
at the creek, and many agreed that they
wanted to do something about it. As a result
they decided to hold a creek cleanup before
Fukudome's arrival.

The creek cleanup marked a turning
point in the participatory process: it was
the first creek-related activity initiated and
organized by the community. The first place
the residents cleaned up was Ever-Fortune
Bridge, an old stone arch bridge. Constructed some fifty years ago by a master
mason named Jung who was now a senior
villager, the bridge was abandoned when a
concrete bridge was built next to it, and it was
now covered in vines. However, the BPRF
planning team discovered that Ever-Fortune
Bridge was a particularly important spot on
Chu-Keng Creek. Jung had built the bridge
on two rock outcroppings on either side of
the creek, and the creek's deepest swimming
hole happened to be located between the
outcroppings; thus, the bridge had served as
a diving board for many villagers. Hands-on
work on the creek and its environs stirred up
people's childhood memories of swimming
in the creek and catching shrimp and frogs
on its banks.

Once all the garbage was hauled out and
access paths were formed by weeding and
trampling, a "clean creek" appeared, and
the community shifted into full action mode.

Within the two weeks remaining before the scheduled demonstration, the BPRF helped organize the residents into different working groups in charge of materials and equipment, food and drink, and publicity.

Moreover, a few residents didn't wait for the foreign guests to meddle with their creek; they drove backhoes into the creek and created a series of ponds for swimming. They then filled a natural pool at the bottom of a waterfall so residents could enjoy a cool spa experience there. Right over the spa is a high spot by a road that overlooks the creek. Here they placed large rocks and boulders to serve as tables and stools, planted trees, and hooked up lights they recycled from abandoned houses in a neighboring village that had been damaged by the earthquake. This spot became so popular that by the end of the summer it was crowded almost daily with villagers chatting, playing chess, and drinking tea until midnight.

Construction and Aftermath

On construction day the village was in a barn-raising mood. When the Japanese guests arrived at Kuo-Hsin, housewives in the Mama's Classroom had prepared a wealth of local delicacies that were presented in front of the earth-god shrine. The crowds and media were waiting, and the backhoe drivers and volunteer workers were ready to pitch in.

The construction site was located next to a masonry bank that Jung had built next to his own property. Over the years down-cutting at this spot had caused the bank's foundation to be exposed, endangering the bank and the property. Fukudome had only discussed this particular problem briefly with Yang and seen a few pictures of the site the day before. There were no design drawings except for a sketch proposed by Yang. But once the master stood on the creek bed, he knew exactly what to do.

Fukudome's idea was to construct a lateral arch structure downstream of the masonry bank so that in time it would raise the bed upstream and form a deep pool immediately downstream from the structure. To convey this plan across the language barrier to Jung and other villagers, Fukudome made a miniature model out of cobblestones. Jung, a veteran mason in his own right, responded by moving the stones around to illustrate his own concerns, giving rise to an intensive "conversation" between the two masters. The debate around the model was a crucial step in smoothing out the entire construction process. Over the next four hours Fukudome, Jung, the backhoe drivers, and the core working group, wet with perspiration in the midsummer mugginess, began to implement the scheme.

The villagers watched with interest and came forward when called upon to help deposit cobblestones and gravel between the precisely positioned large rocks. This step, crucial for structural reinforcement, was also fun for the crowd. As the backhoe drivers scooped water toward the completed structure—a way to tighten the rockwork as well as a ritual to cleanse the construction— all cheered with joy and opened cans of beer. The villagers presented Fukudome with brush, ink, and red paper so he could write some words to be inscribed on a commemorative tablet.

After construction was completed, the villagers continued actively to shape their version of the ideal creek. More swimming ponds were built, such that the creek was soon choked by the series of ponds. These small projects were not ecologically sound, and within two months the lowered water level had caused the ponds to become stagnant and murky, and swimmers did not use them. Now that the villagers felt empowered to take action to improve the creek, the project team saw a need to educate them in basic concepts of stream morphology. However, the team was not particularly concerned that the villagers' limited attempts at transformation would do lasting damage to the creek; the mountainous creek is too energetic to be confined by those misplaced rocks for long. Plus, the team believed that through their new engagement with the creek, the residents would learn what the creek "liked" and what it did not.

Eight months after the construction demonstration, Chu-Keng Creek proved the team was right. After a heavy storm all in-channel construction done by the villagers was washed away, and only the nature-friendly grade-control work remained intact. In fact, Fukudome's new construction had already achieved exactly what it was intended to do:

the upstream bed had risen significantly, so that the exposed bank foundation was now halfway buried, and a deep pool had formed under the rock weir, where various kinds of fish now gather.

In the years since the earthquake, Kuo-Hsin has come a long way. Chu-Keng Creek is a living demonstration of how to use nature-friendly stream-enhancement techniques. The village now has a master plan that sees the stream as an asset sought after by tourists and cherished in villagers' daily lives. To fully realize this vision, however, Kuo-Hsin still has a long way to go. The community has neither the funds to pay for high-quality planning services nor the technical capacity to do its own planning. Moreover, there is a need to teach the villagers about crucial ecological concepts and to teach stream-restoration techniques to local masons and construction workers. Without this foundation of knowledge, the master plan and the ongoing work of grade control will not take root.

A less visible yet undeniably real outcome of this process is the remarkable increase in the community's sense of its own stewardship and self-reliance. It has flexed its muscles against incompetent contractors and destructive community members. More villagers now believe that no matter how bad things seem, something can be done. This shift in attitude encourages the BPRF team to believe that although severe economic burdens and political constraints continue to fetter Kuo-Hsin, the village is now better equipped to grapple with them.

Growing Urban Habitats:
A Local Housing Crisis
Spawns a New Design Center

KATIE SWENSON

A developer's plan to displace longtime residents mobilizes a new community design center to search for a better solution.

Charlottesville, Virginia, recently ranked the number one place to live in America by *Cities Ranked & Rated*, offers small-town ideals, a top public university, a strong sense of history, and abundant cultural and environmental resources. Like many medium-size cities around the country, Charlottesville is grappling with the gentrification spurred by urban growth and the associated challenges of maintaining affordable housing and preventing the loss of low-income families to outlying counties. A growing discrepancy between incomes and the cost of city living has resulted in housing costs doubling in Charlottesville over the past five years.

These issues flared into prominence when Sunrise Trailer Court, a low-income housing site in Charlottesville, was put up for sale. Although the trailers perch on impermanent cinderblock foundations, the residents' bonds run deep within the community. Marion Dudley has lived at Sunrise for twenty-five years and she describes the community in terms of the closeness of people and their willingness to step in and help:

There are only a very few of us that have been here a long time, the others have come in within the last five to ten years. But, you know, the minute they pull their mobile home in they're automatically family. We're all here to greet them when they start moving stuff in, and we let them know that if there's anything they need for us to help them with, let us know. And everybody that's moved down here has always been nice. That was one of his strict rules—that you had to go by certain guidelines to live here—and Sunrise has been a very quiet, very respectable trailer court. You never heard of things going on in this trailer court. You still don't.

Sunrise residents were shocked when a private development group put a contract on the site stipulating that all residents be evicted 120 days after rezoning. Not only were residents facing the loss of their community, but also they had few options for relocation within the city. Many trailers were too old to move, there were few suitable sites, and affordable housing was virtually nonexistent.

Fear and anger motivated Sunrise residents to join with the Belmont-Carlton Neighborhood Association to oppose the property sale.

After protesting the loss of neighborhood low-income housing and the impending displacement of community members, the Sunrise and Belmont-Carlton residents won a victory when the developers withdrew their plan and offered the contract to Habitat for Humanity of Greater Charlottesville for development. Habitat for Humanity (HFH) purchased the property in November 2004 with the promise to build mixed-income housing and provide affordable housing options to all Sunrise residents.

HFH's stated intention allayed residents' worst fears, but new issues quickly arose. How could the site be developed with affordable housing? How could HFH ensure that the development wouldn't displace low-income residents? How could the new project respect the values and needs of the existing community while tripling the density of the site?

Community Design Comes to Charlottesville

The Sunrise project was in development when I was at a critical juncture in my own career. I was finishing a three-year Rose Architectural Fellowship with local affordable housing developer Piedmont Housing Alliance (PHA) and embarking on the creation of the Charlottesville Community Design Center (CCDC). During my tenure at PHA, I learned that designers had a critical, if often overlooked, role to play in the field of community development, which often regards good design as secondary (or even superfluous) to the utilitarian goal of providing affordable housing and community services. I became acutely aware of the widespread need for high-quality, sustainable, affordable housing, and I sought to work on this issue in Charlottesville and beyond. The Rose Fellowship had provided me the tools and models to pursue my goal by allowing me to both work locally and travel throughout the country and observe national community design models.

As I introduced the idea of a community design center to local architects, planners, and residents, I was met with a groundswell of interest and support. I also found a partner in Jim Kovach, a young local architect with strong ideals and the desire and ability to work for a better community. With a band of local design professionals and students, Jim and I founded the CCDC in September 2004.

Our mission was to bring together design resources and citizens for the creation of equitable, sustainable, and beautifully designed communities.

The redevelopment at Sunrise Trailer Court was the CCDC's first big project. I approached HFH with the idea of promoting the Sunrise project as a design competition, because I anticipated that the redevelopment of the 2.3-acre site would be challenging for the nonprofit organization. Unlike HFH's typical projects involving the construction of single-family homes with a volunteer component, Sunrise was larger and involved the development of higher-density, mixed-income housing on a mixed-use site. Beyond generating redevelopment plans for the parcel, it was our intention that the design competition would produce replicable prototypes for multifamily mixed-income housing that considered the needs of the existing residents while creating sustainable, equitable, and beautiful communities.

To ensure resident participation in the development process, CCDC joined with HFH and the residents of Sunrise to convene the design competition, named "Urban Habitats." The competition sought realistic, innovative, universal models for multifamily housing that prevented gentrification and displacement. The design competition was launched through the CCDC's Web site and was aimed at students, design professionals, and construction professionals. CCDC sought to explore and bridge the gaps between disciplines in hopes that any resulting dialogue would establish a new sense of understanding and respect between the various design communities. By requiring entrants to address the social, economic, and environmental aspects of community development to the same degree as the formal site design, Urban Habitats sought to balance design innovations with responses to residents' needs.

From the earliest stages the competition's focus never drifted from the realities of Sunrise. Brainstorming sessions, on-site community events, and public visioning processes elicited residents' hopes and engaged their senses of ownership and leadership of the project. The community meetings resulted in a set of clearly articulated convictions that were incorporated into the Urban Habitats program requirements. The expression of these values engendered new strength and confidence within the Sunrise community.

The program requirements suggested that entrants strive to achieve the following goals with their entries:

1. Design a vibrant, attractive urban neighborhood.

2. Generate a culturally and climatically responsive architecture.

3. Implement a sustainable continuum, from site development to energy-efficient unit operation.

4. Create a community that integrates mixed-income and mixed-use principles.

5. Design a diverse range of market-rate housing and commercial space using compact floor plans.

6. Develop and utilize economical, innovative building technologies.

Prize Jury Brings
All Stakeholders Together

The competition drew more than 160 entries from all over the world, from which a nine-person jury selected three finalists over the course of one tiring but satisfying July weekend. The jury was composed of internationally renowned architects, city government officials, HFH board members, and local residents, and the review process was successful precisely because the group understood that the vision for Sunrise went beyond the physical qualities of the site. The real issue was how design would engage the needs, desires, and history of the community. The diversity of the jurors' positions and outlooks—along with a sense of mutual respect and admiration and ability to listen—made for a vibrant, constructive conversation and a jury process that was a true community-building event.

Because the jury was drawn from a variety of backgrounds, differences of opinion emerged during the selection process. For example, while the residents tended to prioritize social aspects of the proposals—such as green space and livability—the developers and architects seemed to focus more on the practical and technical challenges. One juror, a local architect, noted that the jury process "seemed driven more by ideas than by a hard look at reality." Despite differing views of "reality," the honest and open discussions led a number of jurors to comment on the comfortable dynamic that developed over the weekend. The warmth and ease with which jurors formed relationships led Sunrise resident Dudley to comment that "from day one, they were like family."

A long-time Charlottesville resident and a natural leader within Sunrise, Dudley admitted to being shocked when she was first asked to be a juror. She took on the responsibility, however, because "it wasn't just me—it was the whole trailer court that I was doing it for." Unlike development projects that present communities like Sunrise with established plans at the first public meeting, Sunrise residents were involved in the project from the outset, which provided residents the rare opportunity to shape their future. Dudley's participation as a juror further solidified her community's influential presence. She informed the other jurors about the area's

subtleties, elaborated on the community's roots, and grounded the jury in reality if the conversation drifted too far into design theory. As nervous as Dudley might have initially felt about accurately representing her community's views, she was absolutely delighted when she learned that a couple of her neighbors had favored the entry that wound up being the first-prize winner.

When asked about the Urban Habitats Competition's first-place winner, Dudley responded, "This one said 'home' to me. It's more like our own home that we have now than any of the other entries." These two honest, simple sentences speak volumes about the winning entry, designed by architects Susanne Schindler and Christopher Genter, especially regarding the designers' efforts to preserve and reinforce the site's history by retaining the location of the main street, renamed "Green Street" in the new plan. This central road now serves as both a traffic artery and a social space; the winning design thus affirmed and redefined its community significance. While the architecture itself draws from a modern vocabulary for house and garden, the plan uses an architectural vocabulary of primarily detached housing with front porches and private outdoor space, which is familiar to the community, while increasing the density to accommodate more residents and increase affordability. The winning design is the one that best recognizes and incorporates the site's existing orientation while addressing the residents' desire for shared open spaces where they can gather and garden.

Jurors awarded second place to the entry submitted by the Metropolitan Planning Collaborative, a multidisciplinary group from Washington, D.C., New York City, and San Francisco. The relaxed Southern personality of their site plan offers a wealth of both communal and private space, responding directly to the residents' stated desire for the feel of a tight-knit neighborhood where people watch out for one another. The jury also noted that the Metropolitan Planning Collaborative's attention to phasing would not call for current residents to be displaced from their trailers until well into the construction process, thereby successfully addressing a crucial component of the program guidelines.

Left
Sunrise residents dance at a barbecue.

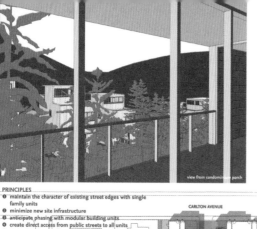

view from condominium porch

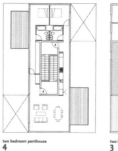

two bedroom penthouse
4

two bedroom atrium unit
3

PRINCIPLES

- maintain the character of existing street edges with single family units
- minimize new site infrastructure
- anticipate phasing with modular building units
- create direct access from public streets to all units
- create direct access from all units to community open space
- provide every unit with private open space: yard, deck or roof
- build sustainably using low-tech measures: density, cross-ventilation, grass parking and green roofs.

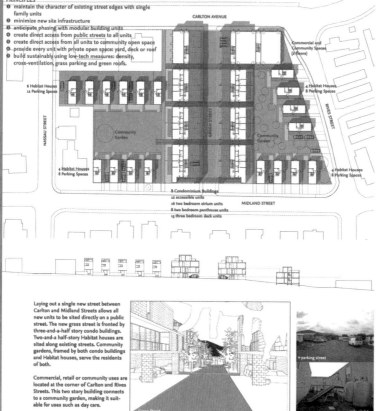

CARLTON AVENUE

Commercial and
Community Spaces
(2 floors)

6 Habitat Houses
12 Parking Spaces

4 Habitat Houses
12 Parking Spaces

NASSAU STREET

GREEN STREET

RIVES STREET

Community
Garden

Community
Garden

4 Habitat Houses
8 Parking Spaces

4 Habitat Houses
8 Parking Spaces

8 Condominium Buildings
12 accessible units
16 two bedroom atrium units
8 two bedroom penthouse units
15 three bedroom deck units

MIDLAND STREET

Laying out a single new street between Carlton and Midland Streets allows all new units to be sited directly on a public street. The new grass street is fronted by three-and-a-half story condo buildings. Two-and-a-half-story Habitat houses are sited along existing streets. Community gardens, framed by both condo buildings and Habitat houses, serve the residents of both.

Commercial, retail or community uses are located at the corner of Carlton and Rives Streets. This two story building connects to a community garden, making it suitable for uses such as day care.

Green Street

←parking street

side yard →

☐ **60457**

Each condo building, or Double Wide, comprises
nized around a central scissor stair ❶. Residents
along the street ❷. From here, they arrive to thei
on a walkway connecting to the community garde
has a different porch | deck configuration based c
building ❸ and incorporate green roofs ❹. With
units can be cross ventilated. The material is CM

DOUBLE WID

TRIPLE HIGH

In the Habitat House, or Triple High, residents als
community gardens: they park in their side yard ❶
open space beyond. When the car is away, this str
comes a play area. In addition, by reducing the nu
increase the size of their yard. The building's cent
and out of the house and culminates in a porch ❻
house is stick built and wood clad.

☐ **60457**

Above
Susanne Schindle
and Christopher
Genter
Double Wide, Tripl
High, first-place
winner of Urban
Habitats Competiti
sponsored by the
Charlottesville
Community Design
Center. 2005

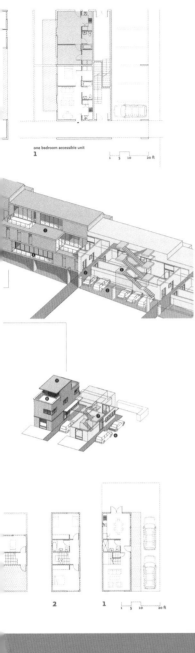

one bedroom accessible unit
1

2   1

When asked about the Urban Habitats Competition's first-place winner, Dudley responded, "This one said 'home' to me. It's more like our own home that we have now than any of the other entries." These two honest, simple sentences speak volumes about the winning entry, designed by architects Susanne Schindler and Christopher Genter, especially regarding the designers' efforts to preserve and reinforce the site's history by retaining the location of the main street, renamed "Green Street" in the new plan.

SUNRISE | Charlottesville, Va

Responding to the context:

Urban design proposal:

SUNRISE Context Diagrams:

SUNRISE Program:

SUNRISE Budget:

Efficient site plan and program:

Flexible framework:

ID# 60301

ID# 60301

Jurors awarded second place to the entry submitted by the Metropolitan Planning Collaborative. The relaxed Southern personality of their site plan offers a wealth of both communal and private space, responding directly to the residents' stated desire for the feel of a tight-knit neighborhood where people watch out for one another.

Above
Metropolitan Plan
Collaborative
SUNRISE, second
place winner of Ur
Habitats Competit
sponsored by the
Charlottesville
Community Desig
Center. 2005

Guided by a Vision of Equity, Beauty, and Sustainability

Even after investing so much effort and time to organize and hold the competition, the most challenging phases lie ahead. As one juror suggested, in any successful development group, one needs "the money, the management, and the vision." While all parts are integral, the vision must be the element that guides the entire process. Luckily, Urban Habitats' vision is established and unwavering. Through the leadership of the HFH board's chair, Lynne Conboy, HFH has engaged the further architectural services of the first- and second-place winners. HFH will work with those teams to turn the competition's schematic designs into fully developed plans, while keeping the residents involved, invested, and represented throughout the process. In the meantime CCDC will employ symposiums, exhibitions, and publications to disseminate the redevelopment prototypes generated by the competition throughout the city of Charlottesville and beyond.

The CCDC has positioned itself in the area as a loyal partner in community design efforts. The scope and scale of this ambitious project forced the organization to develop and grow. We have become trusted advocates for sustainable, affordable housing, and we now serve as a resource to many local nonprofit groups. We have since facilitated community processes for neighborhood planning, public park redesign, and innovative housing projects, and we are a local leader in green building and sustainable-design assistance and education. The Urban Habitats project also has given CCDC a national and international presence, granting us access to the best community-design projects around the world as models for Charlottesville, and allowing us to share the lessons of Urban Habitats with other communities striving for equity, beauty, and sustainability.

The success of Urban Habitats lies in its affirmation of the value of community-based collaboration and design.

Last year neighbors were fighting the development; this year they are part of the redevelopment team. The local residents are learning that change can be positive when the community works together toward the best outcome. Dudley says, "I know these places that they'll put down here will be a welcome change—they'll be nice places—but it's going to take me a long time to adjust to it." Change is never easy for an established community. Yet when it improves the quality and quantity of affordable housing while respecting a place's inherent history, values, and culture, change is a positive force. The Sunrise project is empowering its participants as it creates sustainable new communities of lasting value.

Traditions, Transformation, and Community Design: The Making of Two Ta'u Houses

When participatory design is put into action, the results can be true discoveries, revealing the complex relationships between cultural identity, design solutions, and change.

If the public housing is so bad, why don't you just move back to the traditional houses?

JAMES SOONG, former Taiwan provincial governor

In 1994 representatives of Taiwan's indigenous Ta'u tribe, dressed in traditional warrior outfits, met in Taipei with government officials to protest the conditions of government-built housing on their island of Pongso-No-Ta'u. From the 1970s to the early 1980s, in a move intended to "upgrade" the tribe's standard of living, the Taiwan government under the Kuomintang Party eradicated four of the six traditional Ta'u villages and replaced them with rows of concrete barracks. This seemingly benevolent effort to modernize the lives of the Ta'u caused profound and traumatic changes on the island.

The transformation in Ta'u life went beyond the loss of their villages. With the removal of the traditional dwellings, an entire generation of Ta'u was uprooted from a social system in which building practices were intricately tied to social norms and rituals, local environmental management, and continuity of knowledge. Now, as the younger generation of Ta'u goes to Taiwan for education and jobs, they bring different lifestyles back with them when they return. On the island today the most popular type of house is modeled after the country villas in Taiwan, many of which are built by indigenous workers like the Ta'u, who provide cheap labor in Taiwan's construction trade.

Governor James Soong's suggestion that the Ta'u move back to their traditional houses seemed ignorant on its face, as the government had already destroyed most of the original Ta'u dwellings. Nevertheless, the question touched on a profound generational and cultural rift within the Ta'u society. The Ta'u now had a younger generation who would no longer return to the old way of life, even if they could. This situation created a perplexing challenge for the designers and planners who were assisting the Ta'u with the rebuilding of their homes.

A History of Distrust

The island of Pongso-No-Ta'u ("land of people") is located at the northern tip of an archipelago stretching between Taiwan and the Philippines. The Ta'u tribe, with a population of about three thousand, is an Austronesian group that has historical and kinship linkages with the Bataan Islands of the northern Philippines. Pongso-No-Ta'u was annexed by Japan in the late nineteenth century and has been governed by Taiwan since the end of World War II.

In the 1970s and 1980s the government undertook its demolition of traditional Ta'u villages, replacing them with concrete housing. Then in 1994 the Provincial Bureau of Aboriginal Affairs contracted with a group of design professionals at National Taiwan University (NTU) to develop a plan for further physical improvement of living conditions on the island, a decision prompted by the history of conflict and distrust between the Ta'u and the Taiwan government. In the early 1980s the government had built a nuclear waste depository on the island without informing or consulting with Ta'u residents. At around the same time the Ta'u had protested against plans to create a national park on the island, fearing that the park would give the government an opportunity to take control over Ta'u ancestral land. The NTU team had worked with the Ta'u on the campaigns against the national park and the nuclear waste depository, so the government chose the team for the project to improve living conditions on the island, despite the team's known advocacy approach to planning.

The NTU team already knew that the government's public-housing project had had a profound impact on Ta'u culture. Team members soon found out that the actual structures also posed an immediate physical danger to the residents. The use of beach sand in the concrete had caused the rebar to corrode, which made many of the ceilings and walls burst open. Most families lacked the money for repairs and continued to live in these dilapidating buildings. With houses on the verge of collapse in an earthquake-prone region, the Ta'u as a people were in danger. The NTU team quickly invited structural experts to evaluate the buildings and organized a series of public meetings to inform the residents about the danger of living in them.

Ta'u leaders decided to stage a protest in Taipei to demand compensation and reconstruction of their homes.

For two consecutive days images of Ta'u representatives dressed in traditional garb dominated the nation's newly liberalized media, leading to a meeting with Governor Soong and other government officials. Under the media spotlight the officials promised to survey the structural conditions of the houses and provide subsidies for the rebuilding of damaged homes. After the protest the project for physical improvement of Ta'u living conditions became a project for reconstruction of the island's six villages. It then became the NTU team's task to plan the rebuilding of Ta'u homes and communities in the face of the profound social and cultural transformation the Ta'u had undergone.

communicated by means of a variety of details, such as the house's size and the number of doors it has. The layout of dwelling clusters reflects clan hierarchies, personal relationships, and the history of adjustments to the village's social situation.

The design of traditional Ta'u dwellings embodies both cultural values and strategies of environmental adaptation to the island's unique climatic and physical conditions. A typical unit consists of four primary components, with the occupants migrating seasonally from one space to another. The *vahay* (main house), submerged and protected by stone walls, shelters occupants from fierce winter winds. The half-submerged *makarang* (tall house) is occupied in spring and autumn. The *tagakal* (cool house) is where occupants live in summer. High above the ground, it provides ocean views and breezes. The *inaorod* (front yard) is a stone-paved open area in front of the *vahay*. The *vahay* is the most elaborate and sacred of all the structures, but the *makarang* and *tagakal* are also used for ceremonial and casual gatherings, and the *inaorod* serves as a place for important rituals and ceremonies, boat-building, drying of the sacred flying fish, and daily family activities.

Out of the original six traditional Ta'u villages, only two—Iraralai and Ivarinu—escaped the demolition crews of the 1970s, because residents fought to keep the bulldozers out. In Iraralai and Ivarinu public-housing structures were instead erected alongside traditional dwellings. But even here reinforced-concrete houses built by villagers have begun to replace traditional dwellings as the housing of choice for new construction. For some time almost all new houses have been built above ground. Reinforced concrete is used to provide structural resistance to the wind. Concrete also allows for taller residences that provide better daylight. Many of the new concrete houses have also incorporated elements of the traditional dwellings, creating a hybrid form. This hybridity is also evident in some new public buildings.

The transformation of traditional dwellings in Iraralai and Ivarinu inspired the project team to look for ways to integrate historical forms with the needs of contemporary life. Though these aims were theorctically sound, the process of implementation was

Above
A traditional Ta'u dwelling consists of multiple structures for seasonal adaptation. Foreground, the *vahay*; left, the *makarang*; right, the *tagakal*

Tradition and Transformation
The NTU team began its work by closely studying traditional Ta'u dwellings. The team wanted to incorporate traditional building practices and local culture into their plans and use the original homes to inform the design of the new houses that would be built.

The island's traditional dwellings are perhaps the most important artifacts of Ta'u culture. A dwelling represents the social status of its owner; this information is

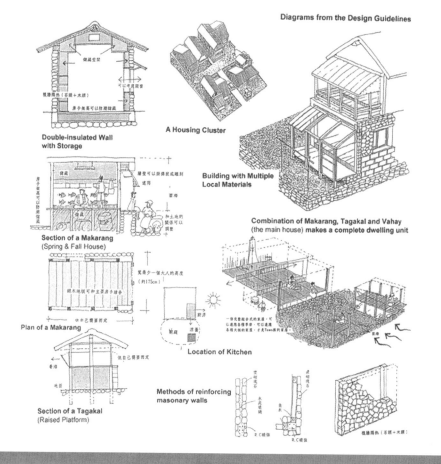

Diagrams from the Design Guidelines

Left
Building and Plan
Research Founda
Design studies for
Ta'u houses. 1995

Double-insulated Wall
with Storage

A Housing Cluster

Building with Multiple
Local Materials

Section of a Makarang
(Spring & Fall House)

Plan of a Makarang

Combination of Makarang, Tagakal and Vahay
(the main house) makes a complete dwelling unit

Location of Kitchen

Section of a Tagakal
(Raised Platform)

Methods of reinforcing
masonary walls

not simple. First, the provincial government demanded that the team produce a standardized design for all houses to facilitate planning and construction. To avoid repeating the mistake of imposed standardization, the team refused to meet this demand. Another challenge occurred when the team attempted to engage local residents in the design process. In the Ta'u culture it is taboo to tell others about one's plan, because it is feared that once a plan is revealed, it will be sabotaged by evil spirits that roam the island. Nor did residents respond favorably to the project team's recommendations, even though the team's work was based on careful analysis of traditional building practices. For example, to preserve ocean views, the team recommended setting height restrictions and regulating roof forms, as had been done in the past. However, most residents opposed this recommendation because they wanted larger and taller

buildings. Some even saw the height restriction as an attempt to revive plans for the national park, which would have also imposed design restrictions on some buildings. Nor did the residents respond favorably to the suggestion of wood construction. Instead they preferred reinforced concrete, both for its structural strength and as a symbol of prestige.

One Community, Two Kinds of Design

Many months passed while the project team built prototypes, conducted workshops and interviews, and negotiated with provincial officials. Eventually an opportunity to move the project forward presented itself: an elementary school was planning to build a cultural classroom and museum on school grounds. The team convinced the school principal that the classroom and museum should be housed in a demonstration dwelling that would be designed in accordance with ideas that had been generated in the design process. The construction of the dwelling would also provide an opportunity to engage local residents in further dialogue on dwelling design.

The design was an experiment in the integration of traditional morphology and contemporary functionality. The main building is half submerged in the ground, similar to a traditional *vahay*, but the two-story structure is taller and can provide more space and natural light. It is also oriented toward the sea, to establish a relationship between the dwelling and the larger landscape. A stand-alone *tagakal* was included, built in the old way to revive and preserve time-honored building techniques. The *inaorod*, an important outdoor element of the traditional dwelling, features prominently. The use of reinforced concrete is limited to the post and beam elements, and a system of hollow wall units made of wood was modeled after traditional construction practices and provides insulation and storage space.

A local resident was hired to erect the building and collaborate with the design team to refine the plans throughout the construction process. Months later, when the new building was completed, the school and the community organized the enactment of traditional rituals to celebrate. Pigs were slaughtered and meat was distributed to all villagers and guests. A singing ceremony was held inside the new building through the night and into the morning.

Meanwhile, now that government subsidies were being distributed, many villagers were busy rebuilding their own homes, turning the entire village into a large construction site. As the new residences took form, traditional elements began to appear in ways both expected and unexpected: windows and railings in the shapes of traditional icons and motifs, concrete columns evoking ceremonial wooden posts, and *tagakals* built entirely out of concrete and sitting on top of new buildings. The interior spaces of these new homes were utterly contemporary, with tiled floors, electric appliances, painted walls, and, in some cases, double-height ceilings. Sometimes the spaces between buildings evolved incrementally, resembling the organic forms of traditional dwelling clusters. Although the villagers had rejected the project team's recommendations, their designs reflected similar interests in integrating traditional morphologies with contemporary functions.

Despite the contemporary appearance and amenities of these new homes, they still play an important role in Ta'u society, just as the traditional homes once did. In times past, a Ta'u household would spend years collecting building materials, cultivating fields, and undertaking other activities to prepare for construction of a dwelling and the ceremonies related to it. A completed dwelling represented an ultimate personal achievement and served as a symbol of social status and prestige. Today the new houses still signify the culmination of years of hard work by the members of Ta'u house-holds. Ta'u men, and often entire families, spend years working elsewhere in Taiwan. Many of them hold jobs as manual laborers at construction sites and factories in hopes of saving enough money to someday return to the island and construct a new house. While other aspects of Ta'u culture have been significantly altered, the tradition of the social importance of home-building has remained alive and well, despite the use of different architectural forms and construction practices.

What Does "Community Design" Mean?
The two types of house—the demonstration dwelling and the actual homes of residents—represent two modes of community design that took place on the island during this period. The former mode attempted to follow a comprehensive approach to rebuilding the community and its future, using a community-oriented process to carefully design spatial forms and physical structures. The designers saw rebuilding as an opportunity to revive Ta'u traditional culture, including its construction practices. They looked for features of custom-ary dwellings that could be integrated into new designs with renewed functions and meanings. They focused on social processes and the mechanisms of rebuilding, and not just on the design. They talked and listened to the residents extensively, and tried to create a meaningful participatory process. In all these ways they followed the established norms for the practice of professional community design.

Above
A traditionally
built *tagakal* was
a key feature of
the demonstration
house. 1997

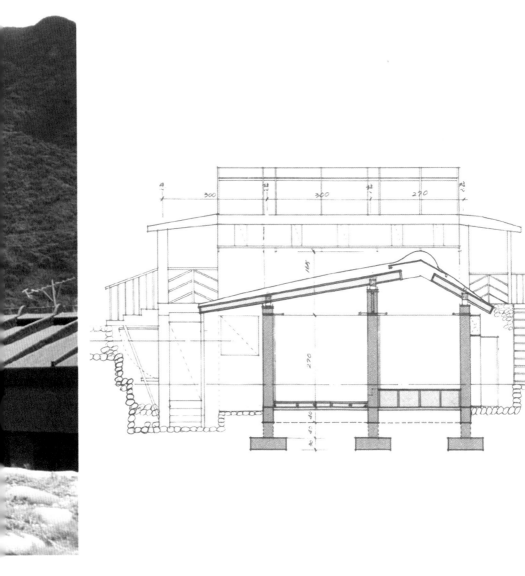

bove right
uilding and
anning Research
oundation
ectional drawing
 the demonstration
ouse showing
e incorporation
 traditional
welling elements

The houses built by the residents, on the other hand, provide a starkly different expression of what community design means. The demonstration house may have had some influence on the structures that residents erected, but the final products clearly reflect residents' priorities for their own homes. Against the project team's recommendation, the homes were constructed almost entirely out of reinforced concrete, using imported cement and local gravels and sand. Each building was an attempt to be taller than the next. Outdoor spaces are almost nonexistent, given the large size of the new buildings. There is a seeming lack of hierarchy and coherence among the buildings and building elements, and no particular relationship exists between the dwellings and the larger landscape. Nevertheless, each building is a projection of the image of success in contemporary Ta'u society. Though visually quite different from the traditional houses, the new buildings still represent the residents' cultural identity. The designs have a vocabulary and language of pragmatic ingenuity similar to those of the old homes. In their own way, the new houses embody the evolving cultural practices of the Ta'u.

The striking contrast between the two outcomes highlights a set of challenges commonly faced by community designers when they attempt to "assist" local communities that are facing social and cultural changes. Can design rescue or resuscitate culture and tradition? How can community design critically respond to forces of change? How can the common good and community-oriented processes be reconciled with individual decisions?

In indigenous communities experiencing profound economic and social change, designers need to be aware that notions of tradition and culture have become destabilized, increasing the volatility of the process by which individual and collective decisions are made.

Designers also need to recognize and validate the subjectivity of local residents. Despite Governor Soong's suggestion to the contrary, younger Ta'u don't want to move back to the traditional houses. Instead they have shown a preference for building new homes that embody their changing identities and values, and that reflect their individual and collective decisions.

Below
A new house in Iraralai incorporate a *tagakal* on the rooftop. 1997

Claiming Public Space:
The Case for Proactive,
Democratic Design

PETER AESCHBACHER AND
MICHAEL RIOS

There is a need to
rethink citizenship
in contemporary
society. One
democratic act is to
claim both physical
and political space
for the public good.

What makes a space public ...is not its preordained "publicness." Rather, it is when, to fulfill a pressing need, some group or another takes space and through its actions makes it public.

DON MITCHELL, *The Right to the City:
Social Justice and the Fight for Public Space*

The challenges to democracy and full participation in society that we face today require a proactive stance toward constructive social change and a new conception of how design contributes to democracy. Design is an expression of human intent in the material world. Its artifact—the built environment—reflects the contemporary state of our society. Designers play a vital role in giving form to what is and imagining what can be, and their roles must extend beyond disciplinary boundaries to directly engage the material production of space through active citizenship.

Critics contend that current trends in the United States are an attack on much of the social, political, and environmental progress made during the twentieth century. Some identify a historic ideological restructuring of the relationship between the state, civil society, and its citizens.[1] This trend toward neoliberalism is characterized by an embrace of market forces and private enterprise; the dismantling of democratic structures and public investment; deregulation that externalizes environmental and social costs; and the privatization of state-owned enterprises and services.[2] In addition, military and foreign-policy objectives are being used to justify state surveillance of everyday life, the sharing of private data between corporations and government agencies, the bureaucratization of dissent through government-sanctioned "free speech zones," and the institutional monitoring of public communications. The Patriot Act, the Clear Skies and Healthy Forest initiatives, and attempts to privatize entitlements are seen as retreats from the government's role in safeguarding intellectual freedoms, environmental protections, and social safety nets. The twin agendas of neoliberalism and militarism use the rhetoric of "individual

responsibility" and "national security" to override the public good and citizens' rights, engendering a true crisis of the commons.

One result of these trends is citizen disempowerment through reduced access to the means required for social progress. The increasing marketization and monitoring of social life discourages people from participating in social spheres, erodes their sense of cooperation, and limits their capacity to help foster equality and democracy. The issues facing us all seem to be beyond the capacity of any one individual to change.

How can people—including designers—engage with the roles and responsibilities of citizenship and begin to effect positive social change? To begin with, we claim that there is a need to profoundly rethink citizenship in contemporary society. Active citizenship begins with the recognition that the public realm is a political and physical terrain of struggle that is produced contextually, relationally, and through dialogue; that is incrementally negotiated over time through democratic participation; and that is manifested in material form.

Based on these propositions, we argue for a claiming of public space that encompasses:

Spaces of recognition
Individuals and groups need to assert their roles and responsibilities in defining shared claims and rights, creating positive models of identity and community, and building solidarity across group differences.

Spaces of engagement
Emerging models of democracy provide new arenas for collective action. Social networks of communication and exchange are the building blocks of civil society, but association without mobilization remains mere potential. The true value of these local and global networks resides in what they can achieve through constructive engagement.

Spaces of materiality
Physical spaces are a major component of the creative commons that reflects civil society's values. They are the material artifacts of democratic projects, providing a vehicle for citizens to communicate about their worlds

1 Philip G. Cerny,
"Globalization
and the Changing
Logic of Collective
Action," *International
Organization* 49, no.
4 (1995), 595–625.

2 Bob Jessop,
"Liberalism,
Neoliberalism, and
Urban Governance:
A State-Theoretical
Perspective,"
Antipode 34, no. 3
(2002), 452–72.

Top
Through the Cent[er]
for Community
Engagement, Miam[i]
University architec[ture]
students worked
with the photogra[pher]
Jimmy Heath to ra[ise]
questions concern[ing]
neighborhood
gentrification, hou[sing]
abandonment,
and homelessnes[s]

Bottom
Examples of the
work of Yellow
Arrow, a global
public art initiative

3 Guillermo
Gómez-Peña,
"The Multicultural
Paradigm: An
Open Letter to
the National Arts
Community," in
Gerardo Mosquera,
ed., Beyond
the Fantastic
"London: Institute of
International Visual
Arts, 1996), 187.

4 Miami University
Center for
Community
Engagement in
Over-the-Rhine,
www.fna.muohio.
edu/cce.

5 This conception
differs from
antagonistic and
insurgent models
of citizenship.
For the latter, see
James Holston,
"Spaces of Insurgent
Citizenship,"
Planning Theory 13
(1995), 35–52.

6 Donald A.
Schön, Sanyal
Bish, and William
J. Mitchell, eds.,
High Technology
and Low-Income
Communities'
Prospects for
the Positive Use
of Advanced
Information
Technology
Cambridge, Mass.:
MIT Press, 1999).

7 Counts Media,
nc., "Yellow Arrow,"
www.yellowarrow.net.

and share their visions. Designers play a critical role in giving physical form to citizenship and engagement.

The Space of Recognition: Envisioning Citizenship

Taking action is a central right of citizenship. Active citizenship constructs new political and geographical boundaries beyond traditional licenses of sovereignty and legal status. It requires a definition of the rights, roles, and responsibilities of individuals and groups, and the promotion of values and ethics as a basis for personal action. Empowerment is grounded in the envisioning of citizenship.

Designers will gain from redefining themselves as "citizen-designers," for they are both members and enablers of communities. Designers are well situated to emphasize their role as citizens, because they already intervene directly in the world, stimulate dialogue, create physical and social spaces for others, and in some cases seek to redefine asymmetrical power relationships. Citizen-designers can play multiple roles in a broad democratic movement, including those of social thinkers, educators, and even "counter journalists, civilian diplomats, and human rights observers."[3] Such diverse engagement counteracts the typecasting of designers as service providers and the myth of the impartial expert.

Education plays an especially vital role in empowering a new generation of responsible citizen-designers. Particularly valuable are university programs and design centers that focus on social responsibility. For the past twenty-five years, one such program, Miami University's Center for Community Engagement, has been devoted to collaborating with neighborhood organizations in inner-city Cincinnati that struggle for human rights and social justice.[4] The center's site-specific installations, called Agit/Prop, draw attention to issues of public significance, reorienting consciousness and challenging the boundaries of claims to citizenship.

Unfortunately, such programs are the exception. The design and planning disciplines are too often complicit in the enclosure of the commons. Traditional norms of disciplinary expertise limit designers' capacity to frame projects and isolate them from the conse-

quences of their work. A politically engaged design that works toward justice will attempt to circumvent boundaries that impede democracy and will lay claim to a central role as an active agent within the community. Such work will be well served by working at multiple scales with communities and networks.

As citizens we have a personal obligation to define our values and ethics as the foundation for participation in the public arena. As citizen-designers, we must define the role of the design and planning disciplines in an increasingly pluralistic and global culture. Crossing boundaries of discipline and scale is the first step in enabling emergent forms of collaborations to flourish. The act of transgression allows for the co-creation of ideas in a participatory and dialogical fashion.

The Space of Engagement: Dialogical Participation

People are most effective in their role as citizens when they act as members of communities. A community may be best understood as a socially and politically specific group identity that is constituted by individuals who have a common set of values, concerns, or visions. The value of the community is twofold: it constructs a shared vision of the common good, and it creates new, alternative centers of power.[5] Communities also function as multiple and simultaneous centers to build associations and networks oriented to larger common goals.

Some argue that the mobile, networked nature of our society has led to isolation and placelessness, but we can turn this scenario to our advantage through the innovative use of network technologies to facilitate participatory democratic practices. Affordable Web-based tools have the potential to become a form of empowerment, particularly for the most disadvantaged populations.[6] For example, Yellow Arrow, a global public art project, takes advantage of ubiquitous communications technology to enable people to "point out what counts." Coded yellow arrow stickers placed in public spaces allow participants to view site-specific text messages on their mobile phones.[7] At the leading edge of what the geospatial web can do, Yellow Arrow initiatives have created psychogeographic maps, recounted public histories, and engaged community members in discussions of issues of common concern.

The Space of Materiality:
The Creative Commons

Designers materialize claims of citizenship in the public realm, bringing into form the confluence of social relations and material relations, practice and theory. The result is a breadth of material expressions rather than a singular hegemonic ideal. These artifacts embody the multicentric reality of civil society, and they act as snapshots of dynamic democracy. The built environment is recast as a collective resource: the "creative commons."

Public spaces in particular can materially express an embodied aesthetic comprising multiple identities and relations that all citizens have the right to claim.[8] The work of landscape architect Walter Hood emphasizes the accommodation of multiplicity. The investigations in his book *Urban Diaries* focus on the everyday activities of a full range of neighbors, from children to gardeners to the homeless, and propose an improvisational strategy of positive coexistence for the design of public spaces.

Material spaces reveal hidden social ecologies, express identities, and offer a means for deeper self-understanding. Public spaces can provide a basis for dialogue with others that can lead to the exchange of knowledge and the creation of understanding. Among the Northern Cheyenne in Montana, the explicit construction and expression of cultural and spatial narratives have been used as ways to build community and identity. A multiyear collaboration between the Indian reservation and Penn State University has resulted in the design and construction of public spaces, educational facilities, and a child-care center.

8 Don Mitchell, *Th Right to the City: S Justice and the Fig for Public Space* (New York: Guilfor Press, 2003).

Local youths, artists, and other community members have worked alongside university students and teachers to plan and execute projects that pass on indigenous forms of knowledge to younger generations. The tribe's traditional uses of the reservation landscape have served as inspiration for the design of public spaces, linking identity to place and strengthening ties to culture and the physical environment. For example, in the design of a courtyard symbolic of a Cheyenne campfire, words inscribed into stones were chosen by youth as a form of self-expression. Built environments also reveal the rich complexity of fluid, hybrid, and trans-local forms of citizenship and engagement. In the best circumstances, the built environment embodies the highest common aspirations and ideals of a community's citizens. More often, however, it reflects dominant values or the lowest common denominator of agreement. For this reason it is crucial to claim a space for engagement through participation and design.

Community gardens are an example of a production of space that springs from the direct involvement of citizens in everyday landscapes. The Union Avenue/César Chávez Community Garden, the second-oldest community garden in Los Angeles, represents a local vision to sustain a center of community for gardeners, schoolchildren, the elderly, and other residents. Designers make a vital contribution to such efforts by enabling self-expression and making material the values of self-determination and active citizenship.

Toward Democratic Design

Claims to spaces of recognition and engagement establish invested, critical roles for individuals and groups while proposing that a multiplicity of centers, sectors, and scales allows more effective action. In taking action, individuals seek a personal, collective,

Below
A courtyard on the campus of Chief Dull Knife College in Lame Deer, Montana, is symbolic of a Cheyenne campfire, where knowledge is imparted through storytelling.

and sometimes competing vision of the common good. The recognition of multiple publics challenges us to dispense with the convenient myth of a unified, liberal public that deliberates on issues of common interest and concern in a public forum.[9] The popular conception of the agora postulates an idealized public sphere of equal power relations in which a rational consensus can be reached. Conventional models of public decision-making such as "deliberative democracy" or "communicative planning" take as givens the existence of a singular public, the value of rational deliberation, and the capacity to reach a broad consensus.[10] Upon closer scrutiny, though, history reveals a public divided by gender, race, and class, leading to a broader recognition of the limits of deliberative democracy.

An alternative model, *agonistic democracy*, proposes that the existence of multiple publics and centers requires a conception of democracy that embraces difference and is realized through dialogue between adversarial parties.[11] In this model power is relational, and a "vibrant clash of democratic positions" is celebrated. Agonistic democracy values a democratic process in which multiple centers and identities advocate for their own interpretation of the common good. Importantly, this model seeks to avoid the worst-case endgame of achieving consensus by imposing an authoritarian order.

As the political theorist Chantal Mouffe succinctly argues, "The prime task of democratic politics is not to eliminate passions from the sphere of the public, in order to render a rational consensus possible, but to mobilize those passions towards democratic designs."[12] Planning theory has recognized the value of multiplicity in democratic discourse:

The organizational counterpart to this epistemological commitment is a structure for radical practice that consists of a large number of autonomous (or quasi-autonomous) centers of decision and action whose coordination remains loose and informal. Such a structure encourages a better fit with local environments, a great deal of local experimentation, a maximum of social mobilization, a self-reliant practice, and a non-dogmatic view of the problem. It is the very opposite of planning by the state, with its single-track

vision, its remoteness from people's everyday concerns, its tendency to gloss over differences in local conditions, and its hierarchical ladders.[13]

The aim of such network participation is to develop "emancipatory practices that seek to create a space for the collective self-production of life."[14] The result is change in societal and institutional structures as roles and responsibilities are redefined and enacted.

Democracy, as a system of decision-making and a mechanism for public action, can provide the means for the design and production of space. Multicentrism, agonistic democracy, and competing visions of the common good provide a perspective from which to consider an alternative practice of democratic design. Full civic participation in the creation of the built environment inspires competing visions of the common good. Within a reinvigorated vision of agonistic democracy, participation enables empowerment and bestows responsibility for realizing a vision of the future.

The quality of a democracy is ultimately determined by the ways in which power is distributed and used in collective decision-making.[15] How can we, as the planners and designers of the public realm, manifest agonistic and dialogical spaces that reflect a multicentric, dynamic vision of citizenship? Designers have long recognized that social problems cannot be solved through physical solutions alone. To that end we have created a newer field of practice that extends beyond professional technical assistance to include participation in efforts to enhance the social and economic well-being of cities, towns, and communities. In the United States this movement is called community design; it strives to discover "how to make it possible for people to be involved in shaping and managing their environment."[16]

Since the 1960s community designers have developed a range of strategies to improve the built environment while also building the capacity of groups and individuals. A core value of community design is advocacy, a multisectoral and multiscalar strategy in which coalitions organize around issues such as community development, affordable housing, or environmental justice. This proactive practice links participatory

9 Nancy Fraser, "Rethinking the Pu Sphere: A Contribu to the Critique of Actually Existing Democracy," in Fra Barker, Peter Hulm and Margaret Ivers eds., *Postmodernis and the Rereading Modernity* (New Yo Manchester Univer Press, 1992), 197–

10 Pauline M. McGuirk, "Situating Communicative Planning Theory: Context, Power, and Knowledge," *Environment and Planning A* 33 (200 195–217.

11 Chantal Mouffe, "Deliberative Democracy or Agonistic Pluralism *Social Research* 66 no. 3 (1999), 745–

12 Chantal Mouffe, "Deliberative Democracy or Agonistic Pluralism," *Reihe Politikwissenschaft Political Science Series* 72 (2000), 1

13 John Friedman, *Planning in the Pub Domain* (Princeton Princeton Universit Press, 1987), 395.

14 Ibid., 392.

15 A seminal work on the topic of citiz participation and power is Sherry Arnstein, "A Ladde Citizen Participatio in Richard T. LeGa and Frederic Stout, eds., *The City Read 240–52* (New York Routledge, 1996).

16 Henry Sanoff, "Origins of Community Desigr *Progressive Plannir* (winter 2005), 14.

17 Ibid.

techniques, which enable local groups to define problems, with design assistance to help them envision appropriate solutions. However, this conception of the designer-advocate still emphasizes professional and technical contributions. Henry Sanoff, a pioneer of community design and one of its leading educators, calls for a broader view: "The community design movement now faces a new challenge: to create a wider civic vision that crosses social and physical divides and promotes a broad understanding of social and environmental justice."[17] The creation and implementation of this wider vision are the aims of claiming public space.

Claiming Public Space
There is a crisis of the commons in contemporary society, a crisis inextricably linked to our vision of democracy and its expression in the built environment. Critiques of the predominant methods for production of space are growing, yet substantive dialogue and reflection are still lacking. Efforts to claim public space face an urgent need for the dissemination of useful knowledge, effective practices, and information on exemplary works.

Claiming public space will require simultaneous creative engagement by a broad array of citizens, groups, and networks. It will require retaking and critically reevaluating the spaces of recognition, engagement, and materiality. Designers can make a vital contribution to democratic design and the public realm through critical analysis, intellectual discourse, and knowledge production. This collective creative commons of projects, tools, and templates for action will expand the horizon of possibilities for improvement. Perhaps most importantly, designers can produce and valorize democratic social relations by making thoughtful contributions to the physical spaces where collective experiences occur.

Envisioning citizenship, redefining democratic participation, and building the creative commons are strategies for realizing an ethical involvement with democratic design. As an evolving project, claiming public space represents a form of design intelligence—a process that will give material expression to tomorrow's spaces of democratic engagement.

PUBLIC-INTEREST ARCHITEC-TURE

Mobilizing Mainstream Professionals to Work for the Public Good

JOHN PETERSON

**What strategies
can the traditional
architecture firm
use to contribute
to architecture as
a public service?**

Left
David Hecht for
Public Architecture
Rendering of Folsom
Street sidewalk
plaza, South of
Market area, San
Francisco. 2007

Ten years into my practice, I found myself in the same position that I imagine many firm principals do: yearning to provide a richer experience for myself and my staff, one that extended beyond the high-end residential and commercial jobs that constituted the bulk of our commissions. I wanted to work on projects that would engage a wider range of clients and have an impact on a broader segment of our community. Thus, looking for opportunities outside of our normal clientele, I did what so many of us do: I considered having our office enter an open design competition.

As I perused the available competitions I began to think critically about the nature of design competitions. Consider the hundreds upon hundreds of proposals submitted to each competition, representing countless ideas and thousands of hours of labor. The vast majority of this work ends up on storage-room shelves or in rarely seen portfolios. Even the winners often get little in return for the time they spend, with many competition projects never being realized.

Why is our profession so willing to accept such a meager return on our investment of that most precious resource, our time? Is this the most effective allocation of our energy and ideas? In response to these concerns, our firm decided to identify a design opportunity closer to home and with a greater chance for real impact.

For our first effort we focused our energies on developing an open-space strategy for San Francisco's South of Market area. Originally a light-industrial zone and now mixed-use, South of Market possesses little recreational open space for its growing and very diverse inhabitants and users. Our proposal sparked a dialogue within multiple city agencies; it directly influenced the development of the city's Rincon Hill plan; and it became the subject of an unprecedented day-long workshop that included more than thirty-five city agency and community leaders.

The need for public open space in urban places like San Francisco's South of Market is not new. SoMa, as a light industrial/warehouse district, has always been home to thousands of workers as well as residents who could have benefited from such spaces. The area was not, however, planned with open space in mind, and existing public areas are limited in number, size, and accessibility. Today the need for open space is even greater. The future health of this diverse urban fabric depends, in large measure, on open-space development.

Public Architecture's open strategy proposes to reconfigure Folsom and Howard as two-way streets, while still accommodating intensive traffic. Additionally, Folsom would be more pedestrian-oriented, with generous sidewalks creating new spaces for a variety of outdoor activities and urban amenities. The incremental installation of diverse public amenities, keyed to the particular conditions of SoMa's varying uses, makes for a responsive, rather than prescriptive, urban plan. The plan quickly earned support from the San Francisco Planning Department, the Redevelopment Agency, and the Transportation Authority, and funds are being sought to implement a series of sidewalk plazas along Folsom Street.

The positive impact of this effort begs the question, shouldn't there be an organization that positions designers to be problem identifiers as well as problem solvers? That question inspired the creation of Public Architecture and, soon after, our 1% Solution program, which was subsequently renamed "The 1%."

Pro Bono: For the Public Good

The phrase "pro bono" is shortened from the Latin *pro bono publico*, which means "for the public good." Pro bono work is generally defined as services rendered free of charge or at a significant reduction in fees for people in need or charitable organizations supporting underserved communities. Architects regularly field requests to do pro bono work from communities, non-profit organizations, and religious groups. Unfortunately, very few firms have institutionalized ways to respond to these requests, and even fewer have set expectations for these projects on par with their regular fee-based work.

Pro bono work includes architectural services for projects leading to construction as well as any activity that engages public policy, such as service on volunteer boards and commissions, participation in community design charrettes, and advising public-policy bodies. It can also include speculative work and other forms of research, provided that these efforts benefit the public or otherwise engage positive change in the public realm.

Liability issues often make architects reluctant to perform pro bono work. Liability is a reality of architectural practice, whether or not we are paid for our services. Professional liability insurance plans cover pro bono work, but the professionals involved should fully understand their coverage as well as their level of exposure. This exposure can be limited by including provisions in the contract that reasonably share the legal responsibility with the client. Liability issues should be addressed and resolved as early as possible in the process of doing pro bono work.

For all of its challenges, pro bono work can render a number of benefits to the service provider. In the setting of a firm it can function as a recruitment and retention tool, a professional development and mentoring opportunity, and a way to gain exposure to new markets and project types. Young architects may find pro bono projects to be particularly appealing, as they can yield direct client interaction, valuable portfolio material, and early built work.

The fact of the matter is that architect registration creates a virtual monopoly for architects and fosters an economic hierarchy that makes architectural services less available to a large segment of our society. We believe that professionals have an obligation to provide pro bono services, and that this obligation arises from the economics of licensure as much as it does from the ethical imperative to provide for those in need.

For architects the vast majority of awards, press coverage, and practice resources are geared toward fee-based jobs. Pro bono work is mostly done on a catch-as-catch-can basis, slipped in between paying projects. The primary cause of this laissez-faire approach is that there is no professional support or recognition of public-interest work in architecture. This is not to say that architecture firms and professionals are not already generous with their time; but the profession as a whole has never viewed pro bono service as a fundamental obligation of professional standing or as an integral component of a healthy business model.

Going Public with Public Architecture

Within our own firm, Peterson Architects, we discovered that our vision for pro bono work was greater than what we could create on our own. This realization inspired the establishment of Public Architecture, a nonprofit organization that puts the resources of architecture at the service of the public interest. Public Architecture acts as a catalyst for public discourse through education, advocacy, and the design of public spaces and amenities. Rather than waiting for clients or funding, we identify and solve practical problems of human interaction in the built environment. Our first three pro bono design projects were the open-space strategy for San Francisco's South of Market area; design interventions for day-laborer gathering spots; and an initiative to add small secondary dwelling units to single-family lots. In some instances Peterson Architects provides pro bono services, as in the facilities we designed for Homeless Prenatal Program. In other cases, including the Day Labor Station and the Accessory Dwelling Unit, Public Architecture acts as the catalyst to bring other talented architects and designers to focus on a particular need and issue.

The contributions of day laborers typically go unseen, and the inability of most cities to accommodate them within the urban infrastructure is highly visible. Because of their role in the informal economy, day laborers have been forced to occupy spaces meant for other uses, such as street corners, gas stations, and home-improvement store parking lots. A relatively small number of officially sanctioned day labor centers have appeared in recent years, but the informal gathering sites remain the norm and are far from ideal. Their presence in spaces designated for other uses means they often lack even the most basic amenities, such as shelter, water, or toilet facilities.

The Day Labor Station is a project that we are developing to address the needs of a community that traditionally has not had access to well-designed environments. The station is a simple, flexible structure that can be deployed at these informal day labor locations. It is a self-sustaining project that will utilize green materials and strategies and will exist primarily, if not completely, off

the grid. Our design is based on the realities of the ways in which the day labor system operates, and responds to the needs and desires of the day laborers themselves, as our clients. As such, the structure will be flexible enough to serve such varied uses as an employment center, meeting space, and classroom.

Another Public Architecture design effort addresses the accelerating need for affordable, multigenerational, sustainably designed housing. Accessory Dwelling Units (ADUs)—more commonly known as in-law units, secondary apartments, or granny flats—are viable mechanisms for filling this need without dramatically changing the character of existing neighborhoods or communities. Recognizing this fact, the state of California recently revised crucial legislation to encourage such development, and similar efforts are under way in municipalities across the country. To date, no group—be it homebuilders, buyers, or owners—has capitalized on the potential of ADUs. However, it is only a matter of time before ADUs become the norm rather than the exception.

In 2003 the city of Santa Cruz invited Peterson Architects and six other firms to design a variety of ADU typologies. Peterson Architects developed a 500-square-foot detached single-story ADU using alternative materials and construction techniques. The proposal makes use of low-cost, high-performance, and often unconventional building systems in a simple and direct, low-gable, backyard structure. The wall system comprises prefabricated insulated aluminum panels developed for commercial refrigeration buildings. The primary fenestration is glazed garage doors that enable the small dwelling to open to the adjacent private garden. The planted roof offers low runoff, high insulation, and is a nod to the rear-yard context.

Public Architecture is a new model for architectural practice. Supported by the generosity of foundation, corporate, and individual grants and donations, Public Architecture works outside the economic constraints of conventional architectural practice, providing a venue where architects can work for the public good. Rather than waiting for commissions that represent well-understood needs and desires, we

Above
Patrick Perez for
Public Architectu[re]
Rendering of
Accessory Dwell[ing]
Unit prototype. 20[

take a leadership role, identifying significant problems of wide relevance that require innovative research and design. We seek needs and desires that are palpable but poorly defined, in circumstances where both client and financing must be imagined in new ways. Each of the designs described above was conceived as a prototype for adoption in other cities across the country, a criterion for every Public Architecture project.

The 1%

In an effort to engage other architects in public-service work and to develop a stronger culture of pro bono service within the profession, in 2005 Public Architecture launched a national campaign that came to be called The 1%. Supported by a grant from the National Endowment for the Arts, the campaign challenges architecture firms to contribute a minimum of 1 percent of their working hours to pro bono service. The 1% focuses on firms rather than individuals in recognition of the fact that the policies and practices of firms are crucial in making it both possible and desirable for individual employees to undertake pro bono work.

One percent of the standard 2,080-hour work year equals twenty hours annually, which represents a modest, but not trivial, individual contribution to the public good. If all members of the architecture profession were to contribute twenty hours per year, the aggregate contribution would approach 5 million hours per year—the equivalent of a 2,500-person firm working full-time for the public good.

The goal of The 1% program is to increase significantly both the quantity and quality of architectural services performed in the public interest. By making public-interest work a regular part of architectural practice, The 1% enhances the profession's engagement with the community, bridging a widely perceived gap between the two. By sharing guidelines and documenting model efforts of public-interest practice, the program increases the effectiveness of architects' contributions to society. And by demonstrating the value of architectural services, The 1% has increased popular awareness of the value of design in the built environment.

To Start a Nonprofit or Not to Start a Nonprofit

One thing I would like to make clear is that forming a nonprofit organization is probably one of the *least* efficient ways for mainstream firms and professionals to do public-interest work. The solution for the dearth of public-service work in architecture is not more nonprofit organizations, but more and better public-interest projects. Don't start a nonprofit unless you feel the work you are planning to do absolutely requires a separate organization or nonprofit identity to be effective. In general, there are no special opportunities exclusively available to nonprofits. Even pursuing grant or foundation money that requires nonprofit status can be easily addressed by using a fiscal sponsor or partner.

Working within your existing firm or employment structure offers other advantages: there's no need to create or manage a corporation with a board of directors, and a private firm is likely to be more flexible with its money and mission. In short, there is virtually nothing that a nonprofit like Public Architecture can do that you can't do right now.

Managing Pro Bono Clients

Like all clients and projects, pro bono clients and projects deserve and require a significant amount of attention. Also, like many paying clients, pro bono clients may have little or no experience with the process of selecting or working with an architect. The good news is that all of the same "rules" apply to pro bono and paying clients alike.

The best way for your firm to handle pro bono clients and jobs is to give them precisely the same level of care that you do your regular paying clients and projects. Designate a single contact on your staff, and ask them to do the same. Make clear the value that your work brings to their organization, perhaps even in terms of time or money. We strongly recommend "invoicing" your pro bono clients against an agreed upon budget of time that you are providing. This will help build the client's understanding of the work you do and their appreciation of the value of your time. Most important, it reinforces the fact that your time is not limitless.

Initiating Projects, with or without Clients
One of Public Architecture's guiding principles is the belief that architects should be proactive, particularly in situations where clients and financing must be imagined in new ways.

Here are five suggestions for how your firm might go about initiating and pursuing a project, with or without a client:

1. Create a competition of one.
Traditional competition structures can be used to facilitate an intra-staff exploration of social issues.

2. Use your insight to start a dialogue.
Developing and illustrating solutions to age-old social issues can be a powerful and rewarding effort.

3. Partner with others.
Use a pro bono project as an opportunity to collaborate with artists, community leaders, contractors, city agencies, and even firms that normally would be competitors.

4. Adopt a nonprofit.
You can be a great asset to an organization or community group struggling to deal with physical-facility issues.

5. Seek recognition for your cause.
Editors and publishers are always on the lookout for public-interest stories, particularly ones that include a graphic vision.

What You Can Do Personally
There are countless things you can do as an individual to expand your work and be more active as a citizen-architect. Take it upon yourself to identify a problem in the public realm and pursue a solution. You can choose a known problem, or you might expose one that has been overlooked. Do it alone or build a team. You may not have all the answers, and that is fine; just be prepared to do what it takes to move the idea or project forward. If your proposal resonates with people, you may be surprised by how much interest and support your efforts generate.

Design: The Center of It All
I am proud of the design work that my firm and staff have generated over the past decade. Our projects have increased in quality and complexity, and we have had multiple return clients. Starting Public Architecture, however, is undoubtedly our most far-reaching endeavor. Although I did not initially set out to establish a nonprofit organization, Public Architecture has the potential to become far more important as a vehicle for shaping the built environment than anything I could ever do in private practice. Still, the act of designing our surroundings remains my foremost passion, and I have worked hard to keep that focus at the forefront of my efforts as a leader in these two related but very different organizations.

The Community Design Collaborative: A Volunteer-Based Community Design Center Serving Greater Philadelphia

DARL RASTORFER

A long-standing, successful community design center connects communities in need with experienced professional volunteers for win-win results.

The Community Design Collaborative's long history and high level of sustained engagement may seem surprising given the fact that the services it offers come through the volunteer efforts of design and construction professionals. The Community Design Collaborative (the Collaborative) is, nevertheless, a productive, smoothly operating contributor to the Philadelphia region. One key to the organization's enduring success is the narrow scope of assistance it offers.

Collaborative volunteers singularly focus on the initial steps of a project, providing community-based nonprofit clients with predevelopment services. Volunteers evaluate sites, survey buildings, assess structural, mechanical, and electrical systems, analyze space and accessibility needs, write requests for proposals, design conceptual plans, and offer opinions of probable cost. This scope of work lowers a formidable barrier faced by many nonprofit organizations. Typically, nonprofits are not well funded; they must raise money for projects involving construction. They can successfully do this *after* a thoughtful and credible plan is in hand, but nonprofits rarely have both the expertise to find appropriate professionals for predevelopment planning and the finances to pay for the service. It's a catch-22: there is no capital funding without predevelopment, but there can be no predevelopment until there are resources to hire design professionals. Enter the Collaborative volunteers. Their pro bono contributions get nonprofit projects moving and direct them toward cost-effective, competent, community-oriented conclusions.

Currently more than six hundred volunteers in Greater Philadelphia and southern New Jersey contribute community service through the Collaborative. Volunteers work in teams of two to six individuals over a six-month period. Traditionally, the teams comprise individual contributors drawn from firms and disciplines within the architecture, construction, and engineering industries. More recently, area firms have internally assembled teams to work with a Collaborative client. In 2006 alone, thirty-one design firms and eighty-seven design professionals volunteered to deliver more than $550,000 in pro bono preliminary design services to forty-seven nonprofit organizations throughout Greater Philadelphia.

All of the Collaborative's predevelopment projects culminate in the production of a report that includes drawings, photographs, a narrative, and a cost estimate. The report gives the nonprofit's governing board solid information upon which to base decision-making regarding a proposed project's feasibility. If the nonprofit decides to move forward, the report will be essential to its community organizing and fundraising efforts. The Collaborative's services have enabled nonprofit organizations to obtain funds (typically in amounts ranging from $30,000 to $100,000) for further planning, resource development, and physical improvements.

Nonprofits that seek preliminary design services apply to the Collaborative. The staff project architect screens applications and conducts site visits, offering an early consultation and determination of an appropriate scope of service. Grants are awarded by the Collaborative Project Selection Committee on a quarterly basis, and the staff tailors and recruits volunteer teams based on the scale of the approved project. Following an orientation meeting with Collaborative staff, teams work directly with the client. To ensure the quality of the work performed under the Collaborative's auspices, each group of volunteers is assigned a leader and undertakes two peer reviews during the course of the project, one at the midpoint and one at the conclusion. Upon the project's completion, the team presents its work and reviews the final report with the client.

Community Design Collaborative volunteers have completed nearly five hundred predevelopment projects since 1991. Collaborative clients include community development corporations, housing providers, park associations, childcare providers, public libraries, community recreation associations, economic development corporations, and the public school system. Three recent projects are profiled in the following sections.

Infill Housing for the
Allegheny West Foundation

Ron Hinton, Jr., is the president of a community development corporation in North Philadelphia, the Allegheny West Foundation, which focuses on comprehensive community-building through programs that include education, career counseling and placement, community organizing, and housing rehabilitation. Hinton first approached the Collaborative in 2002 because he wanted fresh ideas for contextual residences he was seeking to build on vacant lots created by row-house demolition. He was particularly intrigued with the design possibilities that might emerge if two narrow lots were combined into a single property.

The Allegheny West Foundation's request encouraged the Collaborative to recruit its first project fully staffed with volunteers from a single firm. The predevelopment service was staffed by employees of Francis Cauffman Foley Hoffmann, Architects, a multidisciplinary practice of 135 professionals that provides integrated architecture, planning, and interior-design services. Participation in the project presented the firm with an opportunity to offer professional development for its associates, allowing them to earn credits toward the National Council of Architectural Registration Board's Intern Development Program in-house.

The volunteer architects were asked to explore design options for fourteen vacant mid-block lots on Somerset and Garnet Streets. Seven volunteers participated through two teams, each led by a registered architect. The prototypes they developed used a traditional row-house vocabulary of bay windows, cornices, and zero setbacks, but they took advantage of double-wide lots to offer off-street parking, decks, and spacious living rooms.

The staff of the Allegheny West Foundation was impressed with the volunteers' research and with their ability to design architecturally interesting affordable housing. Allegheny West Foundation presented the volunteers' conceptual plans and elevations to the Redevelopment Authority, Philadelphia's Office of Housing and Community Development, and the Pennsylvania Housing Finance Agency. Together the three agencies allocated $1.2 million to redevelop the fourteen lots

into nine units for home ownership. Allegheny West Foundation constructed all nine homes, which are now occupied.

Two years after the Collaborative provided its first pro bono service grant to Allegheny West Foundation (valued at $26,000 [320 hours]), Hinton returned to the Collaborative for site-specific assistance for the 2700 block of North Gratz Street, also in North Philadephia. (Nonprofits apply to the Collaborative for a service grant just as they apply to foundations for financial grants.) A volunteer team provided a pro bono service grant of $8,200 (110 hours) that generated schematic designs for new housing on vacant lots at the end of the block.

The Allegheny West Foundation is currently working with Blackney Hayes Architects, a firm it hired to develop house plans for additional double-wide lots in the neighborhood.

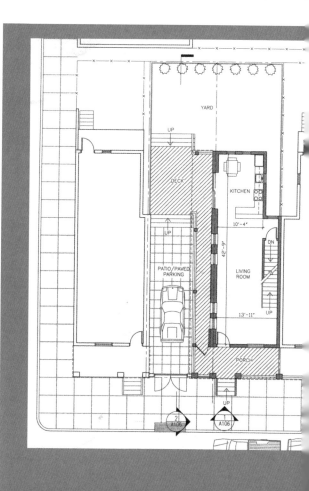

Cedar Park Renovation

Cedar Park is a leafy destination for residents near Baltimore Avenue and 50th Street in West Philadelphia. Though not large—about 45,000 square feet—the triangular park boasts mature trees and a handsome World War I memorial. Despite these attributes, crumbling paths, hazardous play equipment, and a growing number loiterers congregated, called for the removal of a waist-high chain-link fence that encircles the park, resurfaced existing pathways, widened the walkway between the actively used playground equipment on the east end of the park and the war memorial on the west end, introduced more seating along that path, and softened the memorial plaza with new plantings.

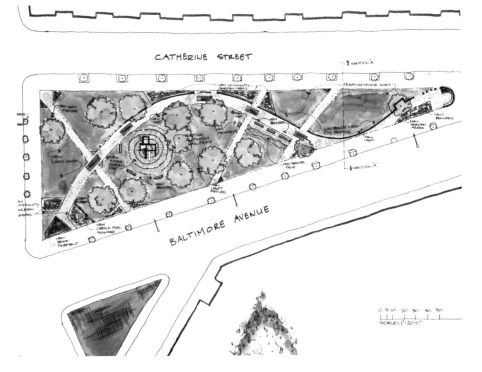

of loiterers concerned local residents and members of Cedar Park Neighbors, a local association. Members took action by launching an effort to restore the park. They hoped funding would become available once a professionally prepared plan was in place. Cedar Park Neighbors contacted the Collaborative for assistance, and Collaborative volunteers worked with the association in early 2004.

The Collaborative's team visited the park and met with a small group from Cedar Park Neighbors to learn about the client organization's concerns and ambitions. The team developed a plan, presented it to the association, and revised it based on comments from community members. The final proposal added lighting where

Collaborative volunteers accompanied representatives of Cedar Park Neighbors to the City of Philadelphia Recreation Department's meetings to present the renovation scheme. Based on the plan, cost estimates, and the team's presentation, the Recreation Department pledged $100,000 toward the total renovation budget. The Collaborative's services represented an in-kind value of $10,700 (131 hours), and the association raised approximately $70,000 more from private foundations. Maureen Tate, the president of Cedar Park Neighbors, acknowledges the seminal role that design volunteers played in the project, stating, "The Collaborative helped us move from a broad vision to a credible plan."

The City of Philadelphia Recreation Department hired Lager Raabe Skafte Landscape Architects to develop and detail the Collaborative's conceptual plan and manage much of the park's transformation. In November 2006 Cedar Park Neighbors hosted a rededication ceremony for the newly renovated park. The community group recently received an additional $100,000 state grant for the installation of playground equipment.

As stewards of public open space, Cedar Park Neighbors has demonstrated that it is focused, persistent, and adept at drawing others into their project as they realize the improvements that the Collaborative helped develop.

Woolston Child and Family Center: An Adaptive Reuse

The Preschool Project is a nonprofit provider of affordable child care, an advocate for high-quality child care, and a provider of child-care training. For years the organization leased office space for its staff and training activities, but it wanted a building of its own. In 2001 the Preschool Project learned that facility funds were available through the regional office of Head Start if they could submit a credible building plan before the funding deadline.

Also in 2001 the diminishing congregation of the East Baptist Church allowed the Preschool Project to purchase its building in the Fishtown neighborhood for $1. The church's offer and the Preschool Project's ambitions seemed to be a perfect match, but the deadline for Head Start's funding program was fast approaching. As part of the funding application, the Preschool Project needed an architectural survey of the church building and qualified assurances that the structure could be converted into a preschool center with an after-school program, staff offices, and a training facility. With no money for predevelopment services, the nonprofit turned to the Community Design Collaborative for help.

Three Collaborative volunteers measured the church, prepared drawings, and created timely application materials that secured the Preschool Project's grant. As the business manager for the Preschool Project explained, "We didn't have any money to hire design professionals, yet we needed

professionally done drawings in order to attract funders. The Collaborative's work was essential in allowing us to approach funders." "It was not a big project," observes Michelle Robinson, the volunteer architect who led the effort, "but it was a key project at a crucial time." The Collaborative's in-kind service was valued at $2,500 (40 hours).

In the second phase the former sanctuary (which is one story above ground level) and its balcony were reconfigured to house staff offices, storage for training material, a space for preschoolers and their caregivers, and activity areas for an after-school program. The first phase was completed in 2003 with $800,000 provided by PNC Bank, the Philadelphia Department of Human Services, Head Start, the William Penn Foundation, the Nonprofit Finance Fund, and other funders. Phase two was completed in 2005.

In all its undertakings the Collaborative aims to help its clients build neighborhoods, and together the Collaborative and its clients have become successful neighborhood developers.

Many factors contribute to the Collaborative's success. First and foremost its volunteer service is confined to predevelopment assistance. Second, the organization continually adapts its way of practicing to better serve evolving needs. For example, when recruiting midlevel and senior professionals to volunteer teams became challenging, the Collaborative began asking single firms to volunteer. The firms assembled a team within their ranks that included midlevel and senior staff. The Collaborative is driven by a skilled staff and board of directors, close ties with the Philadelphia chapter of the American Institute of Architects, and an enthusiastic, knowledge-able volunteer corps. An established force in its region, the Community Design Collaborative offers a worthy model for community-conscious design and construction professionals everywhere.

Above
AK Architecture Woolston Child and Family Center. The former sanctuary and balcony now house staff offices and activity areas.

A funding flow began, and the church's conversion was divided into two phases. The Preschool Project hired AK Architecture LLC for both phases, but the Collaborative was involved only in phase one. During the first phase the overall structure was stabilized and four classroom spaces were created on the ground level for fifty-four preschoolers.

Invisible Zagreb

DAMIR BLAŽEVIĆ

**Guerilla tactics
activate an
abandoned
city and inspire
the potential
to claim space
for public use.**

Platforma 9.81, the architecture and media collective that I coordinate, is focusing right now on the empty spaces in the city of Zagreb, the capital of Croatia. We have been mapping these abandoned spaces in an ongoing project called Invisible Zagreb. We say "invisible" because these spaces—empty lots, empty buildings—are totally unnoticed by the city; they are not used by the citizens or the public, so we have been using different tactics to render these spaces visible. Ten or 15 percent of this activity is architectural design, and most of it is something else.

Croatia was a part of Yugoslavia, which was part of the Communist bloc. Before 1990 people didn't own their apartments, the government did. Many of the users of these apartments had tenants' rights or something similar. It was a "supercollective" state, where private property was neglected and unimportant. Until 1990 there were no "No Trespassing" signs in Croatia, though you can see them there now.

The government and the municipalities—the almighty state—were the planner, executor, financer, investor, and designer of all types of space. The implementation of building projects and every subsequent decision were carried out by the all-powerful state. So the planner—the state—relied on its own power to expropriate the land, tear down the houses, and build whatever was good for the collective. However, after the war in Croatia and the change of the social system in the 1990s, after which the state was no longer so powerful, the number of state-built dwellings decreased. Most development activity went into private hands; we now call it a "superprivate" development model. The first shopping mall in Croatia was built in 1995. As you can imagine, it was a real shock to a country that had had a supercollective state.

The new private-development model has influenced the public domain. Zagreb has approximately 6.5 million square feet of buildings, and two-thirds of these, or 4.3 million square feet, are residential. The city has only 3,000 square feet of high schools, however, which is about two or three classrooms. The recent increase in residential construction generated the need for school space for 13,000 pupils, which

equals 0.23 square feet per pupil in the high schools. Private kindergartens started popping up all over the place, like in the garage of a small apartment building. This is an example of the privatization of public space.

There are about sixty empty lots and buildings in Zagreb, many a consequence of unresolved ownership issues. Some of them are owned by the government, some by the city, some by private investors. Because they are owned they cannot be developed, so these spaces are abandoned and unused. We have claimed many of these spaces, even though we, as a nonprofit organization, do not have the legal right to manage them. Strengthening the public domain through the use of public space is the most important thing an architect can do in Croatia today. This is probably also true in most of the other transitional countries in Europe, such as Bulgaria, the Czech Republic, Poland, and Romania.

Our first step in claiming some of these unused spaces was to begin making a map and a database of them. We made the information public by publishing the map in national newspapers. The project is ongoing; we will also publish the map and the database on the Internet so the public can use it.

Zagreb has a very active cultural scene. When the war was over, all the nongovernmental and nonprofit organizations that had been devoted to wartime initiatives and peace movements shifted into the cultural sphere. So we have many independent organizations that are receiving international recognition but are not properly supported by the national or municipal government. They have grown strong, yet they do not have their own spaces to work in and their future is in jeopardy.

On the other hand, Zagreb has a lot of empty space.

We said, "Okay, let's give them space to work in, and let's fill the empty spaces with cultural programs."

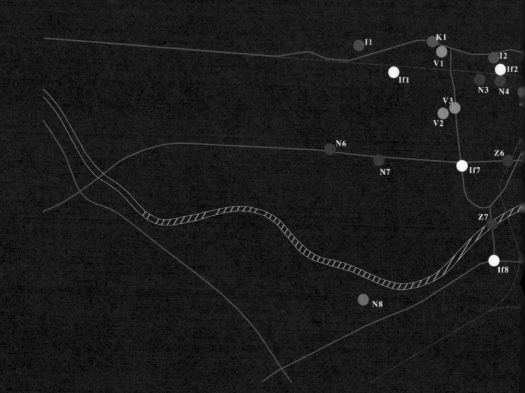

industrial
industrial private
cultural
cultural private
infrastructure
commercial
commercial private
military
unreserved chamber
unreserved chamber private

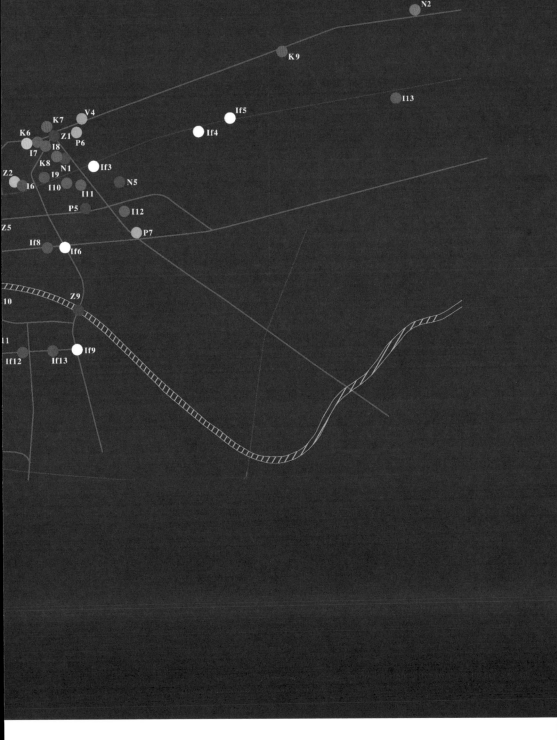

We reached out to these organizations to demonstrate what the spaces were about and how they could be used for their cultural activities. Then Platforma, collaborating with a variety of organizations, started to colonize these spaces, outsourcing work in areas where we as designers had limited knowledge.

Last year we had fifty or sixty different events in these spaces. At a former slaughterhouse we organized concerts; at a former textile factory we organized a theater production. We moved an existing art exhibition—a very formal and very popular one—from an institutional government exhibition setting in the city center to one of these empty spaces on the outskirts of the city. We claimed the space in another unused factory building, got permission from the owners, and came up with the exhibition design. In the process we collaborated with many different sources, communicating with the artists and the organizers of the show. We asked the national army to lend us some equipment, and borrowed shipping containers from a bankrupt company that didn't need them anymore; each container housed a different piece of art. This was all done more or less for free.

In another instance we worked with Swedish artist Mihel Von Hausfelf. He went into an old liquor factory and designed a light installation; we were unable to use the space in any other way because the building was in bad shape and we couldn't get a permit or meet fire regulations.

We also used a former cinema as the location for a symposium. We met with the organizers of the symposium and let them influence the design for their event; and we as designers, in return, influenced their program. We wound up creating a sort of hybrid program that could be used for the symposium and then the same space was utilized afterwards for a dance, followed by an electronic music event. By covering the floor of the old cinema space with white plastic, we transformed it into a dance floor. Upstairs on the balcony we showed movies made by some of the independent video artists who participated in the earlier symposium. The soundtrack from their videos was broadcast on headphones.

With these events, we wanted to create a spontaneous experience that could be organized quickly, gathering people together in one place to emphasize the physicality of shared space. We wanted to create a public space, even if was for just one night. By creating temporary public events around the city, the public domain is strengthened.

The concerts we organized in the abandoned slaughterhouse attracted four or five thousand people. In the same way that we achieved a critical mass of empty spaces, we were able to generate a critical mass of people who wanted to participate in the events held in these spaces, by heavily publicizing the events on national television or in the newspapers. This gave us the power to influence the decision makers and the owners of the spaces.

A lot of the spaces on our map actually overlap with places the city owns and, thus, where it can control a public architectural competition or the designs for a master plan. This overlap has allowed us to become consultants, in a sense, for the city of Zagreb. We will sit on juries for the major competitions, and be present at the meetings of those who make decisions about the city's master plan and the type of uses that will be assigned to these spaces. This will allow us to strategically influence the future development of the city. We can make our analyses and demonstrate the cultural potential of different plans. We can show how the public domain can be included in new schemes, whether a space will be residential, commercial, or put to a different purpose altogether. We hope to include permanent public spaces in all these plans.

I do not know if we will succeed. If we have sixty open spaces around the city, I think it will be an achievement to secure public domain in ten or fifteen of those sites. We will see.

Editors' note: This article is adapted from the transcript of a lecture delivered by the author at the fifth annual "Structures for Inclusion" conference, held on April 2, 2005, in New York City.

Top and bottom
Mihel Von Hausfe
Light installation
in a former liquor
factory, Zagreb

cityworksLosAngeles:
Making Differences, Big or Small

ELIZABETH MARTIN AND
LESLIE THOMAS

How can we
create standards
of practice to
address the
challenges of
delivering pro
bono architect-
ural services,
especially in an
urban setting?

Left
Chantal Aquin
and Rocio Romero
Service Spot,
downtown Los
Angeles. 2001

A few years ago, immediately after the too-early death of Samuel Mockbee, a memorial to Mockbee and a subsequent series of roundtables inspired by the work of the Rural Studio brought together a startlingly high number of Los Angeles professionals, academics, and students who admired Mockbee's work but were frustrated by the lack of perceived opportunities for them to contribute to their communities through pro bono design and construction efforts.

The strong attendance at the roundtables made clear that while many projects were under way to provide pro bono work to clients in need, these efforts tended to be both smaller and more complicated than anyone wanted them to be. The vast amount of labor that it took to complete each project seemed out of proportion with its modest outcome, especially when compared to the work produced by the Rural Studio. That group consistently produced four or five new buildings from the ground up each year, but community design projects in Los Angeles seemed limited to community gardens, street furniture, interior renovations, facade upgrades, and projects of similarly size.

The roundtable participants realized that there was a lack of infrastructure to support meaningful community-level pro bono work in an urban setting, and discussions quickly blossomed to encompass a larger desire for constructive social engagement by architecture/design professionals, the building industry, and students. The collegiality created during these discussions led to the creation of a grassroots organization called cityworksLosAngeles. The cityworksLos-Angeles group began its task by asking the question, "How can we apply the Rural Studio's successful philosophy to an urban setting?"

Assessment

The major issues discussed by group members fell into two categories: design and construction. In the design category there were three main issues. First, design schools could not consistently find architecture and engineering firms that were willing to stamp their drawings so that they could complete working drawings. Second, it was difficult to partner with potential pro bono clients because such clients generally did not work on an academic timetable. Third, professional firms of architects and engineers were so afraid of errors-and-omissions liability that they could not take on the projects.

In the construction category four issues emerged. First, academic administrators did not feel there was room in the curriculum to devote full studio time to design/build projects. Additionally, schools did not permit students to do on-site construction because of health-insurance liability. Third, individual professionals who wanted to do construction and had their own insurance could not organize a coherent, consistent team that would see a project through to the end; and they generally could not build a project on their own, either. Finally, contractors doing nonprofit work who might otherwise have been interested in partnering with schools did not want students on their construction sites for liability reasons.

The attempt to merge activism and design in an urban setting is fraught with complications. Many of the activities involved in the Rural Studio's ten years of noble and elegant projects are thwarted on multiple levels when brought to the environ-ment of the megalopolis. For instance, rural communities often have no permits, inspections, or enforced building codes, allowing academics and professionals to use their best judgment in architectural planning and structural design, which can lead to an efficient process and an elegant outcome. In the city of Los Angeles, however, there are thousands of pages of enforced codes, a lengthy review process, and many specialty review boards.

The discussion highlighted other challenges. For example, the cost of land in urban areas is completely prohibitive for most potential local clients, in contrast with land in rural areas, which tends to be much more affordable. The culture of litigation in the urban environment is also a dilemma. Clients are potential legal adversaries if a project does not come to a mutually satisfactory conclusion. If there is a failure in the built product, the stamping architect or engineer is responsible and can be easily sued. Finally, the cost of living in rural areas is low enough that students at Auburn University in Alabama, for instance, where the Rural Studio is located, are often able to extend their time in the program for an additional year to complete their construction work. The cost of living in a major urban center would make similar extensions impossible for most students.

After several months of discussions the group decided that members of Los Angeles's design and architecture schools should loosely affiliate into one big urban studio, in order to provide support for members of the community trying to work in the pro bono arena, both in design and in design/build.

Urban Testimonials

One participant in the early cityworksLos-Angeles discussions was Jim Bonar, director of Skid Row Housing Trust, an organization that provides permanent housing and support services for the residents of Los Angeles's Skid Row neighborhood. Bonar talked about the design of the Housing Trust's new service center, the Service Spot. Located on the ground floor of one of the organization's single-room-occupancy hotels, Service Spot needed to be a user-friendly center that would offer case management, support group meetings, educational opportunities, and service referrals for Skid Row residents.

Project designers Chantal Aquin and Rocio Romero sought to make their design reflect the open and friendly relationship that the Skid Row Housing Trust has with its clients. "When it comes to designing for the homeless or mentally ill, there's typically a sense of fear there, because it's sometimes difficult to anticipate their behavior," explains Aquin. "The design usually has lots of barriers and a very distinct separation between public and private spaces. But we wanted users of our design to feel a sense of ownership of these spaces. We also wanted the residents to feel as though they were given something precious, not just services contained within blank walls." The designers proposed a mix of public and private spaces, with corridors that promote free circulation.

While planning the renovation of the Service Spot, the designers conceived the idea of creating a furniture-design studio that would provide the Service Spot with custom-designed furnishings. With funding from the Los Angeles Department of Cultural Affairs, furniture-workshop students from the Southern California Institute of Architecture (SCI-Arc) undertook the studio as a community-service project under the leadership of SCI-Arc senior faculty member Randall Wilson. Wilson led an intensive summer studio that included a rigorous design process, after which students built and installed computer workstations, filing trolleys and file cabinets, stacking conference tables, kitchen cabinets, and a copy center.

Though Bonar was skeptical of their ability to furnish the space, students received material donations from Home Depot, Anderson Plywood, and Häfele, and they were able to outfit the entire 2,000-square-foot space. "These projects often become more inventive through the help of architecture students," Bonar says, "which is a powerful tool for creating well-designed spaces for everyone."

Building on his work in fabricating furniture, Wilson spent the next summer with his SCI-Arc students producing furniture for a counseling center for battered women and their children in south-central Los Angeles. Wilson always starts off his classes by assuring that the students understand what they are making before they attempt to reinvent or re-create it. Wilson insists that the objects meet their functional requirements: a chair must support a seated person, and a cabinet must safely store its contents. Wilson's classes are heavily weighted with social discourse, but he also says that making beautiful objects for a person in need is important. To fulfill the course agenda, his students must be "practicing creativity while building community." For Wilson, the marriage of these two elements is what makes a project successful.

Publicity

The first stab that cityworksLosAngeles took at strengthening the partnership between Los Angeles–based designers and local communities was to organize a competition, which was later developed into an exhibition at the A+D Museum called *Communities Under Construction*. cityworksLosAngeles board member Peter Aeschbacher believed the exhibition inspired designers to do what they do best: to be system thinkers and problem solvers. It also challenged designers to be involved at a personal level, working cooperatively with communities.

An invited jury (which consisted of the architect Ray Kappe, the designer Brian Lane, and the critic Kazys Varnelis) reviewed a wide range of projects submitted by individuals, professional firms, academic institutions, and community groups. The exhibition drew such a broad spectrum of proposals that the jury felt they "could not compare all the projects as equals," Kappe explains. The jury distinguished three separate submission groups: professional firms doing pro bono work, college-level design studios, and a combination of the two. Projects in all the groups provided design services for nonprofit clients. Special consideration was given to schemes that relied primarily on donations and found building materials. The jurors' choices focused on the challenges that the designers overcame in providing high-quality services at low or no cost.

One submission that stood out was the design of facilities for The HeArt Project, a nonprofit organization that facilitates long-term, dynamic learning experiences between professional artists and hard-to-

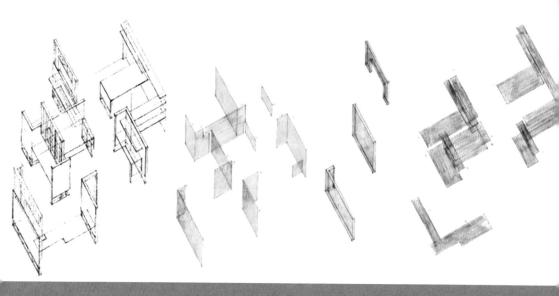

reach teenagers. The building materials were supplied by donations and a single truckload from Home Depot for $197. The organization also benefited from the many, many hours of sweat equity provided by Michael Pinto, who designed and coordinated the project. The drawings Pinto made acted as both design drawings and as a shopping list. All details were chosen so as to minimize waste and to enable a team of unskilled but dedicated volunteers to build the space on a single Saturday. Walls and furniture sizes and shapes were based on the module of a sheet of OSB and plywood as well as 2 x 4 framing for walls. On the day of building out the space, all the HeArt Project employees showed up with rollers, ready to paint. According to Pinto, "when we are working with a successful organization like The HeArt Project, we can assist and even improve their productivity and efficiency through good design."

Overcoming Challenges

While working to pull members of Los Angeles design and architecture schools together into a single urban studio, the founding director of cityworksLosAngeles is coordinating research with legal advisors regarding the roadblocks that tend to stop the progress of these types of projects. The lawyer Eric George, whose practice has represented architects in civil litigation, is working with cityworksLosAngeles to develop a series of practical solutions to the two major legal hindrances to the provision of pro bono services in design and construction: fear of errors-and-omissions liability stemming from faulty design, and concerns about injury and death occurring during a design/build phase.

The first option being explored is a series of legal waivers that would help protect design professionals from litigation and address academic institutions' reluctance to provide services. These waivers would not provide ironclad protection, but they could deter litigation and might lower the risk of expensive lawsuits—particularly those of a more frivolous nature.

An errors-and-omissions waiver would consist of the client waiving the right to bring any legal claims of negligence on the part of the architect or engineer, and would be signed by both the client and the architect or engineer. If a licensed architect or engineer has been brought into the project to stamp drawings produced by an academic institution, the client would also sign a waiver of claims asserting liability against the academic institution. This would allow architecture and

Above
Michael Pinto
The HeArt Project,
Los Angeles.
2003. The material
conservation
diagram enabled
the designer
to catalogue
the amount of
material needed
and calculate
standardized sizes
to reduce waste
and expense.

engineering firms to support the work of academic design programs, which do not have the resources to provide a licensed stamp.

The same waiver structure could be used to help protect students and volunteers during construction services. The types of clients who are served by these projects not only lack funds for design but also need assistance in material procurement and construction. Professional contractors, architects, and students who wish to provide such services do so at their own risk. Fear of litigation prevents many projects from continuing into the construction phase for this reason. By coordinating with pro bono legal services to develop standard documents, cityworksLosAngeles hopes to provide free templates of waivers to those interested.

While the waivers might offer some security, their effectiveness is not guaranteed. A more thorough safeguard would be the creation of legislative protection for those doing pro bono work. Precedent for this type of regulation exists in the Good Samaritan laws, which protect those doing good deeds in the medical field, and architects and engineers would have to work to have it passed on a state-by-state level.

This legislation could shorten the statute of limitations for legal claims against architects and engineers, and increase the burden of proof that would be required in order to successfully prove a claim arising from the provision of pro bono services. It could also give architects and engineers immunity from liability for certain types of legal claims arising from pro bono work. Specifically, the immunity sought might extend to claims alleging negligence in connection with issues such as architectural design; structural failures; slips and falls; leakage and consequent water damage in a building; architectural oversights that are overlooked in permitting, but then recognized by an inspector who requires a rebuild; and selection of building materials, which may subsequently be deemed the cause of damage. This legislation would need to be developed with the American Institute of Architects, plaintiff's lawyers, and a variety of other stakeholders to ensure that it garners broad acceptance.

Another solution simply layers a larger governmental entity, which is inherently at reduced risk of a lawsuit, over the work of the provider. cityworksLosAngeles members employed this method in supporting a student-designed green space for the city. Using the permitting authority of the Bureau of Engineering in a landscape project, qualified bureau staff reviewed and stamped the students' drawings. In addition, construction elements were designed that could be built off-site and delivered to a licensed third-party contractor, thus allowing the students to offer physical labor as well as designs.

If the design community is committed to the establishment of a pro bono tradition, some self-funding may be required. If all state licensing boards would take 1 to 2 percent of the annual licensing fees and pool them into a communal defense fund, that might offer some security for architects being sued. Cases would have to be reviewed on an individual basis, and disbursements from the fund could act as remuneration in situations where the defendant was found innocent after trial. Any additional support that the profession can give would encourage design professionals to offer pro bono or reduced-rate services for worthy clients.

Positive Momentum

Since the founding of cityworksLosAngeles, its members have been involved with a series of community-based projects throughout Los Angeles, ranging from academic research on definitions of "community projects" to hands-on design and construction. Each new opportunity allows the group to work through the complexities of community-based design services and a chance to partner with groups of volunteers, academic institutions, government organizations, and nonprofit clients. The group hopes that this list of works in progress will expand to encompass a full range of design services for all types of communities in need in Los Angeles.

ASSET-BASED APPROACHES

Designing with an
Asset-Based Approach

AMANDA HENDLER-VOSS AND
SETH HENDLER-VOSS

**Shifting the
focus from needs
and deficiency
to strengths
and possibilities
can empower
communities
and designers.**

eft
esign Corps
ummer Studio
tudents and area
esidents build
he framework for
he first bus shelter
n the Shiloh
eighborhood of
sheville, North
Carolina. 2005

Asset-based design is like the classic tale of stone soup. One person starts with just a few stones, another person lends a pot, someone else gives some water, someone donates a carrot, and so on until a delicious soup is made that can serve all. In asset-based design the designer can act as the instigator with the stones, conceiving of a community project that can benefit everyone involved and would not happen otherwise. But the designer does not know what shape the final result will take until the community provides assets of their own. There is no set recipe—just a process of mutual discovery and contributions.

The asset-based approach empowers communities that are not cash-rich but may possess many other resources.

Unlike traditional community development, this approach does not focus on a community's "problems" or "needs." Rather than emphasizing what a community lacks, the process is a celebration of the positive assets they do have, such as their heritage, their local geography, and many other factors that frequently are not financial in nature.

In Asheville, North Carolina, during the inaugural year of the Design Corps Summer Studio, we attempted to adapt the asset-based community development model of John Kretzmann and John McKnight, codirectors of the Asset-Based Community Development Institute and professors at Northwestern University, to a community design effort within the historic Shiloh neighborhood. Basing solutions on the community's capacities rather than its needs, we found that our design strategy could succeed where individual agendas had failed.

According to McKnight, service systems that focus on a needs-based approach can effectively disable communities.[1] Such systems overlook the capacities of citizen organizations to solve local problems and teach communities to focus first on their deficiencies.[2] For example, when low-income

Shiloh residents apply for financial assistance to make ends meet, service providers rarely consider the root problems that lead to underemployment and poverty wages in the community. Even more rarely do caseworkers ask clients what special gifts and talents they possess or what they love about where they live. Instead, service providers come into a community to size up its problems: illiteracy, teenage pregnancy, drug use, and so on. This focus creates codependency between the service "provider" and service "recipient." One must have needs to access the resources of service providers, so residents are positioned as needy.

To some in the greater Asheville area, the name Shiloh evokes a distressed part of the city, a violent neighborhood where drug use is rampant, houses are dilapidated, and many residents rely on welfare. Regardless of how these stereotypes originated, city government and local agencies have done little to shed positive light on Shiloh, which is also an economically and racially diverse area where many residents own their homes, work professional jobs, and are involved in their community. When Bryan Bell, Scott Ball, and Seth Hendler-Voss, the studio cofounders, first arrived in Asheville and went looking for the Shiloh neighborhood, they stopped at a nearby gas station to ask directions. The cashier gave them a curious look and asked why they would want to go to Shiloh. This was their first indication of the general public's perception of the neighborhood in which they would be spending the next eight weeks.

The needs-based approach to problem solving is widely implemented in design school. Designers are taught to conduct a thorough analysis of needs in order to inform an appropriate solution. This approach works well in the private sector, particularly with individual clients, because requests for improvement are typically identified before services are contracted (for example, more parking, better circulation through the atrium, a larger auditorium, more outdoor seating, and so on). But it can be difficult to adapt the private-sector approach to community design, because root problems in a community require a more comprehensive analysis. For instance, providing a design for a job-training center may ultimately help the

Hilary Altman and usan Rans, Asset-ased Strategies for aith Communities Chicago: ACTA ublications, 2002), 4.

Ibid.

members of a community find work, but they will continue to require specialized training as long as they have inferior or underfunded educational institutions.

Designers cannot solve all root problems, but they can help initiate systemic change in a community if they first develop a holistic awareness of the issues. When using a needs-based approach, designers and communities alike are often overwhelmed by an endless list of inadequacies, and the general public appears more comfortable voicing critiques than thinking creatively to identify capacities. In contrast to the private design sector, where time is money, community design allocates adequate time to discover a community's strengths before the design process begins.

Inventorying Capacities
Instead of Listing Needs

Creative neighborhood leaders across the nation are making the shift to an asset-based approach through community organizing, neighborhood associations, art councils, faith communities, and educational programs.[3] Community organizers, for example, often go door-to-door to conduct neighborhood capacity inventories. They ask about the skills and abilities residents possess in the areas of health, administration, construction, repair, food, education, child care, transportation, music, and more. They may find, for instance, that the elder who lives on a fixed income and struggles to pay the bills each month can provide the much-needed child supervision for the single parent who can't find a job due to lack of child care. The elder earns income while enabling the parent to work full-time.

Although the asset-based approach originated within community organizing, other disciplines are beginning to recognize its benefits. In community design this strategy suggests a new way for a team of designers to work with local citizens. It encourages neighborhoods to identify their capacities, use those strengths to achieve an appropriate solution, and articulate community assets through design. Further, it emphasizes the process of design by focusing on the assets of each contributor. This richer process greatly increases the potential for a fruitful outcome.

During the time we spent building a public-transit shelter for the residents of Shiloh, we discovered that the asset-based approach provides two layers of benefit: the potential to build capacity within both communities and the design team. The finished product cannot strengthen a community's confidence in the same way that the process of engagement can. Although the completed shelter is a valued addition to the neighborhood, many residents marveled most at the way they pooled their strengths. The project was Shiloh's first win in steering a project to completion. The public-transit shelter does more than protect transit riders from the rain and wind; it reminds Shiloh residents of their capacity to get things done.

Left
Megan Williams learns welding sk[ill] as part of the bus shelter project.

3 John Kretzmann and John McKnig[ht] *Building Communities from the Inside Out* (Chicago ACTA Publications 1993), 5.

The second benefit of asset-based community design suggests that in the process of challenging area citizens to identify their assets, the individual designer is also compelled to look within to find his or her own talents. The Summer Studio produced no single leader, because the group was inspired to collaborate on specific tasks based on individual strengths.

The studio followed four steps over the eight weeks. First was immersion, then social analysis, followed by the identification of community priorities, and finally design. The first three, however, are not necessarily linear; they often function in a circular fashion, with each step informing the other two as the understanding of a community builds. As design instructor, Bryan Bell discovered that an asset-based approach encouraged group effort. Each student was asked to produce an individual design for the shelter. During design development Bryan challenged the group to identify the strongest elements, or assets, of each proposal and bring them together into one cohesive design. Rather than competing for adoption of an individual design, Bryan asked how the strengths of multiple designs might be synthesized into one.

Designing from an Asset-Based Perspective

. The concept of immersion as a process in social analysis is presented in Peter Henriot and Joe Holland, *Social Analysis* (Maryknoll, N.Y.: Orbis Books, 1983).

The first step in adopting an asset-based approach is immersion.[4] Designers must enter a community filled with the energy to ask questions, listen, and learn. Visiting the home of a neighborhood resident can build personal relationships and provide valuable insight into the culture of a community. Sharing a meal with a client can teach designers more about local dynamics than a boilerplate questionnaire can. During our time in Shiloh we ended each design presentation with a barbecue, which helped strengthen the relationships between the students and their clients.

When we began our journey with the Shiloh residents to design and build a public-transit shelter outside the community center, our student team invited lifetime neighborhood members to share stories of home. Many mentioned the importance of the children and youth who account for a large segment of Shiloh's population. The team took this emphasis as their cue to invite youth participation in the project. Working with a summer camp at the adjacent community center, the design students collaborated with the children to create cement tiles for the shelter floor, empowering the community and producing a culturally enriched design. Shiloh's families now claim the shelter as their own because their children were invested in the process.

The second step in adopting an asset-based approach is social analysis, which involves processing the information discovered in the immersion process. In social analysis there are many key questions to be explored in order to ensure an open, two-way relationship with the community client. It begins by investigating power dynamics, which requires asking such questions as, "Who has the power in this community?" In Shiloh we worked with two neighborhood leaders, Frieda Nash and Norma Banes. Frieda spoke poignantly from the heart, recalling her exodus from Shiloh and her decision to return to contribute to the neighborhood's rebirth. Her candid, no-nonsense personality proved beneficial when the neighborhood faced proposed changes from outside forces. Norma, a quiet and wise leader, had earned the respect of her peers who now looked to her when big decisions needed to be made.

However, just when a designer thinks the power dynamics are pinned down, they are prone to shift. During an exercise in which Shiloh residents discussed the best location for the shelter, a local police officer stationed in the neighborhood (who had chosen not to participate in the earlier design process) adamantly voiced his opposition to the entire project. He thought the shelter would centralize illicit activities, which he had worked hard to disperse during his time in the neighborhood. The resident stakeholders seemed troubled by the officer's mention of increased crime, and they offered little defense of all the work they had done with the students. All eyes were on Frieda and Norma, who surprised everyone with their silence. Then Frieda threw her arms in the air in defeat and yelled out that the project should be terminated. The students were shocked. No one had anticipated how influential the officer's opinions would be in a neighborhood troubled by crime.

After this turning point three of the neighborhood leaders, the policeman, and Bryan went for a driving tour of the neighborhood to look for new sites. They agreed on a new site near a beautiful stream at one corner of Shiloh's central park. The designers had overlooked the site earlier, but it was an inspiring option. As an entry to the park the shelter could provide the three main programmatic criteria requested during the earlier input process: a landmark, a gateway to the park, and a bus shelter. When the group returned to the meeting, the three leaders were able to mobilize the rest of the residents to overcome the policeman's objection to having any transit shelter at all. In the face of the community's will he backed down, and the shelter project went forward.

In a surprising but effective move, three students went out and talked to the drug dealers who frequented the Shiloh street corners. The students asked them if they would start congregating at the new transit shelter once it was constructed, and the dealers said they would not. The policeman laughed at this, but the shelter has been in place for more than a year now, and the dealers have yet to occupy it.

The new location required a bus stop to be moved, and the city transit system, responding to the Shiloh community's input, agreed to alter that part of the route. The city of Asheville issued our building permit in three days.

As another way to examine power dynamics, the student designers took a seminar called "Community Context," where they examined Shiloh in the context of Asheville, attempting to understand the politics governing the relationship between local residents and the surrounding city. They discovered that the residents of the historically black neighborhood once lived elsewhere in the city, on land now owned by the renowned Biltmore Estate, a major Asheville-area tourist attraction. Shiloh residents were displaced to their current neighborhood, which created political and economic vulnerability that persists today. The students also looked at Shiloh in the context of the greater Appalachian region. They explored the grassroots community organizing that characterizes the history of the area, and they considered strategies to work with communities residing on the margins of society. As a group we sought out and visited organizations and communities actively involved in using education and the arts to foster change in other Appalachian cities.

After carefully analyzing the local power dynamics, the design team could then identify priorities. In Shiloh we partnered with Neighborhood Housing Services (NHS), which had an established relationship with Shiloh through a previous organizing campaign and was able to play the role of community liaison. NHS worked with the Shiloh neighborhood to identify the transit shelter as a canary project for the newly formed Shiloh Community Taskforce.

Halfway through the Summer Studio many residents began questioning the importance of the transit shelter. Some members of the community instead desired a park pavilion, a basketball court, or a garden. This is not an uncommon situation, as momentum builds and residents discover their ability to tackle comprehensive projects. The students learned that community priorities can fluctuate, and identifying such priorities can present challenges. In the end the residents held onto the original three goals for the project's built result: landmark, park gateway, and bus shelter.

At the end of the Summer Studio, some students said that this was the most challenging—and thus the most rewarding—experience they had ever had in the field. When using an asset-based approach, both the designer and the community emerge changed. Instead of focusing on the Shiloh community's deficiencies, we sought out their capacities and challenged the design team to walk the community through a process that would encourage those strengths. The community determined what would happen in their neighborhood, and we uncovered capabilities of our own that sometimes took us by surprise. And most students emerged with a stronger sense of their own capacities. Most had contributed a part of the concept and all had made decisions on the final design.

When we returned a year later, we found that our initial achievement had already flourished. The shelter had become the "poster child" for the transit department's effort to increase ridership, which had gone up 20 percent since the shelter had been built. When the police tried to veto our next shelter location in a different neighborhood due to concerns about illicit activities, the success of the first Shiloh project changed their minds. At the ribbon-cutting ceremony for the second project, the mayor spoke of the hope that the first project had given to a depressed neighborhood, and she told the assembled crowd how a grandmother in Shiloh often took her grandchild to the shelter to read books together. Identifying assets is a valuable first step toward building community, which is what community design strives to do.

Communication
through Inquiry

SEAN DONAHUE

**Graphic design
bridges a gap
between visual
and tactile
communication,
allowing the low-
vision community
to use the sight
they have.**

Left and pages 134–38 Sean Donahue Touch. 2002–7. Tactile aids introduce the concept of the hybrid publication to the reader. Here print is used more to introduce each of the colors and the tactile component. Anything rendered in black is also a tactile expression that can be read with touch, and the graphic shows the reader touching the page.

When I told my colleagues I was going to be creating graphic design for the blind, the room fell silent. Undoubtedly, everyone was waiting for the punch line. When I offered none, the room broke out in various levels of laughter. Still not sure how to react, each person settled in and let me proceed to make my case.

My interest had begun with looking at how my abilities as a typographer could inform or extend Braille communication. Was there such a thing as Braille poetry? How does Braille literature represent metaphor through form? Each of these questions in different contexts would be a concern every graphic designer would deal with regularly. Why shouldn't they be appropriate questions in the Braille context as well?

Shaping my interest in this area was my belief that the discipline of graphic design is not singularly defined by the form its artifacts have taken in the past. As vehicles for communication these artifacts become absorbed into our craft but do not predetermine what the discipline is able to do or contribute.

When we take the above statement into consideration, the following words no longer have meanings that result in predetermined form: educate, enrich, enable, persuade, inform, direct, motivate, inspire, and delight. Instead their spirit becomes the basis upon which we redefine what the graphic contribution could be. For a design professional, the limited scope within which these efforts have been exercised in the past is both troubling and exciting. Envisioning new contexts for the design contribution is the core concern upon which I have established my practice.

Separating graphic design from the guises under which it has been applied in the past is the first step toward this goal. Doing so places an emphasis on the discipline's core, which in the most abstract sense fosters connections between cognition and the material environment. These connections are achieved by creating structures that cognition uses to initiate experience and create meaning. These structures are formed by building relationships between textual expression and the imaged world within a consideration of contextuality. This is the language of graphic design. It is the vehicle with which I see the world, organize knowledge, and interact with others. The capacity to

form, understand, and communicate with this language is what makes me a graphic designer; these abilities also ensure that the discipline has a unique and important contribution to make.

The projects emerging from this broader perspective on the nature of graphic design have manifested themselves in many ways. However, those that address issues surrounding the concept of community have yielded the most significant outcomes and are of the most relevance to this essay. The significance of these projects rests in their ability to directly take on the challenges and aspirations of the communities they engage. Each of these projects has given my collaborators and me, as well as the participating communities, an opportunity to reevaluate graphic design's contribution. Instead of communicating to consumers, these projects facilitate connections among city planners, urban developers, sociologists, policy makers, and in this case members of the low- and no-vision community. By choosing to work with what some would call unorthodox, underserved, or nonmainstream clients, I have addressed the core issues of concern for both the communities I am engaging and the discipline of graphic design, redefining the breadth and depth of the contribution that the practice may make.

Touching Graphic Design

Despite the initial reactions to the community I had chosen for my inquiry, I persevered, waiting to decide what I was going to contribute until my exploration revealed opportunities for intervention. Without this openness to discovery my input would likely have been relegated to conventional applications such as designing an advocacy campaign or an annual report. These are valuable contributions in their own right, but the broader context of my practice called for extending beyond these forms. Instead I identified a starting point based on my discipline's strengths. Then, through a direct engagement with the community, I allowed my investigation to help identify where the discipline of graphic design could make the most significant contribution. Taking this position required that I place my work at the center of all parties involved with the subject, allowing it to become a conduit that

contributed what was in the best interest
of the most important client, the low- and
no-vision population.

My research quickly led in new directions,
allowing me to separate the concept of
"blindness" and all the preconceptions
associated with it from the realties of having
no vision. This realization uncovered more
pressing issues. I learned that in many
places, the service providers for no-vision
individuals have become the de facto providers for an exploding low-vision population,
providing counseling, resources, and
education to a group that is projected to
number in the tens of millions by the year
2010 in the United States alone. After
spending time with people who identified
themselves as low-vision, I learned that
even though individuals diagnosed with
low-vision have some level of visual ability,
they are typically classified as "blind."
I realized that this was the place where
I would be able to contribute. My challenge
was to create a vehicle that enabled this
community to use the cognitive structures
that result from having limited visual faculties as an opportunity to introduce tactile
methods of communication, creating
a smoother transition for those effected
by these degenerative diseases to move
through the various stages of vision loss.

The resulting design interventions
consisted of a series of publications called
Touch, which offered a contiuum of material
ranging from tactile photos essays to
information on eye care. The significance
lay in how these publications addressed
the growing communication needs of low-
vision communities. By using both tactile
and graphic forms of communication, the
publications were able to create a dialogue
between tactile language (Braille, line,
texture) and graphic expression (letter form,
composition, pattern). This hybrid language
offered me an opportunity to address the
depression that people commonly experience
upon being diagnosed with degenerative
eye disease. By providing the reader with
self-learning tools that promoted dignity
through a graduated process, I was able
to make the act of reading an opportunity
for education.

The publications were also designed to
allow the communication to function as a

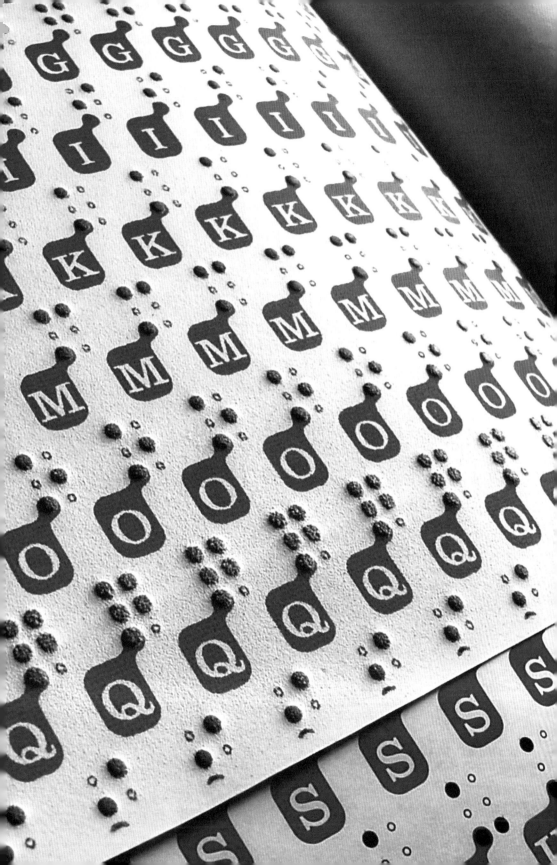

Above
Guidelines for
designing publicati
for low-vision
individuals usually
discourage using
anything other than
established sans se
typefaces. In this ca
however, Donahue

...) of meat you can imagine, the Grand Central Market is a downtown hot spot f...

...reated a vernacular
...le face that exploits
...cale to optimize
...eadability and provide
...he reader access to
...ot only a word but
...lso the spirit of a
...owntown Los Angeles
...eighborhood.

Sprawl
Overdeveloped
Corrupt

congestial

conduit that brought families together. Family members often feel segregated or uncomfortable around loved ones who are forced to use Braille-only books; a family member's inability to understand Braille makes situations even more unpleasant. My publications reinforced relationships between low-vision and sighted family members by addressing the issues within the context of use. At the same time this provided opportunities for the low-vision reader to learn tactile languages. Members of the low-vision community often refuse to learn Braille because they feel it would be tantamount to an admission of blindness. This refusal is exacerbated in many cases because the group most likely to have low vision—people over the age of sixty—often find it challenging to read traditional-sized Braille dots because the poor circulation that is common at that age reduces the hand's tactile sensitivities. To address that need I used larger dots that could be felt

and seen by older readers. This design element also allowed me to design with the element of scale, creating composition hierarchies usually only associated with traditional print communication.

Although these design interventions were the fruitful result of a long-term engagement with the low-vision community, they did not go unchallenged. Each broke from a series of conventions and methodologies established by the way my discipline has been applied in the past, and the reactions were many and spirited. The notion of resizing Braille was met with resistance. Giving readers the option of using visual faculties to begin the process of self-education was dismissed repeatedly. But nothing was more misunderstood than the degree to which I tested the thresholds of existing design criteria established for low-vision readers. My explorations in form and composition were, for lack of a better word, "unsettling" to everyone

Above
Tactile essays introduce the conc of touch as a vehi understand a phys space or subject. Concrete surfaces found in downtow Los Angeles were turned into texture as were the writin collected from its residents. Voice an identity are expres by word choice ar the way in which t word is written.

from service providers to institutions and their researchers.

Reservations were relaxed only after people saw how low-vision readers reacted to the material. When family members and service providers saw readers' faces light up with excitement, wonder, and independence, they understood what the design interventions were speaking to: the pleasures of communication and renewed contact. Access was not solely to the written word but also to delight and discovery. Communication was as much about the pleasure of interpreting a poetic expression as it was about being able to share a sentence with the person next to you. When reading the hybrid publications, the character of a place was revealed as much by the texture and shape of the illustrated buildings as it was by the textual description of them. The concept of "luxury" was expressed as much by the texture of the page as it was by the word itself.

These communicative spaces were designed not to follow rigid rules or specifications but rather to infuse those structures with the spirit of the audience; to go from guidelines to communication. The responses of readers provided a unique lens through which my collaborators could understand my point of view and potential contribution. It enabled them to understand that my role was not to reproduce guidelines verbatim, but rather to use them as a means by which to create communication, reminding each of us that these specifications were the vehicle, not the goal. It was their use in contextual scenarios that made them valuable. This shared perspective became a common ground upon which I was able to engage our mutual interests. A series of workshops, presentations, and long-term partnerships with low-vision advocates and service providers supplied the opportunity to develop resources and flexible guides that continue to speak to the unique issues surrounding low-vision.

This more holistic understanding of the low-vision community enabled my design contribution to move beyond its traditional application, benefiting both the discipline and the group I was engaging. This project focused on providing content that addressed multiple areas of innovation and assistance for the low-vision community, and their issues were addressed within the larger context of interacting in and with a sighted world. In choosing to work directly with this community, I was able to avoid becoming entangled in the trappings of convention. This approach permitted my design to initiate a dialogue that has opened opportunities for vision specialists, policy makers, vision support organizations, and the low-vision community itself to reconsider how those with degenerative eyes disease can and will engage with a breadth and depth of communication not based singularly on guidelines but rather on his or her enthusiasm to know and experience more through a relationship with paper, image, the written word, and the tactile.

This graphic-design approach and its resulting projects are intended to provoke a broadening of the discipline's conceptual and creative scope in order to directly influence practice. These expanded relationships and perspectives have become the foundations for my practice, allowing the graphic-design contribution to move away from the reactionary position of "solving problems" and shift instead into the proactive position of design leadership by enabling design and the designer to identify areas where they can make a significant contribution. However minor this shift may seem, the result is a fundamental change in the use, perception, and practice of graphic design in many capacities. It prescribes the design inquiry a value not dependent on solving a preexisting inadequacy as defined by others and instead positions it as a vehicle for exploration, articulation, and advancement. The profession has the potential to establish a practice well beyond what is acknowledged by most designers and by society at large. We visualize what is invisible, we motivate thought, and we incite others to wonder. But most important, we communicate though inquiry, when we choose to. We need to expand the framework of that inquiry, and we need to hold its results in higher esteem.

Designing Infrastructure/
Designing Cities

RYAN GRAVEL

**An innovative
planning proposal
transforms
abandoned
rail lines and
industrial
wasteland into
a city asset and
suggests a
new vision for
the modern
American city.**

Rem Koolhaas,
Toward the
Contemporary City,"
Design Book Review
7 (winter 1989),
5–16. The present
ext draws from
yan Gravel, "Belt
ine Atlanta—Design
f Infrastructure
s a Reflection
f Public Policy"
master's thesis,
Georgia Institute of
echnology, 1999).

In his essay "Toward the Contemporary City," Rem Koolhaas observes that the modern city was built only in fragments, and the challenge now is to remodel and augment the different parts without destroying them, much in the way Milan or Paris did in the nineteenth century. By working among the different fragments, both the idealism of modern urbanism and the imagery and scale of the traditional city are compromised, but valuable new themes emerge, allowing us to deal with the complexities of contemporary life. Koolhaas observes, "The contemporary city...ought to yield a sort of manifesto, a premature homage to a form of modernity, which when compared to cities of the past might seem devoid of qualities, but in which we will one day recognize as many gains as losses. Leave Paris and Amsterdam— go look at Atlanta, quickly and without preconceptions."[1] If Atlanta may be considered the poster child of the new American city, then we need look no further for the challenges and complexities of contemporary urban life. This metropolitan area, with both uncontrollable suburban growth and extensive inner-city gentrification, suffers most of all from traffic congestion and the ecological consequences of unmitigated sprawl. Real change in the way we continue to build Atlanta will require a significant shift in the attitude of a region that has for too long prioritized the automobile as the primary tool for urban expansion.

The Challenge:
The Mall as a Standard for Growth

Several years ago I went to Savannah, Georgia, with a friend. We were standing on the street near one of James Oglethorpe's famous squares when she said to me, "Does Savannah have a real city?" I didn't know how to respond. After all, Savannah's urban plan makes it one of the most "real" cities in America. She could tell that I didn't understand, so she rephrased her question: "I mean, does Savannah have a mall?"

It is clear that conventional strip-style development has altered our perspective of the city itself. The problem with our sprawling landscape is not just its separation of people (by such factors as income, race, and age), its separation of human activities (home, office, retail, recreation), or its inefficient use of public resources (water, sewer, police, schools). The other problem with sprawl is perhaps even more important, and my friend's comments in Savannah hit upon this point exactly. We now have generations of people, myself among them, who grew up with the shopping mall as the highest standard of how we build our cities. Not only have many of us never gone shopping downtown; many of us have never lived in neighborhoods with people who are significantly different from ourselves, or where we don't have to get in our car to go somewhere. To many of us the mall (or its more recent form, the open-air "lifestyle center") and all of its accoutrements, like highways, outparcels, and drive-throughs, are the physical manifestations of our preferred lifestyle. This is the life we want— or at least the life we think we want.

Fast-growing Sunbelt boomtowns like Atlanta, Dallas, and Orlando have few local examples of high-quality, tightly knit urban growth to which architects can point. Unlike most Northern cities such as Boston or Chicago, or older Southern ports like New Orleans or Savannah, the intense period of development for these new-growth regions is coming at a time when automobiles dominate the design of our urban framework, resulting in cities that are significantly less dense and far more disconnected than in previous eras. This new way of city-building, one defined by regional malls and culs-de-sac, creates a vast periphery of disconnected low-density development that is not likely to go away.

Perhaps more important than the physical problems presented by this style of growth is the challenge of teaching people that their city can be built to better standards. We must set those new standards by finding creative solutions that allow our cities to accommodate the new variables of contemporary living (automobiles, shopping malls, Internet banking) while still maintaining a high quality of life. This is a job for architects. Developing new solutions to the problems created by a sprawl dominated landscape will require a new way of thinking and, ultimately, a new kind of city. We must change not only the city's physical form but also the way we conceive of our city. If we can do that, cities like Atlanta can create a

valuable new identity, one quite different from Chicago, Paris, or Savannah, but equally successful and seductive.

One proven way to influence urban growth is through the careful design of infrastructure systems. In the early 1900s the extension of streetcar lines outward from the central business district facilitated the building of the neighborhoods that are now Atlanta's beloved "intown" area. The model of today's "smart growth," these communities came complete with mixed uses, mixed incomes, mixed housing opportunities, sidewalks, public transit, and neighborhood commercial districts.

Beginning in the 1950s we designed a different kind of infrastructure in America, one that resulted in a very different style of growth. The interstate highway system generated expansive automobile-oriented suburban expansion in the decades that followed and contributed significantly to the subsequent compartmentalization of people by income, race, and activity. If our decisions about infrastructure have such substantial implications for other aspects of our lives, in the future we should consider these decisions thoroughly. If we are spending limited public money on large infrastructure projects like roads, transit, sewers, or parks, we must be deliberate about their design so that their full impact on urban growth is consistent with our other public goals. When the design of public infrastructure directs private action, architecture and planning become political.

The political, of course, comes into play when you have to define what those "other public goals" are. That is not easy to do across a broad spectrum of people, particularly if the goals challenge people to change the way they think about their lives.

The Atlanta BeltLine

Railroads defined Atlanta's origins and continue to influence its spatial relationships. Much like cities across the country that are reestablishing connections to their waterfronts, Atlanta will find its future in its history as a hub of railroad transportation. After the Civil War the railroad companies in Atlanta built a series of "belt-line" railroads circling downtown to expand opportunities for industrial development around what was then the periphery of the city. When the industries used these belt lines for shipping and receiving, they lived in harmony with the growing city around them; but this is not the case today. Virtually all the remaining belt-line area industries have abandoned railroads and shifted to truck-based freight, contributing to blight in many neighborhoods. Also, a number of factors are encouraging industries to leave the belt-line areas, such as growing pressure for residential development in the city, poor truck access to belt-line industrial sites, instances of environmental contamination, and rising land values. As industries depart the sites left behind are ideal for the mixed-use redevelopment that today's intown housing market demands.

The Atlanta BeltLine will make use of these sites in a comprehensive vision for the city's future, creating a twenty-two-mile transit greenway circling downtown and midtown Atlanta. By reusing the loop of existing railroad tracks as a wide linear park with streetcars and paths for bicycles and pedestrians, the BeltLine will be able to connect more than forty diverse neighborhoods as well as schools, historic, and cultural sites, existing transit stations, shopping districts, and public parks. It will organize adjacent abandoned industrial land for transit-oriented development, expand transit service within the urban core, and connect various parts of an emerging regional trail system. The BeltLine will take advantage of Atlanta's intown population growth by creating smart new districts for more than 100,000 new residents and improving the quality of life for hundreds of thousands more.

With the idea that the creative design of infrastructure systems can direct private investment to accomplish public goals, the BeltLine was born as a way to re-invigorate Atlanta's intown communities with appropriate new development and improved transit mobility. The proposal grew out of my graduate thesis in architecture and city planning at Georgia Tech in 1999. My studios and coursework had concentrated on urban design and architectural and urban history, exploring the

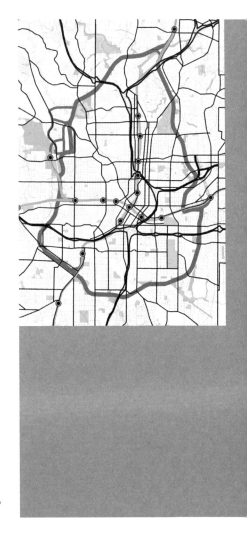

interaction between design, culture, and quality of life. I became increasingly interested in the relationship between the design of public infrastructure and private-market development. In the academic environment, without being tied down by cost or politics, I was free to think boldly about what new vision might take Atlanta toward a more sustainable future. Then I finished my degree, and I put that vision on the shelf.

I went to work for Surber Barber Choate & Hertlein Architects, focusing on several mixed-use projects that happened to be along the BeltLine route. After talking for months about the BeltLine project with two coworkers, we put together a brief proposal and sent out more than fifty copies to anyone we hoped might listen. We got an enthusiastic response from Cathy Woolard, then the Atlanta City Councilmember for District 6 and chair of the City Council's Transportation Committee. Woolard took to the idea immediately and became its most vocal and ardent supporter, kicking off its public debut at a town-hall meeting held in a neighborhood church basement.

Woolard was elected City Council president soon thereafter, and in the years that followed she worked tirelessly to ensure that Atlanta did not miss this great opportunity. Together with her staff and myself as a volunteer, Woolard presented the idea to a wide array of community groups, business groups, and other organizations, and in two short years she had generated broad public support for the project. Our grassroots efforts began to translate into support from other public officials, and early tests of the project's technical merits began to attract attention from regional planners. The project now stands as one of Mayor Shirley Franklin's top priorities. With a study showing a $20 billion impact on the city's tax base, and with a recently approved tax-allocation district that will pay the bulk of the BeltLine's $2 billion price tag, this massive urban project has momentum unlike any other in Atlanta's history.

Getting There

About one-sixth of the Atlanta metropolitan area's population lives within the city limits. After losing residents to the ever-expanding suburbs through the 1970s and 1980s, the city is now growing at a rate not seen in decades. In fact, over the next twenty-five years we will add at least 170,000 new residents—more than one-third of our current population. Most of these new residents will not live in Atlanta's leafy intown neighborhoods; they will live in much greater densities along the commercial corridors heading into downtown and in the redeveloped industrial corridors that line Atlanta's many railroads. This moment in Atlanta's history presents an incredible opportunity to direct the city's future. But with little experience in dense urban growth and a cultural memory laden with highways, parking lots, and pay-at-the-pump gas stations, we have a major learning curve ahead of us if we are going to get it right.

Changes in our culture have caused changes in the way we build our cities. The spatial relationships and systems that

organize and operate the contemporary city are far more complex than the historic monocentric urban model. Today's cities encompass surviving portions of the old city along with profoundly new conceptions like edge cities, international airports, superhighways, and an unprecedented level of communication through cellular and Internet technology. We cannot ignore these changes in city-building and expect to be successful. In other words, we are not going to solve our problems by simply imitating Savannah's street grid; nor can we stay on the path of sprawling disconnection. If Atlanta is going to survive and prosper, it must blend history, technology, culture, climate, and geography in ways that make it unique.

At the seam of the city's goals to protect and revive historic neighborhoods, accommodate an influx of new residents, redevelop available land, and provide alternative means of transportation, we find the historic belt-lines. Atlanta can find "as many gains as losses" and reinvent itself as a twenty-first-century city.

Looking Forward

The current proposal takes us in that direction. By advertising its multiple public goals, the BeltLine has opened itself up to a much larger conversation. What is interesting for Atlanta is that this conversation is actually taking place. In addition to its three major components of transit, greenspace, and economic development, citizens are insisting on a discussion about good design, green building principles, equity, environmental justice, affordable housing, public health, public art, historic preservation, gentrification, urban design, and senior housing—and the list continues. While incorporating these issues will certainly make the project more complicated, they will also make it stronger. In fact these discussions will be the very essence of the BeltLine's success.

As exciting as this conversation has been for those of us who want to educate our communities about good design and have a positive effect on urban development, my friend's question, "Does Savannah have a real city; does Savannah have a mall?" makes the case that we have a long way to go.

Architects must become civic leaders in the design of their city and BeltLine. An architect's nature is to seek solutions through design, and skilled architects can communicate those solutions in ways that teach their clients about the value of good design. We must be able to shift our thinking between the big idea and the small detail, between theory and reality, and between the tightly knit traditional urban fabric and the frenzied demands of the contemporary city.

With the BeltLine, Atlanta has set into motion a long-term project that is bound to have a profound impact not only on the physical conditions of the city but also on the way Atlanta thinks about itself. Atlanta will be forced to confront its lack of urban quality and its range of cultural perspectives. The work has only just begun, and architects have an important role to play in this unprecedented discussion of city-building.

At a press conference held in the spring of 2004 on the BeltLine, just east of downtown, Mayor Franklin said, "Imagine right now we are laying the foundation for the next one hundred years of the city." Indeed, Atlanta's future will depend on its ability to creatively address its challenges head-on and find innovative solutions to building a more sustainable region. We as architects and community leaders must get actively involved. We must discover new ways to build cities where people want to live, within the economic, political, cultural, and spatial conditions of the contemporary city.

HOUSING FOR THE 98%

Mainstreaming Good Design in Affordable Housing: Strategies, Obstacles, and Benefits

KATHLEEN DORGAN AND
DEANE EVANS

Affordable housing
efforts have too
often been hampered
by poor design.
What strategies can
be used to embed
high-quality design
as a core value in all
affordable housing?

Twenty-five percent of all American households face severe housing challenges, including insufficient funds for monthly rent or mortgage payments, maintenance, and repairs; overcrowding, both within individual dwellings and in high-density multifamily developments; and structural deficiencies. These 30 million households include not just the poorest and those without jobs, but also teachers, librarians, firefighters, healthcare workers, and many others who make significant contributions to our communities.

JAYSON HAIT, *Affordable Housing: Designing an American Asset*

The demand for decent, affordable housing far outstrips the supply for an increasing number of U.S. citizens. Design excellence can—and should—play a key role in addressing this critical issue.

In many areas across the country the rapidly escalating cost of land is a major reason for the lack of affordable housing. But there is a subtler barrier: the perception that affordable housing is inferior in quality to market-rate developments. The fear that such "projects" will lower the value of adjacent properties is one of the key drivers of NIMBY ("not in my backyard") reactions to the production of affordable housing, whose advocates must acknowledge that such fears are sometimes justified. Much of the extant affordable housing is of inferior quality, and all it takes is one poorly designed project to negate any goodwill previous successful developments may have generated in a community.

How and why are projects of such inferior quality produced? One reason is that the development process, particularly in the area of affordable housing, tends to place more emphasis on the financial underpinnings of a project than on the quality of the final product. Go to any gathering of housing developers and advocates, and you will see many presentations featuring spreadsheets, but few with pictures of homes. This focus on money is driven by the institutions that finance the developments. These lenders tend to pay more attention to money than to aesthetics or design quality. The result can be housing that provides basic shelter but does little more, to the dismay of its residents and neighbors.

It Looks Good, but Is It Well Designed?
Aesthetics are important, but they are by no means the only component of design excellence. High-quality design encompasses an array of considerations, such as proportion, sense of identity, size and rhythm of openings, circulation, access to light and air, sense of place, and the creation of spaces that are safe, easy to maintain, and suitable for the activities that take place in them. If a development does not address these considerations effectively, it is not well designed, no matter how large it is or how many expensive finishes, fixtures, and appliances it contains.

Design is not simply a commodity that a developer can buy more (or less) of, but rather a process that unfolds continuously over the life of the project and that involves the entire development team. This is good news for everyone involved in the creation of affordable housing. It means that design excellence does not come about by luck or by finding a great architect at a great price, but instead by managing the design process creatively and effectively.

In addition to a good design process, a well-designed development must meet the needs of its occupants; understand and respond to its context; enhance its neighborhood; and be built to last.[1] None of these criteria directly addresses aesthetics, which are in the eye of the beholder. The focus is on outcomes that provide direct, tangible benefits to the occupants and neighbors of affordable-housing developments. For example, Colorado Court in Santa Monica, designed by Pugh Scarpa Kodama, effectively incorporates photovoltaic panels, which contribute to the projects' affordability and ecological neighborliness.

Does Good Design Add Value?

There has been no definitive analysis undertaken to determine whether good design adds value to developments. However, for-profit developers who have faced community resistance to their projects have learned the value of high-quality design, particularly in market-rate developments that are attempting to achieve above-average densities for their locations. Design quality becomes a key selling point for these projects, both for the occupants and for the communities that must approve them. For instance, a project my firm designed in Albany, New York, called Dove Street Independent Housing received unanimous support from the neighborhood association while other projects funded by the same sources were met by lawsuits initiated by neighbors.

High-quality design is one of the most promising— and one of the most under-utilized—strategies available for both improving the asset value and facilitating community acceptance of affordable housing.

Does a Well-Designed Development Cost More to Build?

The short answer is "no." Key components of good design can be achieved on virtually any budget if the process is managed effectively. The most expensive type of affordable housing is the ugly, leaky box that gets torn down after one generation, not the well-designed project that remains a community asset for decades, such as the Children's Village in Hartford, which was constructed in 1925. It continues to be regarded as an example of successful housing, and is a cherished landmark as well. In short, well-designed developments usually do not cost more to build.

The longer answer is "sometimes." While a well-designed development will cost more than the barest code-minimum box, most affordable housing built today costs no less than a typical well-designed development. The cost of truly outstanding

design, however, may be a different story. Judging by anecdotal evidence from across the country, significantly superior design costs slightly more than the typical affordable-housing budget allows. Michael Pyatok, an experienced affordable-housing designer based in Oakland, has estimated that it takes a 3 percent budget increase to go from "a barracks to a landmark."[2] Although this figure may not be applicable in all markets, it appears to be a reasonable pre-liminary approximation of the "extra" costs of achieving very high levels of design and construction excellence.

The good news through all this is that designers and clients who are mindful of design are usually also careful about cost management, and will glean the highest design quality from whatever budget they have. They find donations, use volunteer labor, collaborate with area artists, and sometimes, as Pyatok's team does, even

Above
Grosvenor Atterbur
Children's Village,
Hartford, Connecti
1925

Above right
Pyatok Architects
Willow Court Home
Menlo Park, Califor
1993

2 Michael
Pyatok, personal
communication with
authors, June 13, 2(

Does a Well-Designed Development Cost More to Design?

The short answer is, "It depends whose cost we're talking about." A well-designed project will usually cost an architect more to create, but most clients are unwilling or unable to pay more than the standard rates for this extra degree of service. The result is a system that rewards mediocre design, discourages thoughtful models, and often drives well-meaning, talented designers out of affordable housing altogether. It is cheap to pull old plans out of a drawer, skip project research, drag and drop the same unit plan along each row, accept all the change orders without research, and miss the job meetings. It costs more to explore alternatives, work more closely with stakeholders, investigate pricing, draw all the details, develop a complex solution, train staff, and inspect construction carefully. Unfortunately, clients usually pay the same fees for poorly detailed stock solutions and inattentive construction managers as they do for the best services.

Rehab is a particular challenge. Measuring each structure and keeping track of each unit's needs can be expensive. One-size-fits-all specs such as "repair all defective surfaces" are much easier to prepare than more detailed instructions such as "patch the two-foot-long crack on the upper-right corner of the west wall." It is even easier for the architect to demolish and build anew. These disincentives have caused some questionable determinations about the feasibility of rehabilitation, and deter architects from pursuing creative reuse projects such as Chelsea Court. Thoughtful design transformed this single-room-occupancy hotel into permanent supportive housing for previously homeless and low-income individuals.

Project size is another problem. The fee structure for architectural services is typically based on a percentage of construction costs, which favors the development of larger, more expensive new construction projects. However, smaller projects are usually almost as difficult to design as larger ones. In other words, it takes almost as much thought and energy to create a well-designed infill fourplex as it does to create a four-hundred-unit townhouse complex. This

show up on site to build birdhouses. However, if their care and diligence are not rewarded by allowing them to build a good project, these designers will stop being so conscientious, or they will stop working for a specific developer or funder. In either case, the affordable-housing community loses. It is not uncommon for a designer's heart to be broken by a developer earning multimillion-dollar fees who strips the last elements of quality from a project to save a few thousand dollars. Such "savings" are really false economies. On the next project, the designer will not spend hours sorting through lighting catalogues searching for the best deals. The development of poor-quality projects will necessitate significant expenditures for marketing and approvals—expenditures that could have been avoided by producing better housing to begin with.

problem hurts smaller affordable-housing developments, which often need even more design attention than larger projects with bigger (and probably better) sites. If the design team puts in this extra effort, they are probably doing so on a pro bono basis—an approach that is simply not sustainable over the long term.

What Are the Key Barriers to Good Design?

"Please don't make it ugly. And really make it built well," pleaded a respondent to a community preference survey conducted in the South End neighborhood of Albany, New York.[3] The survey was conducted in response to continuing community opposition to an affordable-housing development proposed by the generally highly regarded Albany Housing Authority. In the same survey neighborhood residents gave high marks to two extant affordable-housing developments in Albany, but they also complained about two other recent projects. One eyesore, located at a key corner, features brick facing peeling from the wall. The development team had failed to propose a model that built on local knowledge of successful design strategies. Why, in three years of community conversations, had the Housing Authority and their private-sector partners failed to identify a set of pertinent facts clearly visible to community residents on a daily basis? The same kind of question can be asked nationally. We know how to do good work, so why don't we just do it every time? The answer is that systemic barriers to the production of high-quality affordable housing remain. In order for those systemic barriers to be removed, each of the players has to take action within his or her own domain.

Funders are in the position to make the biggest difference. This effort should begin with unambiguous support for good design and a rejection of the traditionally low expectations for affordable housing. Foundations, public agencies, and financial institutions need to state their expectations for excellence in all of their publications, requests for proposals, applications, and training materials. Programs that expand design research and literacy are essential. Grant makers should also provide incentives for recipients to secure better sites and hire better design teams, focusing particularly on teams that understand construction costs and know how to manipulate them to achieve maximum value. All funders should also consider a flexible payment structure that increases design fees, as a percentage of construction costs, for smaller projects and rehabilitation. Resources also need to be directed to fixing broken projects so that the relatively few failures don't taint the public perception of affordable housing. Finally, it is imperative for funding allocations to specifically reward good design. If quality confers no competitive advantage, funding competitions become a race to the bottom. Some claim that it is impossible to score design fairly, but the academic and professional peer review systems that evaluate medical care, education, and scientific research demonstrate that thoughtful, knowledgeable experts can provide competent evaluations of both art and craft.

Another barrier to design excellence is the fact that many competitive applications require complete drawings as part of the proposal. This practice favors teams that are willing to simply repeat solutions that are not site-responsive. Even teams with higher aspirations will often do only the minimum necessary to obtain financial support, expecting that their designs will be refined once final funding has been approved. Unfortunately this approach often favors convenience over thoughtfulness, with the result that the core expediency of the winning design remains locked in even as the design is refined.

Affordable-housing developers and sponsors have the most to lose in the battle for design excellence, but this constituency is largely absent from the conversation about good design. Many developers simply don't believe that good design is achievable on their restricted budgets. Furthermore, many tend to be much more comfortable working with pro formas, service agreements, land deals, and financing arrangements, and seem somewhat nervous about dealing with the design side of a project. Until this seemingly deep-seated attitude is changed, the effort to mainstream good design will remain an uphill battle.

3 Monique Wahb "South End Surve Results" (Albany, N.Y.: City of Alban Planning Dept., Dec. 2005), 2.

Right
Louise Braverma
Architect
Chelsea Court,
New York City. 2C

Architects need better tools and training to enable them to serve the affordable-housing market. Many receive no training in residential design, let alone in the unforgiving specialty of affordable housing. Working for a percentage of construction costs means that designers take on more risk for less reward: an unsustainable strategy. There is more and better performance information available for TV dinners, video games, and elliptical trainers than for most building products. Architects face considerable obstacles—some internal to the profession, others external—to their efforts to make accurate cost estimates throughout the development process. Such estimates are always important, but they are especially critical—and the architect's role especially pivotal—in affordable housing. Existing construction-industry systems make it difficult for designers to obtain cost information on materials. Without an accurate idea of what a project is going to cost to

build, in materials *and* labor, an architect cannot be sure that a given product or design approach will be cost-effective.

The capacity of architects to understand and manage costs, never their strong suit, appears to have little prospect of improving in the future. A recent study of architectural internships by the National Council of Architectural Registration Boards found that interns have little problem gaining experience producing drawings, but "bidding and contract negotiation, building cost analysis, and programming were the areas most likely to be reported as somewhat difficult or difficult to get experience in."[4]

4 Beth A. Quinn, "Building a Profession: A Sociological Analysis of the Intern Development Program," *Journal of Architectural Education* 44, www.archvoices.org/downloads/quinnarticleonidp.p

What Needs to Be Done?
Our agenda for mainstreaming good design is simple:

- Affordable-housing **funders** need to demand better design via their request for proposal/request for quotation processes.

- Affordable-housing **developers** need to become more aware of the critical importance of good design and its potential to improve the long-term value of their developments.

- Affordable-housing **architects** must get better at analyzing and controlling costs, and they must make cost analysis and cost control part of the core services they offer to affordable-housing developers. As part of this process, they should support and disseminate research on design strategies that have the potential to reduce development costs.

If the core constituents of the affordable-housing development community can bring all of these "good deeds" to pass, we will have gone a long way toward mainstreaming good design.

Architectural Alchemy

ERIC NASLUND AND
JOHN SHEEHAN

Affordable housing
can be a research
laboratory provoking
creative problem-
solving. As a result,
design solutions
become stronger due
to tough constraints.

Al • che • my:
an early form of chemistry,
with philosophical and
magical associations,
studied in the Middle Ages:
its chief aims were to change
baser metals into gold
and to discover the elixir
of perpetual youth.

Webster's New World College Dictionary, 4th ed.

Americans don't usually expect much from affordable housing. Most view it as important in a social, political, or economic sense, but rarely think of it as a vehicle for good design or great communities. After all, affordable housing is constrained by tight budgets and an overwhelming demand that far outstrips the available supply of units. In such a climate design success is measured by how quickly a serviceable product is delivered. Surely there is no baser metal in the world of architecture. Yet when we as architects accept this view, we overlook a rich source of design inquiry. Affordable housing, as humble as it may be, requires architects to provide dignity, security, and a place to carry out the daily rituals that give life meaning. An architect's job here is to make "gold" from humble ingredients.

As we at the design firm Studio E see it, the gold is already present in what many see as the affordable-housing "problem." Affordable housing offers us a valuable— and mostly overlooked—opportunity to serve as a testing ground for future innovations in housing and community development strategies. Because it doesn't participate in the market-driven mindset of the merchant-built housing industry, affordable housing allows us to focus on issues long neglected in the contemporary housing marketplace, such as environmental appropriateness, strong community structure, and connection to place. The creation of affordable housing can function as a sort of research-and-development activity for the larger housing industry, pointing us toward alternative visions of the future.

The Future as an Extension of the Present

Today's housing marketplace is mismatched with the needs—and the pocketbooks—of most Americans. In Southern California, where we work, many cannot afford to purchase housing; and even if they could, the products available are increasingly irrelevant to their changing requirements. Yet the merchant-built housing industry continues to produce the same products and has shown resistance to innovation and change, for one primary reason: the financing mechanisms that make it possible to build housing are based on borrowed capital. The institutions that lend this capital to development interests have a fiduciary responsibility to their investors and depositors to ensure that loans provide a reliable return. As a result financial institutions often avoid untested ideas and rely instead on past market performance to assess the viability of investments.

While this strategy makes for a more predictable rate of return, it also restricts the marketplace, both at the front end, where initial design decisions are made, and at the back end, where the consumer is faced with loan approval and resale considerations. For these reasons the marketplace often does not generate alternative solutions, and the future can only be conceived as an extension of the present.

An Alternative Vision of the Future

The market-driven housing industry includes a number of stakeholders who play pivotal roles in giving form to the design of housing and communities: market consultants, appraisers, and loan officers, for example. Individuals such as these, and others who are concerned with a project's marketability, greatly influence or even determine the layout of developments, the mix of uses within them, the circulation system, the type of housing to be placed on a given site, and even a dwelling's appearance.

By contrast, most affordable housing is funded from a wider variety of sources, reducing the pull of any one lender, and governments are also usually involved, which reduces the strength of market-based imperatives. Government assistance typically comes in the form of federal low-income tax credits, and local redevelopment funds can also provide gap financing. All of these funds are extremely competitive, but once acquired they do remove the performance burden that borrowed capital places upon a market-rate developer. In addition, the targeted audience for affordable housing is so vast and the availability of that housing so small that the demand far outstrips the supply, rendering the issue of marketability virtually nonexistent.

So what happens when we eliminate the marketing factor from the housing mix? The thoughtful architect will look for other needs that can be met by the form of our communities. When designers avail themselves of this opportunity to explore alternatives, critical issues that are ignored in today's marketplace can be addressed in built form. The result is the construction of prototypes that are available for the larger housing industry to evaluate. Consultants, appraisers, and lenders often require real-world case studies to ease their investment anxieties, so the creation of viable housing outside the market-driven framework is a valuable first step in building credibility for new design and development ideas.

At Studio E we have found two areas where the design of affordable housing has expanded our understanding of what is possible: sustainability and a sense of community.

Sustainability

Although the housing industry is striving to implement more "green" building practices, so far these efforts seem to focus on the use of recycled-content materials and higher-efficiency electrical or climate-control systems. While these are important and necessary first steps, the industry has yet to change land-planning practices or housing designs to reduce the use of energy or resources. Over the life of the home, the greatest cost savings and environmental sustainability are achieved by intelligent land planning and design, but merchant builders rarely consider passive energy measures that work with the local climate. Most production housing is omnidirectional, meaning that no one side of the building is designed for any particular compass direction. This allows houses to be placed anywhere on the site, in any orientation; but that flexibility

comes with a cost. Mechanical systems must be employed to compensate for inappropriate solar orientations in order to maintain a reasonable level of thermal comfort on all but the most temperate days.

In the affordable-housing industry, the luxury of this kind of waste is not an option. The total housing cost for residents is determined by adding utility costs to the rent or mortgage payment. This cost is capped based on the median income of the surrounding community. The higher the utility costs are, the more that the rent or mortgage payment must be reduced to compensate. Thus, there is a real incentive to build savings in from day one by employing time-honored passive techniques for heating, cooling, and daylighting. Once built, homes that implement these efficiencies reap savings throughout the life of the structure, with little maintenance required. Often there are no additional front-end costs for building in this manner, which raises the question of why these passive techniques are not used in all housing.

Sense of Community

In our affordable-housing designs Studio E aims to create a usable and connected public realm that will foster a sense of community among neighbors. By "community" we mean a sense of responsibility and ownership that includes common spaces as well as individual homes. This orientation recognizes that the principal objective in community design is not the individual structures but the spaces between them.

Those spaces between, however, must not merely be the land left over after buildings are placed on a site. For any sense of community to develop, the areas between structures must become figural or primary. The open spaces should at least be conceived in concert with the buildings, if not designed first. Sometimes buildings need to recede in order to allow the voids on a site to assert themselves and have presence. Life happens, after all, in these voids. As the saying goes, what is important about a cup is not the thing itself, but the void it creates. The same holds true in the design of community housing.

Above
Studio E Architec
Indian Wells Villas
Indian Wells,
California. 1996.
East-west paseos
feed into the
central courts,
linking all resider
in a continuous
garden realm.

Case Studies of Innovation in Affordable Housing

A few case studies illustrate how we have attempted to address issues of sustainability and a sense of community in our firm's work.

in our design, and we sought to respect the project's unique desert environment.

The single-story, one-bedroom apartments stretch across 7.5 acres of a former date grove on the edge of Indian Wells. This flat, featureless site has been

Indian Wells Villas

This apartment complex, a ninety-unit affordable senior housing project designed for the redevelopment agency of the city of Indian Wells, California, was built as a deliberate critique of standard development practices in the California desert. The project employs both passive and high-tech cooling techniques to avoid using the wasteful, expensive, and environmentally stressful temperature-control methods so often used in contemporary housing. We paid special attention to place-making

organized into a series of interconnecting pedestrian spaces. The units, grouped into six-plexes, focus on east-west–oriented paseos that feed into courts at the center of the site. These courts are in turn linked along the north-south axis, creating a continuous central pedestrian spine that is anchored by a vestigial date grove at the south end and the project commons at the north end. Automobiles, which play a small but necessary role in these seniors' lives, are stored in attached single-car garages that are accessed through east-west alleys.

The cars are close at hand, yet tucked out of sight.

The housing units are organized according to a thermal and social gradient that becomes more enclosed and cool as one moves into the plan. Private, unshaded outdoor spaces (for winter and evening use) are connected to fully enclosed interior living spaces by a covered outdoor room. This intermediate space acts as a kind of hinge, giving residents summertime outdoor gathering spaces that are socially connected to the paseo/courtyard system. These outdoor rooms function thermally to provide a cool space, drawing air into the units and reducing the mechanical-cooling load. At the center of each unit is a shaded breakfast atrium linking the garage and the kitchen. This atrium provides a second "cool sink" for fresh air. Shading here is manipulable in the form of pull-back awnings that allow residents to completely enclose or open the atrium.

Each unit is passively cooled with a thermal chimney placed at the center of the plan. Inspired by the wind towers of the Middle East, these chimneys allow hot air to vent from the unit while also capturing the cooler night breezes. Openings at the top of the chimney are oriented to draw these prevailing breezes in. The breeze then creates a thermosiphon that induces warm air within the unit to be pulled out the chimney. Replacement air is brought into the unit through deeply shaded outdoor spaces and damp landscape grottos outside windows. This cooling scheme has proven to be extremely effective, allowing residents to avoid using air-conditioning systems on all but the hottest days.

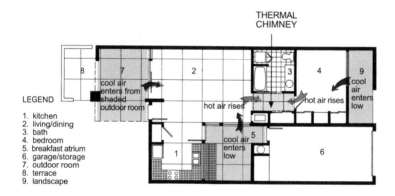

THERMAL CHIMNEY

LEGEND

1. kitchen
2. living/dining
3. bath
4. bedroom
5. breakfast atrium
6. garage/storage
7. outdoor room
8. terrace
9. landscape

cool air enters from shaded outdoor room

hot air rises

hot air rises

cool air enters low

cool air enters low

Left
Every unit at India Wells is passively cooled through the ancient technique of thermosiphoni through wind tow

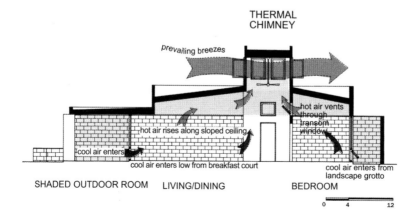

THERMAL CHIMNEY

prevailing breezes

hot air vents through transom window

hot air rises along sloped ceiling

cool air enters

cool air enters low from breakfast court

cool air enters from landscape grotto

SHADED OUTDOOR ROOM   LIVING/DINING   BEDROOM

0   4   12

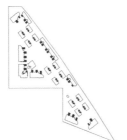

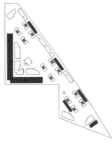

buildings

buildings are placed as "ground" around
the open space "figure." long, thin buildings
shield the site from the freeway.

thresholds

terraces, stoops and walkways overlook
and engage the community space.

parking

cars are pushed to the site perimeter
where they are convenient yet contained.

Above

At Tesoro Grove,
buildings are placed
as "ground" around
the open-space
"figure." Long, thin
buildings shield
the site from the
freeway. Terraces,
stoops, and
walkways overlook
and engage the
community space.

Above right

Simple stucco
boxes at Tesoro
Grove make a
suitable backdrop
for articulated bays
and entrances.

Tesoro Grove

Set on a leftover parcel in San Diego, near
the border with Mexico, Tesoro Grove is
sandwiched between Interstate 5 and the
backside of adjacent properties. As is typical
in affordable housing, for-profit developers
did not consider the site desirable. Burdened
with a frontage of nearly 1,200 feet directly
along the interstate, the site is exposed to
the 300,000 daily vehicle trips that are made
to and from the San Ysidro border port of
entry. In addition, site access requires an
easement across the adjacent sewage pump
station's property. The backyards of several
marginal residential developments overlook
the site. Finally, the south end of the site
fronts Nestor Creek. The creek's flood plain
extends onto the site, and the creek bed is
a protected wetland.

Our solution under these conditions
was to "circle the wagons" and create
a community around a common realm
of open spaces and streets. Parking was
pushed to the perimeter, and the buildings
are located between the common area
and the parking area. The project is
organized around an internal street that
links plazas, common space, and a large
community lawn. Buildings form and
overlook these zones to create a continuous and legible public realm.

The common realm was conceived as
a syncopated experience of alternating
open and enclosed spaces connected
by a small village street. The sequence is
initiated at the arrival point by a plaza and
passes through a grove and a lawn before
terminating at a palm court. Each of these
spaces allows cars to pass but is intended
primarily for pedestrians, and the distinction
between pedestrian and vehicular areas
was deliberately made ambiguous. All
typical clues about driving surfaces (curbs,
asphalt paving, and so on) were dispensed
with, and as a result cars move more slowly
through the complex.

Buildings are constructed of a simple kit of parts and rely on a plastic arrangement of discrete elements to take best advantage of San Diego's quality of light. Construction techniques are simple and cost-sensitive but are enriched by sectional variations and careful placement of openings.

Eleventh Avenue Townhomes

Set in Escondido amid one of north San Diego County's oldest and densest neighborhoods, Eleventh Avenue Townhomes offers all the sunlight, privacy, and attached parking of newer suburban "dream houses" at almost twice the density. These clustered houses sacrifice big front lawns, but they gain a greater sense of neighborhood.

Two spines of attached town-houses front a narrow tree-lined lane. This communal axis serves as a path for automobiles and pedestrians. Midway along its length, the lane breaks open into a protected plaza/courtyard, a space for both formal and informal gatherings. A barnlike meeting hall looks across a tree-filled plaza to an open lawn that includes a colorful children's play structure. The common laundry facility and the resident manager's office are located at this quadrangle. At the far end of the lane, beyond the last two units, is a second common area developed as overflow parking and allotment gardens where residents grow fruits, vegetables, and herbs.

The units are developed as simple, easy-to-furnish plans with a minimum of interior circulation and a maximum of flexibility. An attunement to family living is felt in the provision of small rear patios accessible from the main living area and in the careful attention paid to privacy for the upper-level bedrooms.

While the project responds directly to its immediate site, it is clearly capable of replication. The one-car attached garage could easily be converted into a small professional office or a cottage-industry workshop in another context. Further, its overall width of only 100 feet makes it ideal for insertion into other exurban and urban infill sites.

In affordable-housing design, basic considerations become paramount. The designer must find ways to make poetry out of a very modest kit of parts. Yet we believe that the seemingly mundane activities that consume most of our waking hours can inform the making of meaningful places that are fresh and accommodating. This is how designers can transmute the "lead" of affordable housing into an innovative, sustainable, community-oriented "gold" that can in turn transform the entire housing industry.

Right
Studio E Architec
Eleventh Avenue
Townhomes,
Escondido,
California. 1999.
Porches engage th
drive, making the
lane a pedestrian
space where cars
are the occasional
interlopers.

Competition, Collaboration, and Construction with Habitat for Humanity

ERIK VAN MEHLMAN

A local Habitat for Humanity affiliate teams with a young designer to improve design quality, and lessons are learned by all.

Habitat for Humanity of Wake County, North Carolina (HFHWC), has developed into one of the top-rated affiliates of HFH in the United States. In an effort to develop new designs for Habitat homes, HFHWC joined with the Triangle Young Architects' Forum and the Triangle chapter of the American Institute of Architects to cosponsor a design competition for houses for a new neighborhood in Raleigh, to be named Biltmore Trace. The program called for the design of a one-story, 1,050-square-foot single-family home with three bedrooms, two bathrooms, a living room, a dining room, a kitchen, and a laundry room or utility closet. Required items excluded from the interior square footage included a covered front porch, a back patio or porch, and an exterior storage closet. Among other important criteria were the use of conventional wood framing with a truss floor and roof, standard-size windows, and maintenance-free siding. The hard cost of materials was to be less than $48,000. The site encompassed more than twenty potential lots in a forested area adjacent to an existing neighborhood in the southeast section of the city.

As affordable-housing design already filled a substantial portion of my professional hours, I thought the competition would give me a fantastic opportunity to push beyond the bounds of the "traditional" and "historic" styles of work that my clients usually demanded. Other single-family dwellings I had designed included more opulent custom homes, speculative resort-community homes, historic restorations, and large and small residential additions. Although the competition did not specify a target client, I strove to consider many basic design principles that appear to be largely overlooked in all sectors of the housing industry. These included the house's placement on the site, solar orientation, natural daylight, contextualism, and nonmechanical thermal comfort. Other important considerations that I sought to satisfy in this project included separating public and private areas, maximizing volumes through sharing space, maximizing storage room, and reducing sound transmission. I created the competition entry to include elements that I felt would enhance the physical, spatial, environmental, and contextual design of the home, and eschewed the omnipresent gable-roofed ornamented box. Affordable housing, like all forms of architecture, demands a thoughtful and sensitive design approach.

When the competition results were announced, I received the incredible news that my design was one of two selected for construction. Immediately, HFHWC and I began conducting a dialogue that allowed both parties to come to a better understanding of each other's goals and desires. The short-term result of this collaboration was the construction of a uniquely designed home for HFHWC. The long-term results have yet to be determined; however, encouraging the collaboration between HFH and the design community will prove beneficial to both parties in their pursuit of high-quality affordable housing.

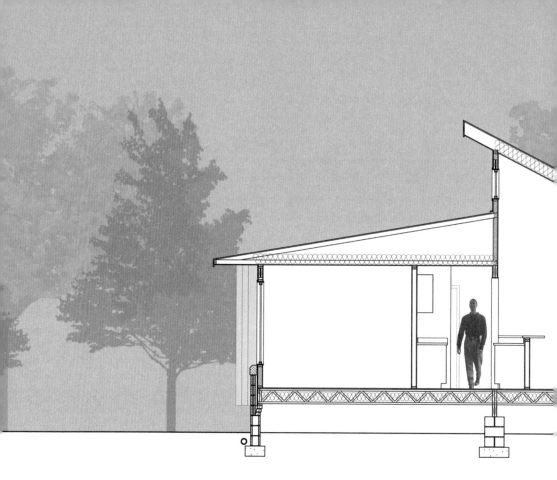

Construction Documents:
Compromise and Refinement

I was pleased that the other scheme chosen for construction was designed by Anna Marich, because she and I had spent some time collaborating on our competition entries. For both of us the honor of winning the competition carried with it the responsibility of completing the construction documents over the next few months. The collaboration that ensued with Chuck Dopler, HFHWC's construction manager, was invaluable. The challenges of and similarities between the two designs would create an important learning experience for us as designers and for the many others involved in the project.

Due to issues regarding ease of construction and other practical concerns, certain compromises had to be made right away. An 8/12-pitched section of roof had to be reduced to a lower 6/12 pitch to provide a safer slope for volunteer roofing crews.

The kitchen layout required revisions to satisfy HFHWC's standard for linear feet of cabinetry and to accommodate the typical appliance package. These revisions were minor, relative to the overall scope of the designs and the excitement with which Chuck received them. "I really like the retro-modern look of both designs," Chuck said. "This is a great opportunity to build two homes that are noticeably different from anything else we have built before."

Anna Marich's design was to occupy lot 1, a prominent corner lot at the Biltmore Trace neighborhood entrance. To provide the appropriate solar orientation for my design, I selected lot 17, one of the few east-west–oriented lots.

In an attempt to reduce our workload Anna and I agreed to develop a similar language for much of the exterior detailing. As we were required to use maintenance-free materials, we considered numerous

Maintaining a certain level of design integrity became a personal matter, and we invested more of our time in pursuing alternate means of compliance. We contacted local masonry representatives and were able to secure sufficient donations of surplus supplies of split-faced concrete masonry units to serve both houses.

By the time I delivered a full set of construction documents for lot 17, I had developed a great rapport with Chuck. I recognized his responsibility to keep project costs in line, and I felt that he recognized my devotion to developing a quality product under the same guidelines.

The Right Homeowner for a Unique Home

The lot 17 plans were presented to potential homeowners along with other house plans approved for the Biltmore Trace development. After some time Chuck contacted me to let me know that the majority of potential homeowners didn't like the design. The typical comment was, "It doesn't look like the other houses." Joyce Watkins King, the director of development and communications for HFHWC, said, "It was a little harder to find 'progressive' homeowners that were willing to be part of the project."

It was close to a year later when Chuck called me to report that a homeowner had selected the home on lot 17. When I later came to know the homeowner, Stephanie Davis, I realized that lot 17 was truly meant for her. Stephanie had consistently rejected a more traditional aesthetic in favor of more contemporary styles. She was thrilled that no one else in the neighborhood would live in a house of the same design, and she was so enamored with her home's uniqueness that she filed the plans away to hide them from her soon-to-be neighbors. Stephanie wanted the home's design to emerge as an ongoing surprise during construction. Chuck later commented, "We offered the unusual design, knowing potential homeowners might refuse it. Of course, once it was built, many of those that passed on it said they wished they had taken it when it was offered."

compositions of masonry, metals, and vinyl. Chuck stressed to us the importance of retaining simplicity in a design intended to be volunteer-friendly, and he requested more concessions on our part. For instance, we were required to reduce window openings to a maximum allowable square footage. Anna and I grew somewhat frustrated because we feared that our designs were slowly being transformed into a product out of Habitat's standards manual.

Some of Chuck's suggested changes were intended to prevent the project from going over budget. For example, in response to the adjacent neighborhood's exterior language, our competition designs called for a concrete masonry unit foundation and veneer wall carrying up to the underside of the windowsill; but when Chuck suggested that we provide Habitat's standard traditional brick foundation terminating at the mud sill, Anna and I finally tired of compromise.

Construction: Volunteers vs. the Weather

Because I had a few years of construction experience, I made the decision to become a regular volunteer in the construction process and see the design through to completion. Once contracted masons had completed the split-faced concrete masonry unit foundation, I headed out to lot 17 on a frosty winter morning to help set the floor trusses. Anna joined me, as she had expressed an interest in contributing to the construction of her design as well, and she welcomed the opportunity to add to her construction experience. That day I met Stephanie Davis and her daughter Kristen, and it was then that I began to realize the true value of the work. What had begun as an exercise in design and construction had become a mission to provide a high-quality home to a family that needed and deserved it.

I was also introduced to general contractor Walt Lewis, who had volunteered to be the "house leader." Walt may have been apprehensive about working with the "designer"; however, I quickly understood that his energy, enthusiasm, and collaborative attitude were a perfect fit for the job. As his knowledge of field construction was far superior to mine, I knew I needed to regard him as a valuable resource. It was vital for me to guide the project rather than to dictate its workings. Anna and I worked and perspired as much

as anyone on the site, yet we felt that our main job was to keep the design intent on course.

Apart from Stephanie, Walt, Anna, and myself, only a sparse crew of volunteers gathered at the site. I learned that lot 17 had an anonymous sponsor and was not affiliated with a church congregation, as are the majority of Habitat projects. The small size of the crew afforded both benefits and costs. There was little need to familiarize new volunteers with the scope of work, as our crew reliably showed up almost every Saturday. However, the general lack of numbers slowed the pace of construction, eventually resulting in volunteer burnout.

Working only on Saturdays also hindered progress, and Mother Nature provided additional delays, as rain fell on six of the first twelve Saturdays. For all of these reasons it took approximately four months to complete the framing, the sheathing, and the installation of the exterior doors and windows.

With the amount of time Anna was spending in the field at lot 17, she had put off completing the construction documents for lot 1—a delay that unexpectedly turned out to be a great benefit. The time we spent on lot 17 gave us a better understanding of the limitations in the volunteers' general construction skills, and Anna was able

below
onstruction of the
ouse on lot 17

As affordable-housing design already filled a substantial portion of my professional hours, I thought the competition would give me a fantastic opportunity to push beyond the bounds of the "traditional" and "historic" styles of work that my clients usually demanded.

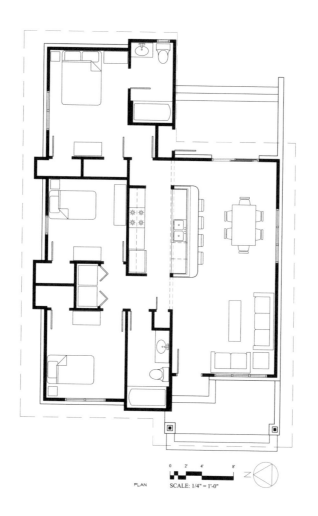

PLAN   SCALE: 1/4" = 1'-0"

0 2' 4'   8'

to simplify portions of the lot 1 design accordingly. For example, the stick-framed 6/12-pitched shed roof at lot 17 proved extremely time-consuming to build because Walt and I were the only crew members willing to work atop the first floor framing. As construction continued, lot 17 often served as a testing ground for on-site detail modifications that served as full-scale examples for the crew at lot 1.

Ground was broken at lot 1 in the spring, and Anna joined the lot 1 volunteers when they arrived. Two church congregations were sponsoring the work on this house, which meant that thirty to forty volunteers were present on the site each Saturday. The home's construction was greatly accelerated, making our experience at lot 1 the antithesis of that at lot 17. The crews at both lots continued their hard work through the summer. Aside from the interior painting, the major volunteer tasks during that period included the installation of roofing, siding, interior doors, trim, flooring, and cabinetry.

From week to week there were exhilarations and frustrations, but Saturdays were always personally rewarding. Anna and I also kept busy securing donated items to enhance the homes. Custom concrete counters were installed in both homes, a laminate wood floor was installed through the living/dining/kitchen area at lot 17, and a special polymyx paint was applied as an accent to a prominent wall at lot 1. As a final gift to the Davis family, I fabricated and installed a library-style ladder system to access the operable clerestory windows. Both homes were completed and formally dedicated in the fall. The AIA Triangle chapter and Triangle Young Architects' Forum sponsored a tour of the homes, both of which were very well received by our guests.

Post-Occupancy Evaluation

The Davis residence at lot 17 is based on a simple design. Three bedrooms are separated from the public living/dining/kitchen area by a utility core containing the bathrooms and kitchen. The kitchen, dining, and living areas share each other's space. The operable clerestory windows above the public area evenly flood the space with north light, and when the windows are opened, they provide a stack-effect

airflow that noticeably cools the home. The windows and the sloped ceiling create a light-filled volume that provides a feeling of grand space in this relatively small area. During construction, visitors, and workers often remarked that the house was bigger than other designs on site, when it was actually one of the smallest.

When I recently visited Stephanie at her home, I felt that I had been successful in designing a house that she and her family loved. She had understood the potential of this modest space the minute she laid eyes on it. "When I saw the plans," she said, "I could imagine sitting in this room [the living room] like it is now, with everything so open, and sitting here with them [her children]. If you're in the kitchen, it's not closed off, like in some kitchens where you can't see what's happening in the living room. I can work in the kitchen and talk to Kristen or watch my shows. She can do her homework or get on the computer, and we can all interact and talk. I think this house is just what we needed."

While I was successful in meeting Stephanie's needs, I was less successful in meeting Habitat's. Chuck has told me that if HFHWC sponsors another competition, it will put a cap on the cost and more emphasis on repeatability of construction, the very areas where Stephanie's home missed the mark to some extent. Before construction was even completed, Chuck asked if I could alter the design for future use by eliminating the high sloping ceiling and clerestory windows. He explained, "The reason I would not build your house again is that we do not need all the extras like the very high volume ceiling, the clerestory windows, and the split-face block."

Chuck is certainly right to say that this house had a lot of "extras," judged relative to the typical Habitat home. In the desire to complete my vision of the home, I went out of my way to secure donated materials that would normally exceed the material costs for a standard HFHWC home. I obtained donated masonry for additional veneer applications and cherry laminate flooring for the public areas of the home. I solicited monetary donations to offset the cost of the casement windows. We benefited from the donation of the manufacture and installation of the concrete kitchen counter. I supplied the rail-and-ladder system for the clerestory windows and spent numerous hours at the site detailing the exterior with maintenance-free materials. We transitioned vertical-oriented siding and horizontal-oriented siding to differentiate between interior spaces and create an exterior rhythm. We ran vertical asphalt shingles to define the roof forms. And we carefully wrapped exterior columns and beams with aluminum coil stock.

Although my intentions were to serve the homeowner by creating the best home possible, it is highly unlikely that a personal design and donation liaison could be assigned to every Habitat house. However, I would eliminate every other "extra" in the design and construction of the dwelling before I would reconfigure the volume of the main space. The sloping ceiling and the clerestory windows together provide the essence of what makes this home special. I would hope that reducing or eliminating the cost of some or all of the other special characteristics of the house would allow these two elements to remain.

Post-Construction Reflections

More than two years after the homes were completed, I asked Chuck if he thought HFHWC had benefited from the design competition and the resultant construction. He said he saw two direct benefits. One was that more students and professionals in construction, architecture, and the technical fields became interested in Habitat as a result of tours of these homes. The other benefit was that HFHWC feels it now communicates and coordinates better with architects, having gained insight into an architect's considerations regarding afford-able housing. HFHWC's Joyce Watkins King also considers the positive exposure from the projects to be a great asset. She said, "I think our affiliate has enjoyed ample publicity from this project, and it has influenced other partnerships [with more architects]."

For me, the competition to design an affordable home became a life-changing experience. I learned a lot about HFH and even more about myself. The sore muscles from a Saturday of hard work filled me

with more exhilaration than pain. I am very pleased to have worked with an HFH affiliate as progressive as the one in Wake County.

Continued collaboration between HFH and the design community will only improve their working relationship. HFH is one of the largest homebuilders in the country; it needs to understand the impact it has on the built environment, and the responsibility this impact creates. Habitat could also benefit from research into long-term savings versus up-front costs, investigation of new materials, and an emphasis on house plans that have a better regard for regional vernacular and site orientation.

For their part, architects must create more volunteer-friendly designs and must work on ways to implement design strategies while honoring budget constraints. A sustained collaboration between HFH and the design community will benefit both parties, our built environment, and the most important stakeholders of all: the families who will live in the homes we design and build.

Architecture and Social Change:
The Struggle for Affordable Housing
in Oakland's Uptown Project

ALEX SALAZAR

**Communities,
activists, and
designers prove
that when people
work together,
affordable housing
can become a
reality even when
challenging the
agendas of the
most powerful.**

There have been significant changes in the affordable-housing field as it has grown and professionalized over the past few decades. Nonprofit developers and the private architecture firms that serve them have increased in size and sophistication, enabling them to compete on larger and larger projects—and causing them to become more distanced from local communities. Perhaps this distancing is the inevitable outcome of the growth and development of stable, well-respected firms that can navigate the inner-city obstacle course of neighborhood groups, affordable-housing advocates, and government departments while creating the award-winning projects demanded by clients and the profession.

Unfortunately the gap between the nonprofit development field and grassroots groups has become too wide to ignore, and some of the people that affordable housing was originally meant to serve are falling through the cracks. To solve this problem a whole new generation of community-based organizations has arisen, led by young, dynamic, politically sharp activists who take race and class issues seriously. They are not designers, and they do not know what "community design" is; but they are challenging established nonprofit developers and architecture firms to reexamine their roots and rediscover why they entered the nonprofit field to begin with. These activists are creating opportunities for young community-design architects and planners to get involved in antidisplacement affordable-housing work in a meaningful way while doing design work for progressive causes that can make a difference.

The dilemma, however, is that very few young architects want to get involved, and those who are interested do not know where to begin. They may have the skills to make a great contribution to the affordable-housing landscape, but the culture of mainstream practice trains young professionals to think of community design only as a method for getting projects approved by city planning departments. The greatest challenge facing today's community-oriented architects is to learn the skills taught and practiced in mainstream firms while putting those skills to work for grassroots organizations. This means taking the time to learn high-quality design and technical skills on large-scale multifamily housing projects, a process that takes years, while also getting involved in organizations that see the lack of affordable housing as an issue not of design and production but of power.

A focus on power is a crucial element in putting design at the service of justice. This discussion is ultimately about power: the power of developers to push out low-income communities of color, and the power of grassroots community-organizing groups to resist that effort.

The Slumification and Jerryfication of Downtown Oakland

Starting in the 1930s Oakland, California, became a point of disembarkation for African-Americans who were fleeing Southern racism and who found employment in Oakland's wartime port economy. By the 1950s a backlash was under way: whites were in full flight to the suburbs, and race-based policies like redlining became part of local planning. For example, redevelopment studies in the 1950s and 1960s documented the African-American population and were used to plan the removal of African-Americans under the guise of improving dilapidated housing.

The failure to meaningfully address political and social inequities in the city, coupled with the decline of Oakland as an industrial center, gave rise to the West Coast civil rights movement and the Black Liberation struggle. West Oakland, in particular, became a hotbed of activism in the 1960s and 1970s, epitomized by the rise and fall of the Black Panthers, who polarized the city and helped contribute to Oakland's reputation as one of the most dangerous places to live in the country.

Not much changed physically in the downtown area until the Loma Prieta earthquake in 1989, when commercial and historic buildings, along with miles of infrastructure, were left in ruins. The quake significantly damaged most remaining single-room-occupancy hotels, forcing thousands of very low-income people, mostly African-Americans, into homelessness. In the vacuum left by fleeing private developers, nonprofits stepped up their advocacy for affordable housing and harnessed state and federal resources to do the job.

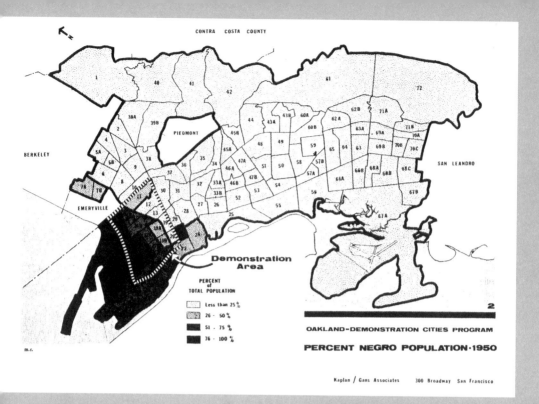

CONTRA COSTA COUNTY

BERKELEY

PIEDMONT

EMERYVILLE

SAN LEANDRO

Demonstration Area

PERCENT
of
TOTAL POPULATION

Less than 25 %
26 - 50 %
51 - 75 %
76 - 100 %

2

OAKLAND–DEMONSTRATION CITIES PROGRAM

PERCENT NEGRO POPULATION·1950

Kaplan / Gans Associates   300 Broadway San Francisco

Oakland's Uptown

Despite the association of the term "affordable housing" with the drug-infested, crime-ridden public housing projects of the past, there is a growing awareness that affordable housing actually increases property values. Downtown Oakland is a classic example. Throughout the 1990s nonprofit developers were the first to produce attractive, high-density buildings on infill sites in the riskiest areas. Projects that revitalized streets and contained social services for extremely low-income residents were often mistaken for market-rate developments. Twenty years in the making, they were the fruit of labor by an active community of advocates and nonprofits that helped generate the financial and political will to address housing inequities.

By the time former California governor Jerry Brown became mayor of Oakland in 1998, however, neighborhood stability had spurred a booming condo market, and gentrification and displacement had become commonplace. Oakland's affordable-housing history appeared to be forgotten, along with Brown's New Age sensibilities and the left-wing talk-show persona that helped him win the election. As mayor Brown was born again, this time as a realist aiming to liberalize Oakland's political economy. During his first year in office he launched several new policy agendas, including the creation of charter schools, the reorganization and expansion of the police department, the promotion of environmental responsibility, and the 10K plan, an effort intended to attract 10,000 residents to Oakland's downtown core.

According to Brown, 10K would create a new "Ecopolis," where an environmentally friendly city could reduce suburban sprawl by producing "elegantly dense" downtown housing linked to public transportation. Brown hoped that a variety of condo projects would help revitalize the heart of the city, providing an upscale twenty-four-hour commercial economy that had not operated in Oakland for more than thirty years.

eft
edevelopment
gency of Oakland
emonstration
ities Program,
map tracking
e distribution of
frican-American
ouseholds in
akland, California,
1950

New Housing Update
- **1,471** units completed
- **350** units under construction
- **1,436** units with planning approval
- **1,712** units in planning

4,969 total units

Telegraph Lofts (Old Sears Bldg.) 53 units

Midtown Lofts 426 67th St. 20 units

Cox Cadillac 125 units

Broadway Auto Row

North Gate

Telegraph Gateway 42 units

23rd & Valdez 204 units

23rd & Northgate 42 units

23rd & Broadway 422 units

Lake Merritt District

Uptown 1040 Units

The Essex 270 units

Uptown

Lake Merritt

San Pablo Triangle

1640 Broadway 254 units

YWCA 50 units

14th & Jackson 50 units

Gold Coast

14th & Madison 76 units

City Center

14th & Harrison 98 units

Swan's Market 42 units

380-388 12th St 10 units

Jackson Center II 100 units

11th & Oak 52 units

Landmark Place (Pres. Park III) 92 units

Arioso 88 units

Old Oakland

Chinatown

251 9th St 29 units

Castro Courts 50 Units

8th & Castro Lofts 18 units

Market Square 202 units

Gem Building Condos 16 units

Wheelink 94 units

New Market Lofts (Safeway Bldg.) 46 units

Phoenix Lofts 21 units

Ironworks District

300 Harrison 91 units

The Sierra 229 units

2nd & Broadway 110 units

Waterfront Warehouse District

Allegro 310 units

Jack London Square

206 2nd St Lofts 75 units

Second St Lofts 100 units

The Landing 282 units

OAKLAND INNER HARBOR

ight
ity of Oakland
ommunity
nd Economic
evelopment
gency
ocation map for
ll 10K projects
2004

While the 10K plan was not entirely at odds with the nonprofit developments that preceded it, attitudes about the scheme changed in 1999, when the dot-com boom caused housing affordability to become a major issue. Downtown rental prices increased 40 percent in 1999 alone. No-cause evictions tripled, disproportionately affecting low-income minorities living in East and West Oakland. This context explains why Brown's infamous "slumification" speech backfired. In a public address to affordable-housing advocates early in his mayoral term, Brown described Oakland's economic future as a choice between 10K gentrification and the "slumification" of downtown perpetuated by new affordable-housing projects. Brown's terminology lent credibility to the view that 10K was a racialized plan serving middle- and upper-class whites, mostly San Francisco commuters, while fostering gentrification and displacement of the low-income minority communities that had lived in downtown Oakland for generations. Brown's rhetoric also fueled downtown residents' desire to fight his plan.

Artists living in the warehouse districts were some of the first to be displaced in the early boom years, and they quickly dubbed the 10K plan the "Jerryfication" of Oakland, a term later embraced by the mainstream media. Advocates for tenants and the homeless organized around evictions and rising rents, creating Just Cause Oakland, a tenant-rights ballot initiative and organizing project that mobilized record numbers of tenants to speak out against displacement. Other concerned organizations, including labor unions and church-based coalitions, began making housing one of their key organizing issues. Amid this resurgence of grassroots housing advocacy, East Bay Housing Organizations, an umbrella nonprofit housing advocacy group, spearheaded the Coalition for Workforce Housing (CWH) to bring activists together with nonprofit housing developers and social-service providers.

CWH made the following demands of the city government:

- Twenty-five percent of 10K housing must be affordable to households earning $35,000 or less.

- The city must enact a "Just Cause for Eviction" ordinance and must not displace residents for the 10K plan.

- The 10K plan must preserve single-room-occupancy hotels and downtown social services for extremely low-income people.

While CWH demands addressed the 10K plan overall, the real target was the Uptown, a 1,040-unit mixed-use development that was the 10K's largest and highest-profile component. Unlike San Francisco and San Jose, Oakland had seen little new market-rate development in the 1990s, so when Uptown came along, city leaders were easily persuaded to give a $60 million sweetheart-deal subsidy to Forest City, Uptown's developer.

This largesse made the Uptown a focal point for advocates, and by the summer of 1999 CWH had launched a three-pronged advocacy strategy:

1. Bring media pressure to bear.
Early in the campaign, CWH held a series of public events that highlighted the lack of affordable housing downtown and in the Uptown project. In March 2001, three hundred Oakland residents of all economic and racial backgrounds came together for a "Gentrification Tour." Homeless and tenant advocates marched near the Uptown site and visited a dozen surrounding locations where residents had been evicted or would soon be at risk. The event raised awareness of displacement and put the media spotlight on city officials' positions on housing issues.

2. Act as a public-policy watchdog.
CWH participated in nearly all city-sponsored meetings regarding housing and used these platforms to promote its demands. In the winter of 2003, twenty residents and advocates took over an Uptown community-design charrette and forced the design team and city staff to hear testimony from local residents and review a presentation of the CWH affordable-housing design proposal.

3. Reevaluate Uptown from a community-design standpoint.
In 2002 volunteer architects and planners developed an affordable-housing design proposal for the Uptown site, demonstrating how the community's demands could be met without significantly changing Forest City's development plans. This organizing culminated a year later with a CWH-sponsored community-design charrette. Approximately thirty coalition activists and community members turned out to study the Uptown's gentrification impact and to give input into the mix of units and levels of affordability in the CWH design proposal. City staff and the Forest City development team participated in the event, which demonstrated to the city and the developer that CWH had the technical knowledge to challenge the development on an informed basis.

Right
East Bay Housing
Organizations,
Oakland
City of Oakland:
Reported 30 Day
No-Cause Evictions,
July 1998–March
2000. The majority
of "no-cause"
evictions affected
low-income
minorities living
in Oakland's flat-
lands, between the
80 freeway and
San Francisco Bay.

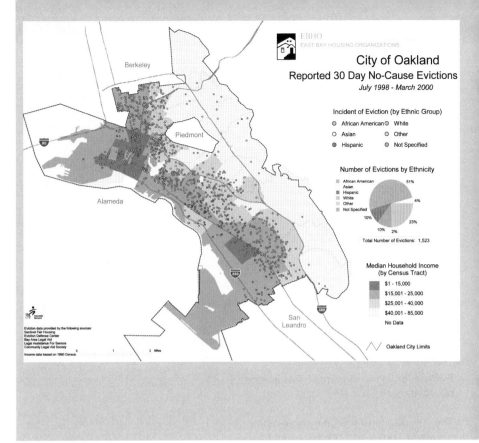

An Alternative Approach

The CWH proposal worked within the Uptown development grid, but it used two of the city blocks to create stand-alone affordable-housing developments with on-site social services. CWH's plan was for these buildings to serve families and extremely low-income tenants, offer social services, and help Forest City make good use of less-desirable land parcels that were risky for market rate buildings. This scheme would utilize a variety of funding sources to produce more than 210 units for residents earning incomes from 20 to 50 percent of area median income (AMI). It also followed many of the design principles promoted by New Urbanists: orienting ground-floor uses like retail stores to the street for a pedestrian-friendly environment; articulating building scale, form, and massing to fit the context of the neighborhood and the particulars of the site; and orienting dwelling units toward the street, with front stoops and windows, in order to increase

safety and create a neighborhood atmosphere. Uptown's affordable housing was to be concentrated in these two city block sites. CWH proposed that Forest City partner with local nonprofits to develop and/or manage these buildings.

CWH's plan to focus on two sites was also strategic, as the organizers knew that once they entered negotiations with Forest City, they would need something to give up in a compromise. This strategy paid off, as it turned out that one of the proposed sites was still owned by the city. As a result of public pressure, the city's redevelopment staff was pulled into negotiations, giving CWH leverage with the developer. Subsequently, CWH gave up one site and in return convinced the developer to set aside the city-owned parcel for a local nonprofit. This affordable-housing development, by Resources for Community Development, is under construction and will be completed in 2008.

The Power of Community Design

The CWH's campaign in Oakland showcases the real power of community design: not as a neutral "method" used in the design profession, but as a tool to help achieve political, economic, and social change. CWH's work was, at its heart, not about designing individual buildings. Instead, it was one step in a process of building neighborhood power.

Indeed, community organizing around affordable-housing issues has since spread to two other major redevelopment projects in the city. New coalitions have formed to take on some of the largest market-rate housing developers in the region. Out of these political struggles, new leaders have emerged and community-design strategies continue to evolve. Community-design campaigns such as the Coalition for Workforce Housing remind us that inclusive, grassroots-driven efforts can ensure that housing developments are held publicly accountable in a meaningful way.

Editor's note: An earlier version of this text was published in Shelterforce, *spring 2006.*

Right
Coalition for
Workforce Housing
First conceptual
elevation of
proposed affordable
housing in Oakland.
2003. Rendering
by Alex Salazar

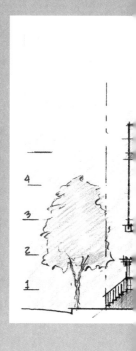

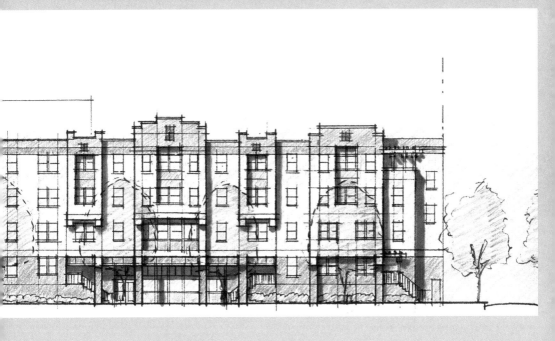

PREFAB-RICATING AFFORD-ABILITY

Migrant Housing

LAURA SHIPMAN

By devoting special
attention to user
needs and the
application of improved
technology, mass-
produced housing
can address the
specific requirements
of small groups.

Prior to the disaster of Hurricane Katrina in 2005, the hurricane season of 2004 was one of the most active seasons on record, as reported by the National Oceanic and Atmospheric Administration, with damages estimated at $45 billion. The paths of the most destructive hurricanes crisscrossed the state of Florida. By November 3, 2004, all sixty-seven Florida counties had been federally designated as disaster areas.

The difficulties of disaster response are especially complicated for the approximately 300,000 migrants who work in Florida's agricultural industry. Annual family incomes do not exceed $10,000 per year, and farmworkers often live in dilapidated mobile homes that are extremely vulnerable to storm damage. The hurricanes of 2004 destroyed or damaged hundreds of units of farmworker housing, exacerbating an already-severe shortage in affordable housing. According to the Federal Emergency Management Agency (FEMA), the fourteen Florida counties most damaged by the storms are home to approximately one-third of Florida's farmworkers, some of whom are undocumented and thus cannot receive housing relief from FEMA.

Advocate Rob Williams of Florida Legal Services brought the situation of Florida's farmworkers to the attention of Design Corps. Working as a fellow on the Design Corps team, I received the assignment. We agreed that as migrant farmworker housing was rebuilt, there was a need to assess the shortcomings of preexisting units and seek a new housing model. We wanted to develop pleasant homes that would withstand hurricane-force winds, be sensitive to the needs of farmworkers, be flexible and adaptable to ensure longevity, and be produced in a way that could be duplicated on multiple sites throughout Florida's agricultural regions, to address the widespread shortage of housing for these laborers.

DeSoto County

After completing our discussions, we traveled to migrant farmworker housing camps in the Arcadia and Nocatee areas of DeSoto County, Florida. These locations had been hard-hit by the storms of 2004 and are heavily populated by migrant farmworkers.

Our overall impression of housing in the area, beyond the immediate devastation wrought by the hurricanes, was the dilapidation and overcrowding that had preceded the storms.

There were three types of housing typically used for farmworkers:

1. Old houses converted into farmworker housing.
This type of dwelling was problematic because the houses were often in pronounced disrepair before they were converted to rentals for farmworkers, and thus were structurally susceptible to storm damage.

2. Concrete masonry unit block housing.
This construction type weathered the hurricanes relatively well, and a few units had only minor window and roof damage. However, their interiors were often stark.

3. Manufactured housing and trailers.
Most of these units were more than twenty years old, and therefore predated many of the improvements that have been made in manufactured-housing construction techniques. They had weak structures and inadequate tie-downs to resist hurricane forces.

Once we had assessed the migrant farmworker housing situation in post-hurricane DeSoto County, we began conducting market research on the best construction practices, with special sensitivity to the culture, needs, and desires of the end users. By including farmworkers in the design process, Design Corps was able to formulate solutions that addressed the clients' highest priorities. In this way even the most limited resources were transformed into the most valued product.

In our planning, we adopted a long-term-value approach rather than emphasizing a short-term emergency response to the crisis. Past emergency-housing models, such as the FEMA type, provided a short-term solution that becomes poor long-term housing. This is directly due to design choices. As the designer of our project, I was charged with creating housing that would gain in value over a thirty-year life span. Manufactured housing built in other states, when designed properly, has already demonstrated this capacity.

Next we conducted initial investigations into possible site configurations, construction types, and hurricane design responses.

The durability of HUD housing bolstered our belief that well-designed and well-constructed manufactured housing was a sound choice for farmworker housing recovery.

With these findings in mind, our design process evolved to pursue a completely manufactured construction process, because of the ease of installation and reduced scope of site work that are typical of modular construction. We are

We researched the use of containers and manufactured and modular building methods. We also considered kinetic structures that could fold down into a hurricane-protection state, and we tried flexible modular units that would begin as a steel structural frame with modular living pods that could plug in as families grew or more space was needed.

One of the unexpected findings after the hurricanes of 2004 was the hurricane resistance of housing built by the U.S. Department of Housing and Urban Development (HUD) after 1994. As stated in a letter from Lori E. H. Killinger, director of governor's relations for the Florida Manufactured Housing Association, to Thaddeus Cohen, secretary of Florida's Department of Community Affairs, dated September 13, 2004:

In sum, the Department of Highway Safety and Motor Vehicles findings were clear that: the newer homes, built since HUD changed its building code in 1994, performed (without exception) admirably. It was not uncommon to see several destroyed homes with the newer HUD homes standing alone with the only damage being from flying debris. To further substantiate that finding, after touring the area, Governor Jeb Bush was quoted as saying that the new construction and installation standards for manufactured homes worked.

continuing to investigate post-manufacture improvement options such as storm-shutter systems and better tie-downs. And while environmental issues are not primary to the rapid response needed by this group of users, we are researching the best ways to ensure that these homes are environmentally sustainable.

Farmworker Focus Groups

A critical aspect of our process involved obtaining input from local migrant farmworkers. By including farmworkers in the design process, Design Corps was able to formulate solutions that addressed the clients' highest priorities. In this way even the most limited resources were transformed into the most valued product. We conducted focus groups as a method of participatory design to ensure that our schemes would be geared toward the intended end users' needs. Juanita Mainster, hurricane coordinator for the Redlands Christian Migrant Association (a farmworker advocacy group), helped facilitate and translate for the focus groups.

Because of the farmworkers' busy schedules, our family meetings were arranged so that parents could attend while their children stayed an extra hour at a daycare center. There were two main components of the participatory-design focus groups: personal information and design input. For the former

> **By including farm-workers in the design process, Design Corps was able to formulate solutions that addressed the clients' highest priorities. In this way even the most limited resources were transformed into the most valued product.**

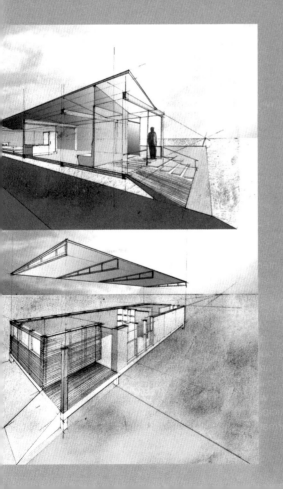

component, we administered a survey to elicit personal information and information on current housing conditions. We learned that the migrant families that participated were all originally from Mexico and had families ranging in size from three to eight members. They worked in the citrus and tomato industries in Florida, Michigan, North Carolina, Ohio, Pennsylvania, and South Carolina. They lived in apartments, rental homes, and trailers; space, light, and outdoor playing space for children were important to them. One of their primary concerns was making sure the housing would be waiting for them when they returned each season.

We also conducted an exercise that gave participants a chance to design desired amenities for the home. Through this process we discovered that the exercise was slightly too complicated and needed to be simplified for future use. However, as we went through the questions individually, we were able to obtain the necessary insights into the family's preferences and concerns.

The second aspect of the group meeting was intended to get direct feedback on designs we had begun to develop based on farmworker research and participatory-design work conducted by Design Corps fellows in previous years. We set up models and drawings, and the participants viewed the designs, asked questions, and gave us their comments. The families generally preferred the two-bedroom design as it was best-suited for family needs. They liked the combined kitchen/dining/living space configuration because the open area made it possible to gather as a family and easily keep an eye on the kids. The participants also liked the sliding shutters for storm protection and off-season security. Many said the design's central housing plan appealed to them because it was reminiscent of the housing designs they had grown up with in Mexico.

Single Men's Focus Group

We also scheduled a meeting with single male migrant farmworkers who had lost their trailer in a fire. They were struggling to find alternate housing because of the hurricane-induced housing shortage, and they had been forced to pay exorbitant rents for substandard living quarters in trailers.

Above
James Sweeney
for Design Corps.
Migrant farmworker
housing, two-bed
version. Rendering
of the manufactured
design. 2007

Their initial input was simply that any housing would be better than what they currently had, but after further discussion specific and valuable input emerged. The men were currently working in construction because the citrus crops had been damaged by the hurricanes. For the rest of the year they worked mostly in Georgia and North Carolina. Their biggest complaints about the trailers were their small size and dark interiors.

When we showed the workers the initial housing-design concepts, they said they preferred the scheme with the covered porch, and they would not mind having four men sharing a big room. They liked the option of having the toilet and shower separated from each other. They strongly favored central heat, as their trailer had burned down because of a space heater. They also jokingly commented that they liked the design's metal siding because it would not burn. Overall, they liked the two-bedroom design best, mostly because its two separate rooms would make it possible to bring in a family member. They also liked the exterior accessibility of the utility room with a sink for washing up after work.

Meetings with Advocates and Growers
Our process also involved meetings with two local large-scale growers, as they have the resources necessary to provide their workers with good housing. One of the growers asserted that providing housing was a fundamental responsibility that his business had to its employees. He was able to give direct advice in terms of possible sites and appropriate construction techniques to enhance longevity and limit maintenance needed on the units. The other grower we met with did not provide housing for his farmworkers, like most large growers, because of cost and the concern with liability. After we presented our designs and discussed the long-term affordability and improved quality of these units, he stated that the company was considering building fifty farmworker units and this design could be one of the models considered.

In addition, we met with other farmworker advocates, such as activists from Catholic charities and organizers at the HUD farmworker forum, who shared with us their opinions on farmworker needs and their thoughts about our designs. We also had a meeting with the manufacturers to clarify our specifications in relation to typical methods of manufactured-housing construction.

Design Development
The two-bedroom unit was the one chosen for manufacture. The central plan allowed for a shorter corridor, creating a more efficient use of space. It was also the design preferred by farmworkers and advocates involved in the process.

The unit measures 56 feet x 14 feet x 12 feet 6 inches tall. Features include:

- a hurricane-resistant structure designed to handle winds of up to 110 miles per hour;

- nine-foot ceilings and increased glazing to provide a well-lit, spacious-feeling interior environment;

- energy efficiency through low-emissivity windows, a radiant barrier to prevent heat gain, and operable clerestory windows to allow for passive cross-ventilation;

- sliding window shutters for storm protection and off-season security;

- a two-bedroom design that can accommodate singles or families;

- a floor plan that allows for a utility room with a large sink adjacent to the exterior entry.

To a designer who had just completed her undergradate architecture studies, the most eye-opening part of this experience was learning just how many non-design factors are involved in producing this type of housing. Collaborating with advocates in other fields, going through the funding and approval processes, and interacting with farmworkers all broadened my perspective on the varied roles the designer must play in order to provide responsive and effective architectural advocacy.

Market Modular

GREGORY HERMAN

Two very different parties—architecture students and a manufactured housing company—combine strengths to yield affordable, well-designed housing.

Left
Students Sheana
Mitchell and Lisa
Skiles on a site
visit to the modular
house factory in
Anderson, Missouri

Pedagogical Objective: A Modular House?

Design/build programs often jeopardize their own viability because of pitfalls inherent in the production process. The desire to create well-designed, affordable housing has become the goal of many architecture programs in recent years, but the inability of these academic groups to engage enhanced processes of production often blocks real innovation. This essay describes a design/build house project recently conducted at the University of Arkansas School of Architecture's Design/Build Workshop (D/BW). The workshop had previously produced three affordable-housing projects, and when I became the sole instructor of the D/BW in 2003, I wanted to continue in the tradition of these successes with a new project during the spring semester.

We set out to explore the conventional, market-produced modular house, inserting ourselves into the construction process as designers, in order to create a house that was affordable and available to an individual or family of low to moderate income.

We chose the modular process because it was well suited to our goal of producing an affordable home for a low-income buyer. By taking advantage of the conveniences and economies of modular housing (for example, weatherproof assembly-line construction), it seemed we might be able to stay within our tight budget of approximately $60 per square foot, including land and all other costs. Furthermore, the efficiency and speed promised by modular producers gave us hope that we would have a finished product by the end of the semester.

As designers our objective was not to fully activate a conventional modular process; the interventions of architecture students would have been unnecessary for that aim. Rather, we wanted to work within some aspects of the conventional modular production process as a learning experience.

A modular manufacturer would construct the house through the framing stages and complete the mechanical, electrical, and plumbing work, providing us with an impressively solid building "carcass" for the project. The students, who shared the duty of making regularly scheduled factory visits to monitor the progress of construction and respond to builders' questions, would then design and install all exterior finish components and materials as they saw fit to make the project meet the needs of the stakeholders—city officials, bankers, realtors, representatives of the manufacturer, and neighborhood advocates. This promising combination of industry resources, stakeholders, and the students' sweat equity provided what we felt to be a unique model for the kind of collaborative work we sought. More important, this scheme allowed each contributing party—the manufacturer and the students—to offer the best of their abilities.

Changes in Sponsorship Cause Changes in the Design Process

Full-cost sponsorship of the D/BW project houses completed in 2001 and 2002 (for which I served as faculty coinstructor) had been provided by a local bank that ultimately also chose and approved the purchaser of the house. Though these projects were successful from both a social and an academic standpoint, the bank redirected its community efforts and decided not to continue sponsoring our D/BW projects. The new project was instead supported by the modular manufacturer and by the city of Fayetteville, which provided Community Development Block Grant (CDBG) funding for the purchase of the building lot and, as the final cost of the house threatened to exceed our initial goal, further discretionary funding.

Design of the house began with a student competition resulting in a team-designed project. We then presented the winning entry to the stakeholders. This was to be a house sold on the market, designed and built without the input of a pre-chosen buyer; under such circumstances the sponsors wanted local interests to have an opportunity to comment on the project, helping to ensure the salability of the constructed house.

Left and right
Design/Build
Workshop
Modular house.
2003. Framing
model by Andy Ki
elevation renderin
by Amy Koenig

All parties in attendance made a number of suggestions and requests. With an eye toward minimizing purchase price, the representative from city hall asked that the cost be no higher than 60 percent of median income guidelines as determined by the U.S. Department of Housing and Urban Development. This demand was a daunting obstacle in Arkansas, where median incomes are low even by regional standards. Additional limitations emerged as panel members offered their input. In a discussion of exterior cladding materials, the direction of the conversation naturally turned toward maintenance costs, and the city representative requested that the house be clad in "maintenance-free" vinyl siding. While vinyl siding was a standard finish cladding material offered by this particular modular manufacturer, the student designers wanted to explore other options. After some consideration they expressed their desire to finish the house in a combination of painted cement-fiber siding panels and corrugated galvanized aluminum panels (the latter is particularly inexpensive in this part of the country, as it is a common cladding material for poultry-raising facilities). The city representative,

still insisting on low-maintenance cladding, offered the following compromise: if we used a painted material, it was to be applied to a height no higher than one person could reach with a roller and without a ladder. We felt we had assisted the city official in coming to a new understanding of what could be considered maintenance-free.

Other issues came to light during the semester, as would happen in any collaborative design process. The manufacturer's representatives expressed some concern about the roof design. The roof of a factory-made modular house is constructed as a group of hinged planes that are folded in upon themselves for shipping. The house arrives at its final site sheathed and ready for cladding, except for areas that will be covered by the roof. The roof is then unfolded and set into place on top of supporting knee-walls. Our manufacturer's houses are always outfitted with low double-pitched roofs, but the students' design called for two major single-pitched roof volumes. When our single-pitched roof was unfolded on site, the unsheathed and unclad tops of the exterior walls directly beneath the ridgeline of the roof pitches would be exposed to the elements.

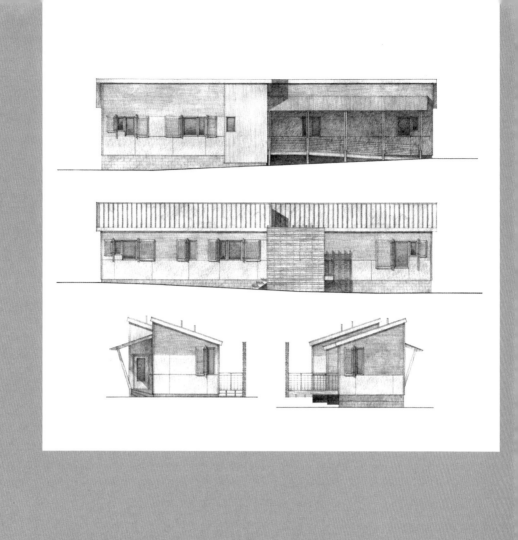

Naturally, these unprotected areas troubled the manufacturer. However, after much negotiation, including our solemn promise to be on site with materials to sheathe and "weather-in" the exposed under-ridge vertical surface as soon as the roof was raised, the modular builder agreed to our single-pitched roof design. The roof profile and the general form of the house turned out to be continuing points of contention. At our meeting with local stakeholders, the bankers and real estate agents implored the students to consider the pressures of the housing market. A more conventional-looking house would be easier to sell than our unusual one. In addition to the corrugated metal siding and single-pitched roofs, we intended to paint the house school-bus yellow. The city had assured us that the low cost of this house would allow it to sell regardless of its appearance, but we took the comment to heart and thoughtfully considered the difference between designing for ourselves and designing for an already-stigmatized market sector.

Success?

In addition to the support provided by the city and the manufacturer, other donating sponsors began to appear as the project gained visibility in the community and our efforts picked up steam. These sponsors, including window manufacturers, finish material suppliers, and metal shops, proved crucial to meeting our design and budgetary goals. However, the ad hoc nature of the donations made us realize that a project of this sort can never be a true prototype, despite our wishes to the contrary. Because academically sponsored design/build projects rely so heavily on material donations, sweat equity, and the fluctuating availability of government funding, each project is unique. This realization led to much debate among the students about whether and how we had succeeded in our project.

As with any construction project, certain design aspects were modified or omitted completely in the field. For instance, the students designed, fabricated, and installed operable cedar shutters for all windows in the house. After we were finished with the project, a field person privately hired by the modular manufacturer's representatives returned to the house and permanently fastened the shutters to the cladding of the house. The same person completed an aspect of the project we had left incomplete: the porch railings had been designed as horizontal cables, but instead they were installed as vertical cedar posts. These very visible changes were like wounds in the design and were frustrating for many of those who had worked on the house, including myself. Throughout such moments we tried to remind ourselves of our larger successes.

Other aspects of our process figured into our self-evaluations. As expected the house sold quickly at the target price of $60,000, although our final cost per square foot (including donations) was slightly more than $60 per square foot. The city covered the cost overage to keep the selling price at the predetermined amount. The owners are reportedly very pleased with their house, and with the subsequent arrival of their two children, they are considering adding a small third bedroom.

If we had not used the modular process, we would not have been able to produce a house of even this limited scope in such a short time. We were satisfied, and even fascinated, with this process throughout our involvement with the manufacturer. In our next D/BW project, we intend to reengage the modular process and investigate its particularities. We will continue our collaborations with the city of Fayetteville and take advantage of the city's CDBG funding as a way of ensuring that our houses sell at or below the projected sale price. We will continue to seek donations as a further means of reducing costs. However, given the constant flux that characterizes our resource streams and the housing market, all we can be assured of is that our design/build efforts must be dynamic if they are to succeed.

ecoMOD:
Exploring Social and
Environmental Justice
through Prefabrication

JOHN QUALE

Beyond hopes
and good
intentions, can
prefabricated
affordable housing
bear out its claims
of fostering
social and environ-
mental justice?

In today's real estate market, ecologically sustainable homes have been mostly reserved for the wealthy. Yet the health concerns associated with indoor air quality, as well as the financial burden of unnecessarily inflated utility costs, point to the need for homes that are both environmentally responsive and affordable for low-income people.

Prefabrication can be a cost-effective method of construction, and highly energy-efficient homes have lower utility costs, making sustainable prefabrication an ideal formula for affordable housing. Currently, however, prefabricated homes are seldom designed for energy efficiency, and most environmentally sustainable homes are expensive to build.

The hypothesis of the ecoMOD project at the University of Virginia School of Architecture is that by combining prefabrication with sustainable design strategies, we can generate a series of housing prototypes that lower operating costs for homeowners while reducing the overall environmental impact of the buildings. As director of the project, my mission for ecoMOD is to demonstrate the environmental and economic potential of prefabrication, and to challenge the modular and manufactured housing industry in the United States to explore this potential.

There are a couple of different ways to simultaneously address social equity and sustainability in a university design program: through design/build projects that offer a direct response to a specific community need, or through speculative design/research projects that seek to have a broader (albeit more abstract) impact. The ecoMOD

research and design/build/evaluate project aims to blend the best of these worlds to achieve results that are both tangible and forward thinking. The project, which is part of the university's curriculum, is intended to create well-built homes that cost less to live in, minimize damage to the environment, and appreciate in value.

A group of students in architecture, engineering, landscape architecture, business, environmental science, planning, and economics are split into teams that participate in the design, construction, and evaluation phases of this multiyear project. We are providing prefabricated housing units through partnerships with Piedmont Housing Alliance (PHA) of Charlottesville, Virginia, and Habitat for Humanity (HFH). PHA provides financial counseling and develops housing units in Charlottesville and the surrounding five counties. The ecoMOD teams also aim to find a modular house manufacturer to produce each of the house designs and to market them to individuals as well as to affordable-housing nonprofit organizations similar to PHA and HFH.

Prefab

Newly built low-income single-family homes in the United States tend to be some variety of manufactured or prefabricated housing. These homes are affordable and easily installed, but they are usually built in ways that waste resources and foster indoor air quality problems. Most prefab homes are sited with no consideration for local hydrology or solar or wind orientation. The buildings themselves are aggressively "siteless"—seemingly adaptable to any environment, yet entirely separate from their surroundings. In contrast, the intent behind the ecoMOD designs is to create site-specific homes using natural lighting and ventilation, nonhazardous materials, renewable energy, and energy-efficient systems to help reduce environmental impact and improve residents' health.

Fully 25 percent of new homes constructed in the United States are prefabricated as manufactured, panelized, or modular units. While this statistic may surprise some, the trend toward prefabrication is likely to continue. As prefab house manufacturers become more market-savvy and start offering more personalized options, a "mass-customized" housing market will become a reality. In a sense this situation already exists. The vast majority of new site-built homes across the country use standardized wood-framing methods. From the simplest HFH starter house to the largest suburban trophy home, the structural system for American homes is largely the same; the only differences are in square footage and finishes. Job sites for most stick-built dwellings are essentially small, temporary factories, requiring equipment and raw materials to be delivered to the house site. Prefabrication simply centralizes this process in a factory instead.

The Environmental Impact of Housing and Design

We have entered the twenty-first century with the knowledge that the construction and operation of buildings is the sector of the U.S. economy that uses the most fossil fuels. Not surprisingly the United States is also releasing more greenhouse gases than any other nation in the world. The average American single-family home is responsible for the emission of more than 22,000 pounds of carbon dioxide each year, due to the use of electricity and oil- or gas-powered appliances and equipment. This is more than twice the amount of carbon dioxide emitted by the typical American car in a year. The reality is that inefficient McMansions are more harmful to the environment than gas-guzzling SUVs.

It is clear that architects and engineers must take greater responsibility for the environmental consequences of their creative efforts. Studies are beginning to demonstrate that building design can affect everything from students' grades to public health. There is a growing realization that buildings, nature, and humans are inextricably connected. I have always urged my students to recognize this interdependence. I ask them to be simultaneously intuitive and rigorous, poetic and practical, artistic and scientific. I believe this is the best way for designers to address the environmental impact of the housing industry. The field of architecture has a hybrid quality that lends itself to this dual focus; successful architects display both intellectual discipline and artistic inspiration.

While it is well known that prefabricated building techniques can save time, money, and materials, their potential environmental benefits remain largely unrecognized. Off-site construction can significantly reduce

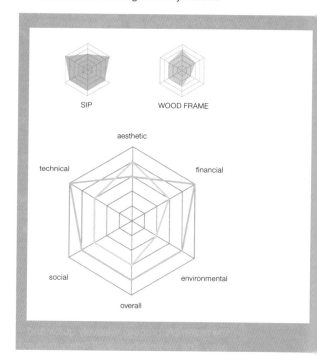

SIP   WOOD FRAME

aesthetic

technical   financial

social   environmental

overall

a building's environmental impact and embodied energy. The inherent efficiencies of centralized fabrication include climate-controlled, year-round construction, better quality control, significant reductions in construction waste, minimized usage of energy and water, just-in-time delivery methods, and fewer trips for fewer people to remote construction sites.

In the design phases of the ecoMOD project, I challenge my students to address issues from a variety of viewpoints and to articulate aesthetic, technical, ecological, social, and financial justifications for their ideas. These justifications are at the center of our complex decision-making process. Any construction project, no matter how conscientiously executed, will harm the environment. It is important to recognize this at the outset of design. Choices are seldom clear-cut, and each design strategy has ecological advantages and disadvantages.

To facilitate the design process I require my students to use "decision webs" when

Right
ecoMOD1 team
OUTin house,
Charlottesville,
Virginia. 2006.
Placement of the
prefabricated
modules on the
foundation

making important design choices. The webs help us track our thought processes and recognize the complex array of issues affected by each decision. The teams do not always agree, and decisions occasionally become compromises. Yet we are constantly aware of the potential danger of watering down good ideas by choosing the strategy that the most people could agree upon. Finding just the right balance between productive collaboration and "design by committee" is an ongoing concern.

ecoMOD1: Designing the OUTin house

The first prototype, ecoMOD1: the OUTin house, was completed in early 2006 in the Fifeville neighborhood of Charlottesville, Virginia. The house was constructed as eight small modules and includes a potable rainwater collection system, a solar hot-water panel, non-volatile organic compound (VOC) finishes, and locally and sustainably forested wood flooring.

The OUTin house combines the best of panelized and modular prefabrication techniques. The primary structural system is structural insulated panels (SIPs), making the assembly process relatively quick and easy. The Virginia-based SIP manufacturer R-Control provided panels with precut windows, doors, and electrical chases. By utilizing wall and roof panels that are

assembled into eight separate modules, the OUTin house takes advantage of the "outsourcing" potential of prefabricated SIPs and the off-site-assembly advantages of modular construction.

In response to the lack of modular systems appropriate to urban lots, OUTin uses modules that are 18 feet long and either 10.5 or 12.5 feet wide. This allows the modules to be transported on narrow streets with tight turning radiuses. The site for the OUTin house, a historically African-American neighborhood with mostly early- to mid-twentieth-century houses, is not accessible for conventional manufactured or larger modular sections. In one of our several meetings with the members of the Fifeville Neighborhood Association, we discussed the possibility of an urban modular system that could be used to bring in more houses at a lower cost, helping to stabilize the neighborhood against the encroaching forces of gentrification. The modular concept and the associated environmental strategies were well received by the community. Surprisingly, no community members expressed concerns about the contemporary language of the house design.

By using smaller modules, turning them ninety degrees from the norm—the long dimensions are side to side on a narrow lot, rather than front to back—and staggering them, the OUTin house takes advantage of the structural opportunity to create outdoor spaces defined by the side walls of the modules. In an attempt to blend outdoor and indoor spaces, the entry deck, which is the primary outdoor space, has direct access to the primary public interior space. By making outdoor spaces part of the modular strategy, the specifics of a given site become integral to the process of laying out any version of the OUTin house.

In developing the prototype, the team made all the decisions about the implementation of the OUTin house. However, if the house design goes into production, the developer or homeowner will determine the final form. To assist with this process, the house is based on a modularity that operates at three scales. The largest scale, defined by the site and other ecological considerations, establishes the orientation of the building, its relationship to the existing topography, and the scope of

ft
coMOD1 team
decision web
ables comparison
the value and
pact of structural
sulated panels
rsus conventional
ood-stud
nstruction.

energy- and water-efficient strategies. The next scale, defined by budget and occupant requirements, determines the number of modules and rooms, and their relationship to each other. The smallest scale, defined by the cultural context and the preferences of the homeowner, dictates the materials, finishes, and other details.

A Three-Pronged Environmental Focus

The OUTin house addresses issues of ecological sustainability through three primary strategies: site specificity, water efficiency, and energy efficiency. To address site specificity the open side of the house faces south to receive sun during the winter, and overhangs shade it in the summer. The house is flexible enough to be placed on a variety of sites and adaptable enough to adjust to climatic and topographic concerns. The house's water-

efficient features include a solar hot water panel and a potable rainwater collection system. The solar panel is an affordable solution for most homes, but the rainwater collection system is cost-prohibitive for most affordable-housing organizations. ecoMOD secured a separate grant to implement the water-system upgrade in the first house. However, the system does demonstrate that the technology it uses is both available and effective.

To achieve energy efficiency, the house uses SIPs for wall and roof construction, a method that is significantly more efficient than conventional framing. A continuous zone of foam installation and properly sealed joints significantly reduces unwanted heat gains and losses. Unfortunately SIPs are a mixed bag in terms of sustainable material selection. The oriented strand board (OSB)

Above
The kitchen of the
OUTin house feat
a work station wit
fold-down table a
countertop. Behir
a custom enclosu
mechanical equip

Right
View of the entry
deck, with rainwa
collection infrastru
and shade trellis t
provide structure
native vines in sur

sheathing the SIPs contains binding agents with formaldehyde, which will off-gas into the living space. To address this concern, all OSB exposed to the interior of the OUTin house is sealed with a product that does not include VOCs. OSB without formalde-hyde and other non-VOC wood-panel products do exist, but they are cost-prohibitive as well. All of these ecological measures also effectively reduce the cost of utility bills, translating directly into more money in homeowners' pockets.

Evaluating the OUTin House

After the project was completed, the OUTin house evaluation team assessed the design process, the financial and environmental consequences of their selected construction techniques and building materials, and the affordability and other financial aspects of the house, among other elements. The team's analysis of the materials used largely supported the decisions made. Despite the off-gassing of the OSB and the petroleum-based expanded polystyrene foam, the energy saved through the efficiency of SIPs made them the right choice. For flooring materials the design team had decided that sustainably forested poplar would have less environmental impact than bamboo. The evaluation team analyzed the overall life-cycle of the two materials and the energy required to transport the bamboo from China to the United States, and agreed that poplar flooring was also a sound decision. Non-VOC paint was a good choice from the standpoint of indoor air quality, but the evaluation team found that non-VOC paint was less durable than conventional paint and would have to be reapplied sooner.

With regard to energy efficiency, the evaluation team found that the design decisions were appropriate within the context of an affordable-house budget. The house will save the family at least 60 percent in utility costs compared to those incurred by a conventional wood-stud structure. The solar hot-water system was noted as a particularly good choice. It was a reconditioned system, causing less of an environmental impact than putting a new one into service, and it will reduce the energy required to heat the water in the home by as much as 80 percent.

The evaluation team questioned the choice of the rainwater-collection system for the home. The choice to install the system led to additional filtration components and the need for regular maintenance. While this system would make sense for a rural site, the team felt that the availability of inexpensive city water made this design element less attractive.

The evaluation team also had doubts about the house's affordability. The design/build team used the financial assumptions of PHA, our affordable-housing partner, who requested a single-family home 1,200 to 1,400 square feet in size that would cost $95 to $105 per square foot. The design/build team almost met these targets by building a 1,390-square-foot home for about $115 per square foot. However, the evaluation team felt that PHA's cost assumptions were flawed because they were based on 2001–2 construction cost and real estate data, when PHA's other similar development projects had begun. Since 2001 average home prices in Charlottesville have increased by more than 60 percent.

Because PHA sells homes at their appraised value, the appraisal was a critical aspect of the financial analysis. While the economics and business students on the evaluation team appreciated the fact that the appraisal came in almost $40,000 higher than an earlier PHA home of comparable size, the high figure created a problem for PHA. We decided to address this problem by finishing off the basement (another 660 square feet) and converting the property to a two-unit condominium. The evaluation team recommended that this kind of multi-unit strategy be considered from the beginning for the next ecoMOD home in the Charlottesville market. While PHA's clients likely would prefer a single-family detached house, the realities of the real estate market indicate that the era of the affordable single-family detached house is over in the city of Charlottesville.

By evaluating the real-world results of the hypotheses of the ecoMOD1 design/build team, the evaluators have helped the first ecoMOD process come full circle, and the knowledge gained has been applied to the next phases of ecoMOD. So far two additional projects have been completed:

ecoMOD2, a single-family detached home for HFH in the post–Hurricane Katrina Gulf Coast region of Mississippi; and eco-MOD3, a two-bedroom home and separate studio apartment rental unit for the PHA, which combines modern modules with a green renovation of a restored historic house. The ecoMOD designs have recently been licensed to Modern Modular of New York City.

As the ecoMOD project heads into the future, we will continue to research, design, and build environmentally sustainable prefabricated homes that meet residents' housing needs and expand the options available for affordable, ecologically sound housing.

Out of the Box:
Design Innovations in
Manufactured Housing

ROBERTA M. FELDMAN

A challenge
is issued for
designers
to reinvest
themselves in
the prefabrication
of housing in
order to tackle
our national
affordable-
housing crisis.

> **The mobile home may well be the single most significant and unique housing innovation in twentieth-century America. No other innovation addressing the spectrum of housing activities—from construction, tenure, and community structure to design—has been more widely adopted nor, simultaneously, more broadly vilified.**
>
> A. D. WALLIS, *Wheel Estate: The Rise and Decline of Mobile Homes*

Over the past decade 30 percent of new-home construction in the United States has used prefabricated components, according to the U.S. Department of Housing and Urban Development. A combination of rising housing costs, limited affordable-housing options, and increases in the size and quality of manufactured housing has contributed to the dramatic impact of prefabricated housing on the national housing market. Manufactured housing is the major source of unsubsidized low-cost housing in the United States today.

Despite their importance as a lower-cost option, manufactured housing and its precursors, the trailer and the mobile home, have been reviled by the general public and government agencies. A house built in a factory has been deemed a threat to property values, even though 95 percent of these homes remain on the sites where they are first installed. Manufactured housing is subject to quality-control oversight in the factory, but many still consider it to be less safe than site-built homes, regardless of the fact that manufactured housing is now required to meet the same building standards. Manufactured housing asks us to reconsider deep-seated values attached to the meaning of home: rootedness versus the freedom to move, dwellings built by hand on site compared to those that are mass-produced, and individuality contrasted with conformity.

Fighting Stigma with Tradition

It is ironic that manufactured housing is so stigmatized, given the average American household's mobility, the increasingly trans-spatial nature of social relationships, and the mass manufacture of virtually all the consumer products and building components that are used in site-built dwellings. The industry's answer to the stigma of manufactured housing is to bring the manufactured dwelling into conformity with the predominant market vision of an ideal of home: rooted in place, with the appearance of a vernacular home. The manufactured house has evolved far beyond the twentieth-century mobile travel trailer, to become a prefabricated dwelling intended as a permanent, site-installed residence.

This process has taken considerable time, however. In the early part of the twentieth century, manufactured housing was characterized by experiments with innovative materials, forms, and construction methods. Yet industry growth was slow, not because of a lack of need but due to insufficient financing, poor quality control, and negative public response. These failures encouraged manufacturers to believe that instead of forging ahead into risky new territory, they would do better to return to the tried and true.[1]

This is exactly what the industry did in the latter part of the century, when manufactured housing experienced dramatic growth. The manufactured house is now designed and constructed as if it were site-built. Stick construction is the norm, and the dominant motifs are reminiscent of historic, handcrafted homes. Despite these relatively upscale design and construction elements, manufactured homes are still more cost-efficient than site-built housing, due to economies of scale in material and equipment purchases, the quality control and continuous manufacture afforded by the factory process, and a reduction in labor costs owing to the lower skill levels required for assembly-line construction.

Socially minded architects once embraced the factory-built house as the answer to shortages in affordable housing. These architects' designs sought to make manufactured homes affordable through machined materials and industrial construction processes. Despite some interesting innovations along the way, architects' interest in social housing through mass production eventually waned, and their role in the manufactured-housing industry became marginal.[2] Architects' ideology of practice and their remuneration structure remain firmly rooted in one-off custom designs, not standardized models or kits of standardized parts.

With housing becoming increasingly unaffordable, recently there has been a resurgence of architectural interest in manufactured housing. Calls for a new prefabrication movement can be read in the pages of the *New York Times*, *Dwell*, and numerous books featuring prefabricated houses designed by architects.[3] These publications targeting the profession and the cultural elite generally emphasize industrial and digital technologies offering mass customization and "high style."[4] The result is a design that brings manufactured housing into conformance with current architectural theories and aesthetic models.

While the affordability of these homes is a consideration, they generally are still not within the economic reach of lower- and middle-income Americans. Rather, most of these designs are intended for a niche market: the "hip" among the middle class who are experiencing the pressures of an unaffordable housing market. Advertisements in *Dwell* tout the advantages and affordability of architect-designed manufactured homes that are available for less than $250 per square foot—a cost substantially lower than that of a similarly architect-designed site-built dwelling, but obviously still beyond the means of most Americans.

What, then, do we do about the millions of families in this country who need safe, decent, affordable housing? How might architects be able to respond to this problem if they reconsidered the design of manufactured housing—especially if they addressed affordability by containing construction costs while sustaining livability? How might these architectural designs foster alternative understandings of the prefabricated dwelling?

Investigating the Possibilities of the "Trailer Home"

Even in the 1930s, when the commercial success of the trailer home was already secure, its value was widely debated. For example, a 1937 issue of *Fortune* magazine reported: "200,000 trailers will swarm on the roads this spring. Whether they betoken a New Way of Life or a plague of locusts is something that makers, taxpayers, hotel keepers, and lawmakers are bitterly disputing."[5] The stigma associated with the trailer home has been so pervasive that, in the latter part of the twentieth century, the industry changed the product name to "manufactured housing," but the name change has done little to alter the public's negative view of this form of housing.

In recent projects eight nationally recognized architects and industrial designers—David Baker, Bryan Bell, Carol Burns, Teddy Cruz, Yolande Daniels, Doug Garofalo, David Khouri, and Ali Tayar—have investigated the design, materials, and manufacturing techniques of factory-built housing.[6] All argue compellingly against the negative stereotypes of manufactured housing, largely by portraying alternatives to the standard manufactured-house design. The diverse proposals are best understood in contrast to the current manufactured housing industry's model: a single-family detached dwelling composed of one or more compact geometric boxes. As in site-built housing, variety in conventional manufactured housing is achieved by modest pushes and pulls of exterior walls and gabled roof heights. Facades typically are made of industrial siding that mimics wood, with small windows punctuating the walls. All of the proposals reinterpret this model, some with more restraint, others more aggressively.

Bryan Bell and Teddy Cruz employ moderate architectural interventions to create visually and theoretically challenging projects. In Double High House, Bell wraps a stack of three manufactured boxes direct from the factory in a rain-screen framework of recycled vinyl siding. This method of screening the rain and sun—peeling the skin from the exterior of the house—transforms the aesthetic language of the conventional manufactured box.

2 Carol Burns St[...] *On the Highway/[...] on the Highway: [...] Manufactured Ho[...] Catalog* (Cambri[...] Mass,: Harvard University Gradua[...] School of Design 1996).

3 See, for examp[...] Allison Arieff an[...] Bryan Burkhart, [...] (Layton, Ut.: Gibb[...] Smith, 2002); Jer[...] Siegal, ed., *Mobil[...] The Art of Portab[...] Architecture* (New[...] Princeton Archite[...] Press, 2002); and[...] *Dwell* (April/May 2005).

4 Ellen Grimes, "[...] Business? New Economies in the[...] Design and Fabri[...] of Housing," in Elva Rubio, ed., *Out of the Box: Design Innovation[...] in Manufactured Housing* (Chicag[...] City Design Cent[...] 2005), 3. Publish[...] in conjunction wi[...] the exhibition *Ou[...] of the Box: Desig[...] Innovations in Manufactured Ho[...] shown at the Fiel[...] Museum in Chica[...]

5 "200,000 Traile[...] *Fortune* (March 1[...] 104–11.

6 In 2005 I curate[...] with the assistance[...] of Dan Wheeler, a[...] associate profess[...] in the School of Architecture at th[...] University of Illinc[...] Chicago, an exhib[...] in collaboration v[...] the Field Museum[...] *Design Innovatior[...] in Manufactured Housing*. Our goa[...] was to counterac[...] the unyielding stigma associate[...] with manufacture[...] housing—commo[...] referred to as "tra[...] homes." The eigh[...] projects presente[...] here were create[...] the exhibition.

What, then, do we do about the millions of families in this country who need safe, decent, affordable housing? How might architects be able to respond to this problem if they reconsidered the design of manufactured housing—especially if they addressed affordability by containing construction costs while sustaining livability?

Teddy Cruz eschews the prefab box entirely with Manufactured Site, and instead transports abandoned houses and construction materials from San Diego to a hillside on the outskirts of Tijuana. With this move he pays heed to the 837 million people who live in the informal settlements that spring up around rapidly growing urban cores in developing countries. To this new community Cruz adds a modest, flexible, prefabricated structural system of metal uprights, platforms, and stairs of vibrant colors, which give the site visual coherence. Both Bell and Cruz illustrate the wisdom of reusing materials and structures that otherwise would become waste in a landfill.

Yolande Daniels and Sunil Bald (of studio SUMO), David Baker, and David Khouri (whose studio is called comma) stretch manufactured-housing technologies to achieve greater adaptability of structure. Daniels and Bald's MiniMax is a high-tech, circuited mesh-covered shell that is expanded both in length and width when installed on the site. Flexibility is achieved by optional program components—such as entertainment consoles, exercise equipment, and home offices—that may be changed or updated as needs require.

Baker extends household choice one step further. In his LaCan Project, "podules," or premanufactured steel frame units, are combined in multiple configurations and transported to various locations. For example, a podule could be placed on a single-family lot, or it could be "plugged" into a "mainframe" high-rise superstructure, allowing a family to move their home from place to place.

Left
David Baker and
Partners, Archite●
LaCan Project. 2○
Rendering

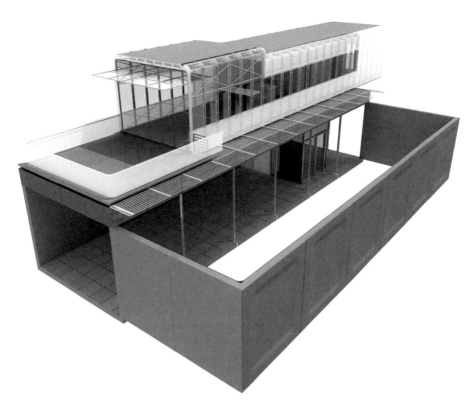

David Khouri's Packed House is a manufactured home packed in a black metal shell that encloses and protects it when the structure is in transit. When the house is installed on site, the shell can be placed in various cantilevered positions below the basic unit to fit different site conditions or to add usable space, such as a partially enclosed outdoor area, a basement, a retaining wall, or a fully enclosed addition.

While all of these projects are innovative, they involve additional costs. Bell's screen of recycled vinyl siding gives greater satisfaction as a formal manipulation than as a cost-effective, functional way to shield the building from sun and rain. Cruz's arresting proposal reveals architects' desire for order, even if it costs more. Is it really necessary to provide more formal organization to a favela? In the Daniels/Bald, Baker, and Khouri projects, budgetary considerations take a back seat to technological and formal invention in the service of flexibility. One could assume that technology will solve the problem of affordability through industrial-

ized production, but this assumption has yet to be supported after a century of experimentation and technological progress.

Ali Tayar (whose firm is known as Parallel Design), Carol Burns (of Taylor and Burns Architects), and Doug Garofalo, by contrast, choose to work within available industrial housing practices while pushing the confines of the manufactured box. Both Tayar and Burns use the basic box, but they organize it in different configurations to achieve variety in form.

Tayar's design, house nine, draws its formal language from the 1950s mobile home, while Burns's Homes Off the Highway uses prefabricated wood and glass-paneled boxes. Both designers slide, rotate, and combine these units to create distinctive house forms that connect the building to the site, and interior spaces to exterior spaces. These straightforward adjustments to the conventional manufactured box promise improved livability and a closer fit with the context without significant additional costs.

Garofalo's CorPod House is a hybrid design that draws inspiration from the motor home/travel trailer industry and the precast concrete manufacturing industry. The CorPod, a compact pod reminiscent of the Airstream trailer, contains a complete kitchen, bathroom, storage, utilities, and optional entertainment technologies. The CorPod is delivered and rolled into a site-erected concrete panel wall-and-roof shell equipped with conduits for electrical and heating systems. Alternative stacking patterns allow for a variety of single-family and multifamily arrangements. The CorPod recalls General Electric's 1950s experiment with a compact utility core, which did not achieve commercial success because it was difficult to repair. With this problem solved, mass-produced compact utility cores like the CorPod could replace one of the more costly components of today's housing.

The Future of Manufactured Housing

Architectural design can play a key role in encouraging public acceptance of a devalued or unfamiliar form of housing. R. Buckminster Fuller, George Keck, and others are remembered for experiments that turned heads and promised comforts and conveniences that were ahead of their time. Fuller's and Keck's prototypes were never manufactured in numbers greater than a few hundred units, but this was because of costly materials, skilled labor requirements, and limitations on available production technologies—not because the public was not interested.

Decades after Fuller and Keck, architects should be ready for the next step: to significantly reduce construction costs while maintaining durability and livability, especially in comparison with the manufactured-housing industry's current cost structure. Available strategies for cost reduction include strategic space efficiencies in the design of the dwelling unit; resource efficiencies, such as economical use of energy and material resources in construction of the unit; cost-effective construction models and assemblies; and reduction of life-cycle costs through energy efficiencies, increased durability, and ease of repair. If they do not devote attention to these and other strategies for achieving cost savings in manufactured housing design and production, architects will remain marginal to the industry and will have little impact on housing affordability for those who need it most.

The number of homeless people and those living in unsafe and crowded living conditions in the United States is at an all-time high—5 million to 50 million, depending on whom you ask—while the number of affordable housing units is rapidly decreasing nationwide.[7] Site-built housing construction costs continue to escalate dramatically around the country, and the availability and choice of housing for moderate- and low-income families continues to constrict.

The current governmental solution to the pressing need for affordable housing is the provision of subsidies, as opposed to the provision of affordable housing. There is little public desire—and hence no significant political will—to fill these needs. Unfortunately, this strategy is unsustainable; subsidies alone cannot meet the demands of all who find themselves squeezed out of ever-tighter residential markets. In fact, subsidies themselves are decreasing at an alarming rate, giving rise to dire predictions for the future of housing.

Manufactured housing is the *only* option currently available for low-cost newly constructed dwellings. If architects want to have a hand in reducing the costs of building homes, they must vigorously pursue the economical design of this form of housing.

Right
Garofalo Archite
CorPod House. 2
Rendering of inte

7 The U.S. Depar
of Housing and
Urban Developm
estimates that 5
million Americans
are underhoused
homeless, while t
estimate of the Lc
Income Housing
Coalition is 50 m

MESHING WITH MARKET FORCES

Finding Balance:
How to Be an Architect,
an Environmentalist,
and a Developer

RUSSELL KATZ

**Can you have
it all—build
strong designs,
with minimal
environmental
impact, and
make a profit?**

I am an architect, and for as long as I have pursued the profession I have been aware of a serious problem. Simply put, there are a lot of fantastic architects out there, all of whom have the ability to design beautiful and even important buildings; but most of them are still waiting for the perfect client to help them realize their potential and enable them to make meaningful contributions to the built environment.

Planning for Success

Ever since I was an undergraduate student at the University of Virginia, I have desperately wanted to find a way to be in control of my work. So I started making a plan for how I could become my own client, in order to focus equal attention on what I considered to be the three most important aspects of building: beautiful design, environmental sustainability, and financial success.

Seven years ago I left my job at a very good firm in New York City and moved home, to Washington, D.C., to start a new business and begin setting my plan in motion. After raising some investment money I bought two derelict and largely vacant apartment buildings close to Metro stations and in transitional neighborhoods that I believed were ready to improve. Then I redesigned and renovated the units and common spaces and rented the units. By the end of the project I had become an owner/architect/property manager.

The endeavor became quite complex. I had to create corporations, do market studies, arrange financing, learn about title law and rent-control law (and the attendant paperwork), open special checking accounts for security deposits, establish a property-management company, set up depreciation schedules, make financial plans with accountants, purchase insurance for every facet of the project, hire consultants for myriad special issues, market and rent apartments, and work according to a budget that was supported by a business plan. The experience taught me how to be a developer and how to put together a financially successful real-estate development deal.

Those first two buildings were not exactly my "ideal" project, but they did provide a positive experience that could serve as a basis for further expansion. Using the knowledge I had gained and the financial strength I had accumulated, I was able to start searching for an opportunity to launch the kind of project I really wanted to work on. After a few months of looking around, I found a good site right in front of me: an empty lot across the street from the Takoma Metro station, only five stops from Union Station. The new site bordered the Metro station on the south, while my first project sat on the northern lot line.

Open-Book Development Policy

The first thing I did after buying the land was to identify the community leaders and call each one of them. These calls were intended to set the stage for a great working relationship with everyone right from the start. I introduced myself and told them I was the new owner of the site that everyone sees when they get off the train in Takoma. I told them my intent was to conduct the development process according to an "open book" policy. I gave each community leader my personal phone numbers and asked them to call me with any questions at any time, especially if they heard something about my project that they did not like.

I began with the idea of a contemporary green building and planned to use what I had learned from my first two residential projects. The design process revealed that the site could afford 68,000 square feet of enclosed space surrounding a courtyard. Eventually, the plans for Elevation 314, as it came to be known, included 52 apartments and two retail spaces.

From the beginning I was aware that a contemporary green design on the most central site in a historic district might be met with some resistance, so I needed to build a lot of support in the community. I had to work hard to gain and keep that support, and I had to make sure small issues or negative rumors did not grow into real trouble. Throughout the development process, whenever I was invited to make a presentation to an individual or a group, I took the time to do it. As my team completed each phase of the project design, I put a copy of the progress prints in the local library. The policy of openness was hard to maintain, but it paid great dividends.

There were bumps in the road, of course. Sometimes I received extremely negative feedback and was harshly challenged. But interesting things happened as a result of those challenges—for one, the design got better. As an architecture student I faced some tough juries, but those paled in comparison to a skeptical community group or an angry neighbor. Hundreds of people gave input on the project, and based on their feedback, adjustments both large and small were made that resulted in tremendous improvements to the design. Most amazingly, some of the building's most vocal, ardent critics became its strongest advocates, often at crucial times such as just before a Historic Review Board meeting or a zoning hearing. The open-book policy is not just a nice and good approach—if done with candor and honesty, it is smart business.

One Project, Multiple Contexts

Throughout the many presentations to and reviews by government boards, community groups, politicians, and community members, I always focused on the contextuality of the project. For people concerned mainly with environmental issues or green building practices, the context of the building is the local ecology of the neighborhood and how that ecology participates in the broader ecosystem of the city and the surrounding region. When a project attracts a lot of attention from the press, its context be-comes even broader, and it can affect what someone else is trying to do elsewhere in the world.

For those concerned with urban history, context refers to the constructed landscape of the neighborhood and city. Most of the energy in this area gets diverted into a study of local and regional "buildings of signifi-cance"; but I find myself focusing on all the structures in the area, from the bridges, train tracks, train stations, and other elements of the infrastructure to the Victorian houses, bungalow homes, 1960s office towers, 1970s postmodern facade renovations—and even the graffiti on a wall. We did a number of studies of this broader context, in one case emulating an Edward Ruscha streetscape photomontage to capture in one image four blocks of the street that the main façade of Elevation 314 fronts. There is also a community

and personal context to consider. This context is hard to define, and it is different for each project, but it has to do with the character, the flavor, and the soul of a neighborhood. Although intangible, the community and personal context does exist, and every individual who encounters a project, especially on a regular basis, has some form of ownership of that place. Acknowledging this fact is the basis for a positive and genuine community discussion, despite the fact that the final decisions lie with the owner.

Balancing Conflicting Roles

Many people ask me how I balanced the conflicting roles of owner, developer, and architect, in addition to those of community member and environmentalist. The owner wants a high-quality building that will be easy to maintain and operate; the developer wants to save every cent possible and get things done quickly; and the architect wants to create a structure that is beautiful and fulfills his or her expectations of good design.

It was not easy to inhabit all these roles, but I am glad I did, if for no other reason than for the efficiency of having my hands in everything at once. To make sure I pulled off the balancing act successfully, I set up a few mechanisms that proved useful. I always referred back to my three-way focus: beautiful design, environmental sustain-ability, and financial success. I analyzed every decision affecting the project accord-ing to these criteria, and the best solutions satisfied all three equally and inseparably. To help make this possible, I selected two project team members in addition to myself, and gave each one primary responsibility for one of the three criteria. Susanne Pollmann, my design project manager, was primarily concerned with the building's aesthetics. Michelle Scurfield, who was hired as the green consultant, was assigned to evaluate every design decision for its impact on the ecosystem. As the owner and developer, I assumed responsibility for the budget, and I framed our discussions in terms of what would be attainable.

Turning a Green Roof into a Courtyard Garden

I am pleased with how the building turned out overall, but I am especially proud of its center and soul: a lush garden located in the central courtyard. The impact of this space on the entire project cannot be overstated. However, we were not originally planning on including a garden in the design. We arrived at the idea from two different directions. First, it is important to understand that sound was the single largest factor affecting the schematic

building design, and questions of sound management persisted as a major engineering problem throughout the process. The west lot line is more than 200 feet long and is shared by the Washington Metropolitan Area Transit Authority and CSX railroad company. Hundreds of trains pass the building every day, ranging from quiet electrical Metro trains to noisy freight behemoths.

One of the first consultants I hired for the project was an acoustical engineer. We did a twenty-four-hour sound test of the site perimeter, and based on the results we decided that while noise was at times intense, the right design would offer enjoyable quiet space for residential use. The courtyard's primary function is to create that quiet space. Every tenant in the building has access to the courtyard, and most of the apartments open onto it. The building

itself creates the buffer for the train noise, and all of the bedrooms, living-dining rooms, and other interior spaces reap the benefit.

The courtyard is a large space, two-thirds of which is on-grade, and one-third of which is the roof of the underground parking garage. Early in the design process we were planning to install a green roof on top of the building and a series of planter compositions on the roof over the garage. However, when we met with the green roof designer, the civil engineer, and the landscape architect to discuss the most environmentally sustainable solutions for storm-water management, we changed our minds. Rather than employ the typical underground sand-filter chambers used in most urban areas, we decided to turn the courtyard into our storm-water management machine. The on-grade garden area was perfect for this use, but it was not large enough to handle all of the rainwater, so instead we brought the green roof down from above the building and installed it on the roof of the underground garage within the courtyard. The green roof would thus no longer be an expense without offset, as the courtyard garden would eliminate the cost of sand filters. Putting the green roof in the courtyard would also give visual access to an aesthetically pleasing installation that is usually out of sight. Meanwhile, the on-grade portion of the courtyard would now be our "bio-retention" area and would serve as an example of the current best practice of water management—which is very important in the local Chesapeake Bay watershed.

In working through the logistics of our solution, we learned that Washington, D.C., had never before allowed a green roof to qualify as a storm-water-management facility, and the city had no way to approve the scheme. Fortunately, the D.C. Department of Health is staffed by a number of progressive-minded individuals, including Dr. Hamid Karimi, who is in charge of the department's Watershed Protection Division. We met, decided that we wanted to set a precedent, and proceeded to do research on other municipalities. Soon enough the Department of Health agreed to a standard for the use of green roofs as storm-water-management facilities, and ours was the first approved.

eft
evation 314,
ew of courtyard
cross green roof
f the underground
arking garage

The courtyard functions as an attractive, cost-effective green space. It is my favorite example to cite when asked the most typical green-building question: "How much more does it cost?" The success of the courtyard at Elevation 314 renders this question meaningless. It adds immeasurable value to the building by making each unit and the building itself a more desirable place to be; it does so at a cost similar to that of a sand-filter water-management system; and it is beautiful.

What Would I Have Done Differently?

When I assembled the team for this project, I was mainly concerned with finding people who had enthusiasm, energy, and commitment. I should have added "experience" to that list. Because I had never found a project overwhelming, I discounted experience as a critical factor in hiring consultants and workers. Having now completed the project, I would weigh experience as heavily as any other factor. My team was great, and we overcame many obstacles together, but halfway through construction problems stemming from lack of experience started cropping up. To remedy the situation, I hired a construction manager who was older than anyone in the group and had decades of multifamily construction experience. He was an extremely valuable addition to the team, and I only wish I had found him earlier.

What's Next?

The question "What's next?" is a tough one because it assumes that all of my prior work is finished, leaving me a void to fill. However, as an investor I hold onto the properties I have developed, which means a "completed" project simply converts from active development to managed property. And one is always busy when one is responsible for a few hundred tenants.

As far as future projects are concerned, I have purchased a 185-acre tract in the fast-developing D.C. suburbs. The land is situated on a lake in an area of farms and forests that are being devoured by suburban sprawl. I am currently studying ways in which to develop a green community on the property with a focus on preserving a natural environment that is under steady pressure. I am also in the early stages of developing and designing an office building for another site in Washington, D.C.

The key to finding a successful project is to be ready when it presents itself, and then to act quickly. But the most important idea I keep in mind when looking for work is knowing when not to do a project. I value my time very highly, and I understand better than ever that nothing is as simple as it first seems. Not starting a project may be the best decision of all.

The process of building Elevation 314 took four years of full-time work, but it is now complete and fully rented. The result is more than I could have hoped for, and the response from the community, tenants, and colleagues has been mostly favorable. Positive feedback from tenants is the most rewarding result of my business, because it reinforces my initial belief that there are many other people who value the things I hold dear: design and the environment.

Bryan Bell has said that in all likelihood only 2 percent of buildings are designed by architects, and I would assume that only a minority of those are green. In my view the reason for both of these facts is that capital investment markets drive the vast majority of construction.

My hope is that more and bigger developers will come to realize that well-designed green buildings make money. I believe that sometime very soon most people looking for a place to live or work will place great value on access to mass transit, bike parking, storm-water management, pedestrian-friendly neighborhoods, affordable utility costs, recycling, good air quality, and so on. When that happens, hopefully we will see that 2 percent turn to 98 percent.

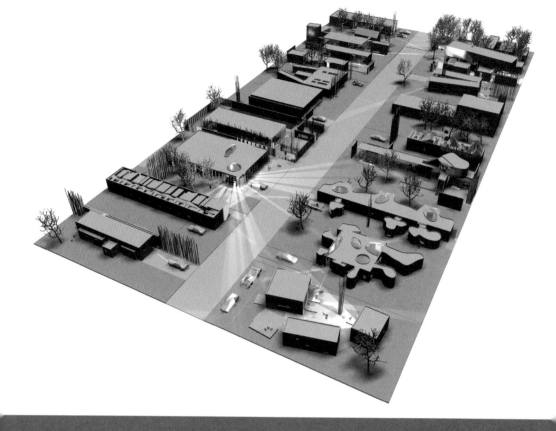

Propositions for a
New Suburbanism

GAIL PETER BORDEN

**Any proposal for
the suburbs must
take heed of the fact
that suburbs are a
product and reflection
of American culture.
In an alternative
suburb, a designer
presents choices
for modest modern
living, a new type
of "plan book."**

Much current architectural attention is trained on those at either end of the income spectrum—the very wealthy and the very poor. Significantly less design energy has been devoted to the middle-income group, although they represent nearly 96 percent of the general population and the largest potential user group. The architectural manifestation of this group in the United States is largely associated with "the suburban." This is where architecture must direct its focus.

The mission of the proposals in this essay is to serve middle-income Americans by illustrating fundamental design principles that can be used to provide well-designed housing within the current parameters of the industry and market.

Our Suburban Culture

The suburban condition has been condemned as ecologically unsound, ergonomically inconvenient, and aesthetically unattractive. But what we need to remember is that the contemporary built landscape has evolved as a manifestation of our culture. The suburban condition is a pure spatial expression of the combination of democracy, capitalism,and America's agrarian geography. Positioned between the density of the old city and the sparse isolation of the farm, the solitary, independent subdivided lot has emerged as the primary spatial building block of housing. For these reasons the greatest housing supply and demand in the United States currently occurs in the suburbs.

The suburban landscape is the new architectural frontier.

Unfortunately, the suburban landscape is devoid of architecture. The suburbs are dominated by speculative builders that subscribe to a single model of development, regardless of family size, geographic location, material quality, or formal meaning. The result is a bleak, monotonous landscape studded with the conventionally bland. To change this situation we must provide for new ways of living in suburbia. By acknowledging and making use of the processes that have given rise to the current housing stock, we can provide the framework for its reconfiguration.

The single-family detached house is still the "American dream" and the standard to which the majority aspires; thus, it is the dominant force in shaping the suburban landscape. However, the current single-family house subscribes to a model that addresses bank-loan guidelines but denies contemporary cultural conditions. In revising this model we still must heed economic realities. The salability of the dwelling provides its value. The current real-estate market accords value to a home based on its features; the home becomes marketable based upon its specific components. These propositions for revising suburban homes subscribe to the necessary programmatic framework of the conventional home (three bedrooms and two and a half baths on the typical (60 x 120-foot lot), but we shift the formal, spatial, and cultural opportunities of their composition.

The following design principles allow for a reinterpretation of the single-family house. In four prototypes implemented through twenty formal iterations (narrowed down from a greater number originally designed), the principles are illustrated through the diversity of the schemes. The prototypes—the Program House, the Porch House, the Tube House, and the Enclosure House—which are described below in greater detail, are not intended as new models to be serially reproduced, but rather as illustrative case studies of how the same systems can be reworked to produce more considered and diverse housing. These homes represent an opportunity for metabolic growth in the suburban landscape—new considerations for a pervasive type.

The proposed principles are as follows:

1. Typologies

The typical house built today subscribes to an image of what a house should look like. The prototype houses suggest what a house could look like. Subscribing to organizational models that emerge from the functional requirements of contemporary home life, the prototypes adopt the same site conditions, basic spatial needs, and building techniques, updating them to affordably augment the experience of domesticity.

2. Service/Served

The typical home scatters service functions such as storage, utility, bath, and kitchen throughout the plan as necessary. The ganging of service functions clearly separates service and served spaces.

3. Public/Private

The typical house is unitary in form, relying on furniture and apertures to articulate space as public or private. By zoning the public and private and articulating their boundaries through formal expression, the prototype houses allow for a greater spatial definition, formality, and diversity with smaller square footages.

4. Day/Night

The prototype houses attempt to blur the solitary functionality of any one space. Employing zones rather than rooms, the single-story free plans allow for a multiplicity of functional interpretations.

5. Indoor/Outdoor

The bounded forms of the typical house deny any connectivity between house and garden. The spatial flow in the prototype houses provides for a fluid movement from outside to inside, connecting and expanding the efficient interior spaces with the exterior both visually and physically. Any increased cost to accomplish this connectivity and expansive spatial perception is balanced by a reduction in square footage.

6. Phasing

The static conception of the typical home requires the construction of the entire structure and all of its amenities at one time. As a result the expense of home ownership is increased, and the market encourages a nomadic attitude by requiring one to move when more space is required. The prototype houses are based on the idea of mutability, allowing the dwelling to expand or contract as needed. The composition established through an efficiency of modularity and sequence provides for segmental construction of the home.

7. Modularity

The prototype houses use conventional construction methods and work to minimize material modification by standardizing structural, cladding, and finish dimensions. This maximization of the modularity of stock materials minimizes both material waste and the labor necessary to modify the material prior to installation.

8. Materials

These houses adopt the same structural systems, construction methods, and materials currently in use in the housing industry, but employ them unconventionally to provide efficiency in cost and effect. Using durable natural materials, the prototype houses simplify the ever-increasing complexity of contemporary systems and rely upon the beauty and intrinsic properties of the material.

9. Experience

The typical home relies on features rather than architecture to fabricate "quality." Subscribing to a compositional connectivity, the prototype houses orchestrate the experience of architecture through a return to the elements of form and space.

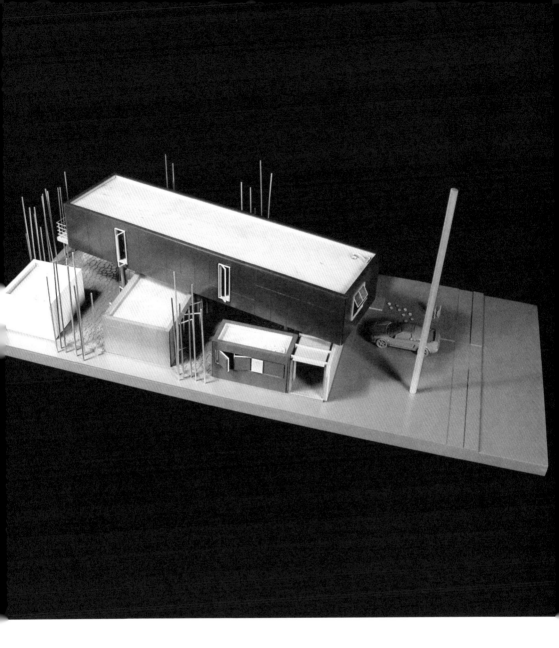

The following are four case studies illustrating these principles, with selected design points elucidated.

House 1: Program House

Each of the eight pavilions has a distinct function, and they are sequenced accordingly. The lower level is publicly zoned (porch, library, living, dining, kitchen, storage, TV), and the upper level is privately zoned (bedroom). The distinct units of the house create thresholds between functions, calling attention to the differences between the uses of each space. The separate buildings are collected on an indoor-outdoor plinth with exterior connections that allow for flexible expansion and interconnectivity of site, space, and function. The spaces between the pavilions expand the house into the site. The discrete pavilions can thus be phased in over time, based on need and affordability.

House 8: Porch House

This design links the landscape to the daily activities of the house by turning the house inside out. Gathering the room pavilions of the home around a central porch creates an exterior room, which also serves as a corridor and a stage. A series of recesses in the ground plane make room for a variety of potential landscape elements—a plunge pool, a bamboo grove, a tulip field, a rock garden. One side of the porch is zoned public and the other, private. The pavilions are articulated by function: eating, living, and sleeping/bathing. They can be pre-manufactured off-site and can easily be phased as needed. Each pavilion has an opaque perimeter shell with openings punched through this outer edge while being transparent and operable to the inner porch and patio. Thus the transparent edge allows for small spaces to expand outward.

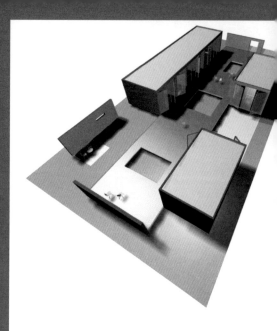

House 19: Tube House

The Tube House is functionally organized along the following chain: garage, entry, kitchen, dining, living, TV, laundry, stair, closet, bath, and sleep. The cycle progresses and reverses relative to the twenty-four-hour cycle of domestic activity. The folding action of the tube separates the house into three zones: a lower living bar that accommodates activities such as cooking, reading, and entertaining; a middle, vertical circulation zone; and a sleeping bar elevated for privacy and security. The house is constructed on a 4-foot material module and clad in corrugated metal to reduce maintenance. The narrow footprint allows for double density on a single site.

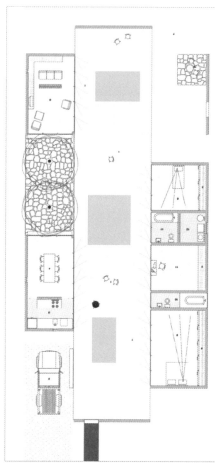

House 37: Enclosure House

The single wrapper of standing-seam metal that encloses this house simplifies construction, provides a low-maintenance privacy shield, and establishes the structure's iconography. A central core contains the house's functional service components and bifurcates the home into public and private realms. Public and private porches are located in the front and back of the dwelling, respectively. The public front has an open floor plan subdivided by furniture configuration, while the private back is compartmentalized into three bedrooms.

**Top and bottom
left
Gail Peter Borden**
Porch House, aerial
rendering and plan

**Top and bottom
right
Gail Peter Borden**
Tube House, model
and rendering of
living room

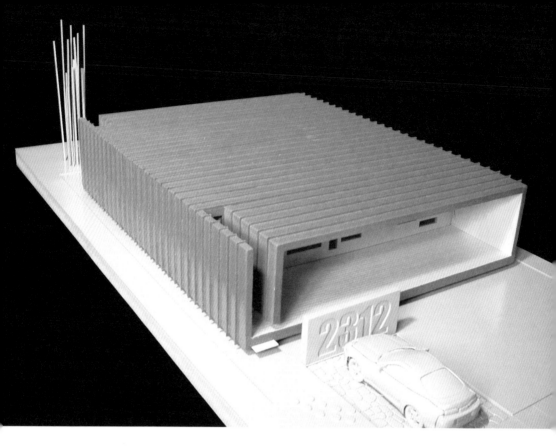

The recessed front wall establishes a public face with functionally choreographed punched openings. The rear elevation is a transparent, operable facade, incrementally studded with colored metal panels for storage. Circulation occurs via a single corridor feeding four zones: front porch, public area, private area, and back porch. Moving from indoors to out, this lateral spine links the various pieces by providing penetrations through the edges of the folding wrapper.

Prospects
The reinvention of the typical single-family home provides opportunities for rethinking the origin and evolution of an entire landscape. The insertion of a new housing model that is not based on mimicry but rather on cultural response, bracketed within the boundaries of current economic and construction systems, provides an alternative to our current direction of development. The house becomes a mediator allowing for a redirection of the system.

The reconfiguration of growth patterns, the evolution of new methods of living, and the cultural revaluation of spatial needs and perceptions are challenges worthy of the attention of this generation of designers. These propositions, rather than abandoning all associations with the current approaches, attempt to transform them.

When we clarify our methods, streamline construction principles, address technological evolutions, and consider the quality of space as governed through light, site, program, and material, only then can we reinvent "everyday" architecture.

Above and right
Gail Peter Borden
Enclosure House,
model and plan

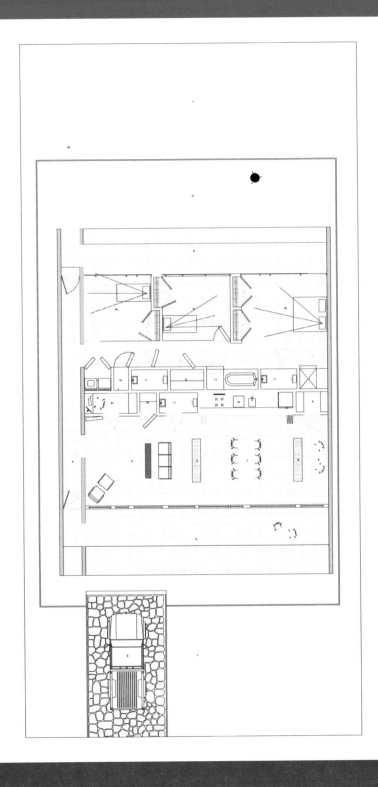

Archepreneurs

CHRIS KRAGER

Build it and they will come. Strong design and strong convictions prove there is a substantial demand for contemporary affordable housing.

eft
RDB
ugar Creek House,
ustin. 2005.
etal-clad SIP
onstruction

When the year 2000 came and went without the onset of Armageddon or at least a global digital meltdown, some were disappointed, but most were relieved. Yet a significant historical milestone passed with little notice: the United States fulfilled its Jeffersonian manifest destiny and officially became a suburban nation, with a majority of its citizens laying claim to their forty acres outside of town (usually something more in the range of one-fourth of an acre).

Fortunately, today's suburbanites don't have to take a grueling, life-threatening journey in a covered wagon to lay claim to their piece of the American dream; it involves nothing more demanding than a forty-five-minute family outing to an outlying suburban tract development in a station wagon or SUV. For the latter half of the twentieth century, a majority of middle-class families in the U.S. have chosen these outlying communities for a variety of reasons: cost, perceived safety, better schools, lower taxes, and better services have played their part, in conjunction with institutional variables such as the interstate highway system and biased lending practices. Add to this the potency of the American frontier mentality, and our current condition seems inevitable.

There has been plentiful discussion of the suburbs in the design disciplines. From excoriation to exaltation, thousands of books, articles, competitions, and design studios have addressed the American suburb—in the realm of theory. Little has been done to engage this portion of the market in practice. While the underpinnings of the growth patterns that have given rise to the American landscape are socioeconomically complex, one thing is clear: architects and planners have not had a hand in the majority of our built environment.

Most Americans live in neighborhoods created by the housing industry. Typical suburban housing is insular and unrelated to the lives of its inhabitants, just as the profit centers that drive the industry are. Builders conform to practices that maximize bottom-line profits, changing materials and methods only as financial targets dictate. Builders and contractors have neither the training nor the incentive to maximize environmental and qualitative factors, except on the rare occasions where such actions are legally required. The fact is that design has been marginalized in mainstream culture. The often-mentioned statistic regarding the small number of homes actually designed by architects (usually cited at around 5 percent or less) illustrates the narrow role played by the discipline. Architects have found very comfortable niches as service providers to the top and bottom 2 percent of the population.

Middle America: A New Clientele

The conventional realms of architectural practice have been civic monuments, homes for wealthy patrons, and service to the economically challenged. Projects of this nature have an impact that is clear and easily understood. They have been, and hopefully will remain, projects where design professionals are seen as a necessity. But imagine the impact design could have if it was brought to middle America, that overwhelming majority of our culture.

Most of us live and work in environments that have received little consideration beyond that of economic necessity. As Winston Churchill said, "We shape our buildings; thereafter, they shape us." Unfortunately, the by-product of recent "shaping" leaves much to be desired. The isolation, homogeneity, and poor quality of our built environment has contributed in many ways to the decline of our culture and communities. This criticism is not directed solely at the suburbs; much of the urban revitalization that is taking place today suffers from an equal level of professional neglect. As designers, architects, and planners, we need to take a more active role in making significant contributions to the creation of our built environment.

Fortunately, the tide has already begun to turn. There are numerous examples of the increased visibility of design in popular culture. Whether it is Michael Graves or Todd Oldham at Target, the slick transformation of the desktop computer, or the advent of the modern-design La-Z-Boy, consumers will respond to objects and places that are thoughtfully conceived and well built. Architecture's small market segment is not the result of a lack of demand, but rather a lack of supply.

KRDB, the develop/design/build firm I cofounded with Christopher Robertson, focuses on affordable modern design, primarily in an urban infill context. We have three main goals:

1. Expand the availability of designed buildings through an entrepreneurial practice.

2. Act as a process and technology laboratory in the service of a better and more economical product.

3. Alleviate the negative effects of recent American growth patterns through the exploration of a variety of density and infill strategies.

Our work at KRDB is intended to propose an alternative housing model for use in the real-estate marketplace. In order to make inroads with production builders and others who fundamentally shape communities, architects and designers must be more pro-active and creative in defining their role. We can do this work. As natural facilitators and complex problem solvers, we possess the qualities necessary to visualize opportunities, assemble teams, and manifest a vision.

Our firm principals had diverse backgrounds in our pre-design days, including experience in construction, real estate, and banking. All of these realms of experience gave us insight into the underlying physical and financial structures required to create buildings, which allowed us to conceptualize our unique practice.

Develop/Design/Build

As a design/build firm we maintain financial and creative control over our process and product. This control is essential to our practice in several ways. Given our chosen niche, affordable modern design, the likelihood of another general contractor being able to execute our designs at the desired price point is slim. Because we are responsible for meeting all budgetary constraints, we pay heed to the financial implications of our proposals from the outset. Far from having a prohibitory effect, this constraint

has forced us to focus on the essentials of good design, imparting a conceptual economy to our work. An intimate familiarity with the construction process helps us understand what can be maximally accomplished with the minimum means.

Rather than relying solely on commission work, we have developed our own projects. From multiunit single-family developments to mixed-use commercial/residential projects, a substantial amount of our business is speculative work. This has been achieved in some cases with the assistance of federally funded municipal programs providing subsidies for affordable housing. Our first two-unit housing project under the city of Austin's S.M.A.R.T. Housing program was so well received that the housing authority went on to offer financing not only for the construction of our next eight-unit project but for land acquisition as well. We were the first design firm to use the program, which previously had been exploited primarily by tract homebuilders and multifamily developers using tax-credit programs. Most cities have homebuyer subsidy programs, and many have complimentary programs to provide incentives for developers and builders to provide affordable housing.

On smaller projects we are able to develop with a limited amount of cash out of pocket, as many banks will lend on the projected appraised value of a project. For instance, if we are selling a dwelling for $100,000 (as confirmed by an appraisal) that only cost $80,000 to build, the bank views it as having a 20 percent equity position and will loan on that amount of equity. Depending on the situation, the lender may want 30 percent equity, requiring an additional 10 percent over the built-in "sweat equity."

As our projects have increased in scale, we have begun to affiliate with a variety of partners in joint ventures that bring a number of different players to the table, such as a developer, an engineer, a contractor, a land owner, or an investor. In these cases we assemble the members of the team, each of whom brings his or her value to the project and contributes it as an equity investment. Each partner's equity stake is determined by the market value of his or her services relative to the overall cost of the project. At the end of the job, profits are divided accordingly.

Right
Factory-built fram panels utilized fo KRDB's Clifford Street project, wh comprises four s family homes in k Austin. 2005

What Is the Market? Who Are the Buyers?

When we first started out, our concept of our target market was more or less limited to people like us. We firmly believed that there were individuals out there who wanted access to good design and would pay for it. We also believed they wanted to live close to the center of the city and were probably interested in sustainability.

Our first open house was attended by approximately 750 people and attracted three news crews. The most interesting thing about the attendees was their diversity. The expected late-twenties and early-thirties creative types showed up (the aforementioned "people like us"), but overall the crowd was as varied as any I had seen in our city. If we had had ten homes to sell that day, I believe we would have sold them all (the two in question presold well before completion). From this event alone we generated an e-mail list of several hundred potential future clients. This local response, in addition to the response we received on the regional and national levels, affirmed our beliefs more strongly than we had dared to hope: the "average" person definitely wanted to live in a thoughtfully designed environment.

Technology, Materials, and Methods

From advances in specific materials to modularity at a variety of scales, we are always looking for better and more efficient means of building that conform to our aesthetic and economic criteria. One of our primary methods has been the use of modularity, which we have pursued in a variety of ways. We are currently using galvalum-clad structural insulated panels (SIPs), which provide a quickly constructed envelope that is both high in thermal efficiency and low in maintenance costs. We have also used factory-built (stick) panels that are assembled on site, significantly cutting waste and decreasing construction time. Both of these panelized methods increase efficiency and improve quality.

For the past three years we have been working toward developing a modular or factory-built housing product. Prefabricated housing has been part of the modernist endeavor since the beginning of the twentieth century, and lately it has been particularly fashionable, but we are approaching prefab in a slightly different manner. Rather than inventing a new prefab system or process, we have contacted modular-housing firms in an effort to operate within that industry's typical standards and methods.

Our manufactured-housing explorations began with research into the industry's existing practices and parameters. We interviewed several different companies to assess the quality of their products and their receptiveness to our concept. Eventually we established a relationship with a manufacturer and began to develop a scheme that would conform to its extant constraints. We embarked on a year-long iterative process that entailed a variety of modifications on both sides of the equation. The privately owned company's smaller size and autonomy meant that its engineers and designers were very receptive to alternative practices and materials, particularly when an approach was identified that would afford them increased efficiency.

To achieve the level of flexibility we hope eventually to allow, we knew the process would need to be incremental. Executing a single model that meets our aesthetic and budgetary goals was the first step. The next phase is to push the process in terms of flexibility and technology. In order to exploit the economies of scale of the manufacturing process, a limited number of modules must be available. These modules can then be used interchangeably in a design matrix that will enable customization and adaptability. We will also be implementing technologies such as metal-clad SIPs and low-impact finish materials to provide an efficient, sustainable, low-maintenance building.

Above
KRDB
Luna modular ho
Austin. 2008.
Rendering

Right
Renderings and
plans of two of si:
modular "building
blocks" that form
the basis of KRD
modular system

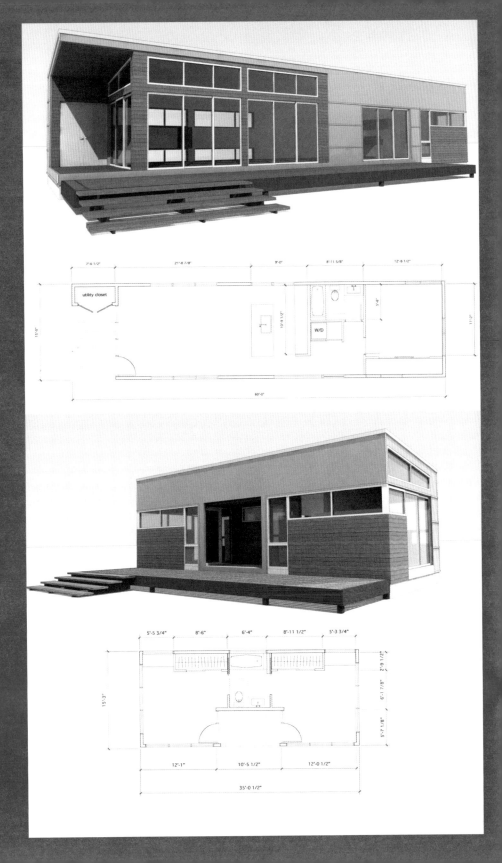

Above
Rendering of KRD
modular for a site
Sawyer, Michigan

Left
Satsuma 53, Aust
2006. This 10,00
square-foot mixed
project was devel
designed, and bu
KRDB in coopera
with Beck-Reit
Construction.

Right
Rendering of KRC
South First mixed
project, South Au
2007

Sustainability

While we make every attempt to create "green" buildings, both through the judicious selection of materials and sensitive siting and design, our primary sustainability focus is on the macro level. The low-density suburban growth patterns that have become prevalent (and not just in the United States) are harmful to our environment and culture and they must be remedied. Having begun our practice with urban infill single-family housing, we soon recognized the need to explore a variety of higher-density options in order to address these critical issues.

Cities are low-density and homogenous as a result of historically exclusive zoning. The infill model we are pursuing is a pocket approach, utilizing relatively small commercial/mixed-use tracts (one-fourth of an acre in size) that are fairly abundant. Many of them are located on the edges of residential neighborhoods, providing transitional opportunities. The buildings, 10,000 to 12,000 square feet, that we design for these sites are compatible in size to the adjacent smaller-scale residential neighborhoods, while providing commercial amenities for bordering communities. This model is an effective bridging element for areas lacking variety of use, but its scale is not necessarily attractive to typical developers. Therefore, we are pursuing this strategy speculatively—developing, designing, building, and selling with a team of like-minded entrepreneurs.

Build It and They Will Come

The creative abilities that allow architects and designers to deliver successful built solutions should also allow the discipline (or individuals within it) to formulate strategies for renewed relevance. This is not to suggest that marquee architects should stop designing museums and start working on tract homes; but if we want to make a lasting impact on society and culture at large, we must begin to transform the mediocre built environment. To accomplish this architects and building designers must act as businesspeople, civic leaders, and activists. Our obligation is simple: our built environment must be improved, and we must lead the way.

If we want to make a lasting impact on society and culture at large, we must begin to transform the mediocre built environment.
To accomplish this architects and building designers must act as businesspeople, civic leaders, and activists. Our obligation is simple: our built environment must be improved, and we must lead the way.

The design of places
is about finding
and forging relationships

Relationships between

people and the
people and buildings
buildings and buildings
buildings and landscape

THE TRANSFORMATIVE POWER OF ARCHITECTURAL EDUCATION

Building Consensus in Design/Build Studios

STEVE BADANES

In the real
world, little
happens without
collaboration.
Design/build
projects are a
great vehicle to
teach a team-
based approach.

In 1968 the Vietnam War was raging, Martin Luther King, Jr., and Bobby Kennedy were assassinated, and all the architecture profession seemed to care about was project fees. In 1969 students shut down the AIA convention in protest. Fed up with the profession's apparent indifference to the needs of communities, architecture students all over America started community design programs in the late 1960s to design and build for clients who could not afford traditional architectural services.

Social Justice in Architecture

When I was in architecture school in the late '60s, some classmates and I opted out of the studios offered by the university. Instead we formed our own community design center, which we called the "People's Workshop," an appropriate name for the times. Our workshop designed housing and built playgrounds in New Brunswick, New Jersey. We felt that architectural education could deal with social-justice issues in a hands-on way that the academic status quo did not allow for.

Many veterans of the design/build studios formed during this period went on to community-service careers or design/build "back to the land" experimental-living scenarios. I bypassed internship and joined some classmates to form Jersey Devil, a group of artists, architects, and inventors committed to the interdependence of design, construction, and energy-efficient building. After gaining construction experience, all of us have taught outreach design/build at such programs as the Yestermorrow School in Vermont, various architecture schools, and international programs in Cuba, Finland, Ghana, India, and Mexico.

By the 1980s the schools had regained control of their curriculums, most of the community design centers were purged from academia, and the style wars—first postmodernism, followed by Decon, leading into Blobitecture—absorbed all that student energy. So it is very exciting to now see the pendulum swinging back to social-justice issues in architectural education. Inspired by publicity generated by groups like the Rural Studio and Design Corps, students are again demanding that their education have meaning and include a hands-on service component. Many schools are starting design/build programs and rediscovering the power—and the problems—of these curriculums.

Since the late 1980s I have run the Neighborhood Design/Build Studio at the University of Washington in Seattle. In my experience the major pitfalls of community-service design/build programs include the following:

• selecting projects that are too large and thus cost more and take longer than expected;

• using a "competition" approach to decide what to build;

• choosing projects requiring students to relocate great distances (the "ambulance chaser" approach). Some programs do this well, but it is much more efficient to work closer to home, where you can be more productive, save energy, and build community credibility with each new project in the same geographic area.

Teaching Design/Build

The traditional design studio reinforces some unfortunate assumptions about creativity, most notably that practice is a solitary endeavor. Students usually design independently and learn to defend their ideas against criticism. In the real world, however, little happens without collaboration. Teamwork is needed to achieve common goals.

That said, I have taught a number of design/build exercises in which individual students or small groups tackle a series of design problems in various media—wood, concrete, and metal—and fabricate their solutions. Before beginning construction, legible dimensioned working drawings must be approved. Subsequent edits and additions to the object are acceptable as long as they incorporate the solution's original concepts. Hands-on construction inevitably yields new information that affects design decisions. These individual and small-group exercises are popular with students. They make students responsible for design, causing them to become more involved; and the difficulties and extra work inherent in a project designed and built by the entire group are avoided.

as shared responsibility and more enthusiasm during construction.

Most students have never designed anything that has been built, and many have no previous construction experience. Students who collaborate on large design/build projects learn that when we work together, we can make our projects happen if we commit ourselves to them. Students gain confidence in the power of commitment, not just in designing and building. We deal with design issues in a practical way, learning construction techniques and detailing, but the real lessons involve self-motivation, courage, self-reliance, perseverance, teamwork, and service to others.

I have been involved in many design/build programs in a wide array of contexts and locations. For the past fifteen years I have conducted a studio during spring quarter at the University of Washington. I co-teach the studio with Damon Smith, a graduate of the university's M. Arch. program and a designer/builder with SHED in Seattle. There are usually ten to sixteen students in the studio, which is open to undergraduate seniors and graduate students in their final year. I feel it is important for the students to complete the project (the clients appreciate this, too), so I select something we can finish in the eleven weeks of spring quarter. Only non-profit organizations are eligible to be clients for the spring studio project. Clients are responsible for securing a grant for materials, and sometimes I help them with the grant application process. Budgets range from $5,000 to $20,000.

The class meets Monday, Wednesday, and Friday afternoons and on Saturdays during construction. If we fall behind, Sundays also become workdays, and exam week is always available for a final push if necessary. On the first day of the studio, students introduce themselves, talk about their construction experience (or the lack thereof), and state their personal goals for the class. The rest of the afternoon is spent on three short, individual projects—each using an 8½ x 11 sheet of paper to build a bridge, a tower, and a foundation—followed by a tour of the shop that focuses on safety issues. An individual design/build problem using plywood is assigned for the following Monday. This assignment allows the students

However, I feel that group projects are worth the extra effort. They can be larger and more service-oriented, and they can provide experience working with real clients. Architecture has always been a service profession, but it has traditionally served only those who can afford it. By working for clients who do not normally have access to architects, students are exposed to community outreach and to the notion of society as our real client.

At the Neighborhood Design/Build Studio, we do our initial design work during studio time, in groups, using a consensus method that includes a facilitator (usually me) and a written "group memory." Discussion proceeds by going around the table, with everyone stating pros and cons. All voices are equal, and we never vote. We break into subgroups, with drawings, models, and people moving from group to group so that everyone shares ownership of the design. In my first attempt at a group design/build studio, at the University of Miami in 1983, we used a competition to decide what to build. This resulted in enormous pressure on the winner and bitterness among the losers, making the construction phase a difficult experience. The consensus method has resulted in more egalitarian designs as well

Above left
Students working
with curved form
Noji Commons

to build something on their own and gain some experience in the shop, and in turn gives me an idea of what they can do.

On Wednesday we generally go to the site, possibly visiting some past projects on the way, to meet with the clients and to commit to returning on Monday of week three with a preliminary design. We return to the studio, share our initial reactions, and begin group exercises if there is time. I always make a little speech about the importance of coming to a group decision. I generally say that if the goal is to build something really cool, maybe I should design it, and they can build it. This of course

is totally unacceptable, so it is a short step from this assertion to get the class to realize that it would be equally silly to build the idea of a single class member. I split the class into two groups and ask them to make a list of the positive and negative aspects of working in groups, which takes about twenty minutes. We then list all the items that the groups came up with, writing them down one at a time on a large piece of butcher paper, alternating between groups. Then the students divide into two different groups and make another list: how to reinforce the good qualities of working in groups and mitigate the bad ones. This also takes about twenty minutes, and the results are also recorded on a large sheet of paper. These lists are on hand in the studio during the group design process to serve as a constant reminder of shared values. I am indebted to Joel Loveland for this exercise. He did it with my class in 1988, and I have done it since then, many times. It gives students a chance to focus on the group process in the abstract before dealing with the problem at hand.

Design work begins by splitting the class into three groups and having them brainstorm. After a few hours (or whatever time period we agree on), we gather around a central table and discuss initial ideas. Often we will assign a scribe to note down important points of agreement (this is an example of written group memory). We search for places of commonality, and usually we can find a few. We then rearrange into different groups—a very important part of the process—and continue designing, using the new points of agreement as givens. The process continues for as long as it takes to reach consensus on the site plan, the structures, and other important features of the design. We only work during class time, and we try to merge gradually into two groups and finally into one.

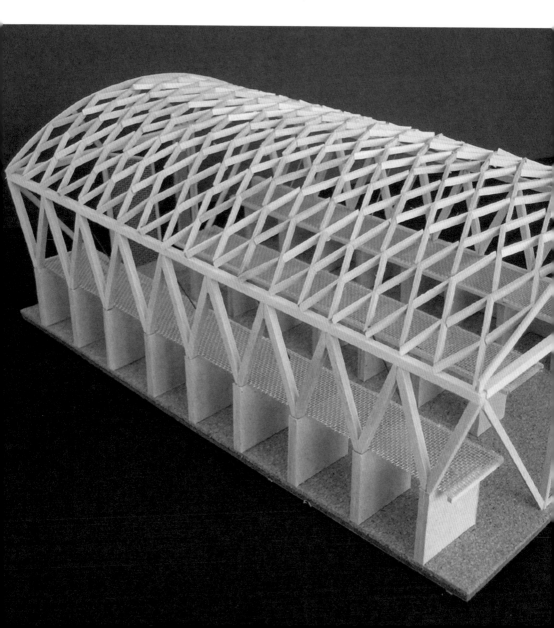

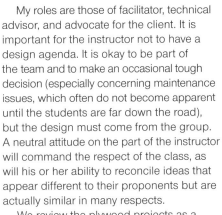

My roles are those of facilitator, technical advisor, and advocate for the client. It is important for the instructor not to have a design agenda. It is okay to be part of the team and to make an occasional tough decision (especially concerning maintenance issues, which often do not become apparent until the students are far down the road), but the design must come from the group. A neutral attitude on the part of the instructor will command the respect of the class, as will his or her ability to reconcile ideas that appear different to their proponents but are actually similar in many respects.

We review the plywood projects as a group on Monday of week two; the atmosphere is informal, the criticism constructive. We usually have agreed on a direction by the middle or end of the second week, allowing us to spend the weekend preparing a presentation for the following Monday (models work best for non-architect clients). At this point the class begins to function as a team or a small design/build office. We do not ask the client to chose from multiple proposals. We may have called the client several times to clarify issues, but when it comes time to make the presentation, we are unified in our approach to the problem.

Drawings, models, critiques, and presentations are all tools for communication, both within and outside the architectural studio. Our focus is on finding common ground, setting agendas and priorities, and managing time, all of which implies communicating more efficiently. The client and community meetings require additional communication skills, as do the occasional presentations to city agencies. We rehearse our presentations because a polished resentation helps mitigate doubts that students have enough experience to build high-quality public projects.

The initial meeting with the client usually goes well. Clients often make some good suggestions that are easily incorporated into the scheme. We spend the rest of the week doing tasks like construction drawings, engineering, material take-offs (lists of the materials that will be needed for the project), and pricing, with the goal of breaking ground during the fourth week. This gives us seven weeks to complete construction.

For the sake of efficiency, the class breaks into groups during the construction phase. Groups are usually self-selected; however, we all work together on big items like concrete pours, and students are encouraged to spend time on all aspects of construction to gain as much experience as possible. There is an inevitable hierarchy that arises on construction sites, as students with more building experience take the lead and teach those with less experience, but we have a group site meeting before each class to cover any issues that arise. Students are responsible for material procurement, fabrication, and scheduling. Damon and I work on-site with the students, but we don't hog all the fun work; we use the opportunity to teach building methods and tricks. I generally give the students a lower budget number than what is really available, because of the inevitable cost overruns. Usually someone in the class takes on the role of the bookkeeper, although I like to keep a close eye on costs as well.

We have always finished on time and have never gone over budget. Low-income clients are generally grateful, which is rewarding for the students. A ribbon-cutting ceremony is usually scheduled to coincide with graduation so that parents and family can attend. Everyone involved with the project benefits from it. Students work with real clients and learn something about building. Clients, who can't even afford the materials, reap the fruits of student labor. Corporate sponsors polish their images by donating materials, and the city and university receive credit for a community-service contribution without having to do much. Community-based design/build studios demonstrate the power of commitment, the value of service to others, and the lasting satisfaction of group achievement.

Above left
Students install la
roof framing for th
Sunhouse.

Teaching Cooperation

AMANDA SCHACHTER

An experimental
master's degree
program features
community collabor-
ation and activism
as core values for
design education.

ft
tent-building
orkshop with
m Corsellis
d Antonella
tale followed
e approach of
eir UK-based
umanitarian aid
gency, Shelter
entre, and was
art of the 2004
eminar "Crisis
elief Strategies."

In the summer of 2003 Alberto Estevez, then the dean of the Escola Tècnica Superior d'Arquitectura in Barcelona, gave me the go-ahead to start a degree program for a Master of International Cooperation in Architecture. The school was eager to be the first in Spain to create such a program. Whether "cooperation" is understood as community design in the United States or as United Nations-relief operations in Africa, Latin America, or Asia, this concept has been receiving greater attention from architects and design students who know that design needs to play a more vital role in the processes of planning, decision-making, and providing humanitarian relief. The new degree program would provide a comprehensive, short-format curriculum to expose designers to a range of cooperative possibilities.

I had originally joined the Catalonian architecture school to teach an undergraduate design studio, sharing the particular experience of my American background with European students. Creating the new master's program was a way to pursue a dimension of design that I felt had been barely present in my American education and completely lacking in the traditional Spanish curriculum; to explore, in an academic setting, how the design process might build more complex relationships among people, allowing architecture to fulfill need as well as desire.

The inaugural year presented all the difficulties one might expect from any start-up program: everything from finding talented, motivated students and freeing up studio and seminar space, to convincing the university administration that a curriculum to be taught in English outside of the university's primary degree track might actually be a worthwhile way to provide common ground to international students and practitioners concerned with these critical issues.

The biggest challenge was to define what a trajectory in architectural cooperation might be. The program strives to teach young architects how to keep design at the center of the creative process while broadening the ends to which design might be applied. "Cooperation in architecture" implies that designers need to collaborate closely with many unlikely people outside the discipline in order to realize meaningful, helpful work.

The program provides a complement to architectural education in that it helps dispel the belief that design is only a self-serving exercise, through the consideration of complex scenarios in need of design rather than the sheer commodification of creative vision.

With a focus on the design process as a way to foster empathy, the degree program addresses topics and issues that are usually handled without architects but are essential in creating the wider built environment, such as sustainability, cultural identity and globalization, disaster-relief planning, the policies of international organizations like UN-Habitat, low-cost design/build processes, and the lasting integration of marginalized urban neighborhoods. Professors and practitioners from specialties as far afield as sociology and shelter construction are invited to investigate the chosen themes with the students in an intensive series of seminars. At the same time the students take on concrete problems in an architectural and urban-design studio. One of the main goals of the design studio is to encourage full collaboration with all parties involved in a given situation.

For the students who enrolled in the program's inaugural year, hailing from countries as distinct as Argentina, Bosnia, and Singapore, "international cooperation" initially meant working with the UN in Africa. Most of the students were frustrated by how their undergraduate degrees seemed to narrow rather than widen their prospects: a desk job in a corporate office turning out commercial projects or a technical career in environmental engineering. Many wanted to do something more meaningful with their education but didn't know where to begin. They had no substantive contact with relief programs seeking designers and had little idea of how to approach a community in need of design services, let alone address a community's design needs. One applicant came to the program believing it would secure her a career-track position with the UN—which she did in fact obtain while writing her thesis—but in the meantime, through the coursework and fieldwork, she also came to understand that "cooperation in architecture" referred to a panorama of design practice far broader than even relief work or infrastructural planning would encompass.

The curriculum's focus on "developing contexts" does encompass UN project sites, but it also includes any part of the world undergoing transformation, even within one's own immediate context, whether purportedly "developed" or not. A student named Medina Hadzihasanović, a recent graduate of the University of Sarajevo's Faculty of Architecture who was working on the postwar restoration of Bosnian mosques, enrolled in our program as an opportunity to learn how to better approach the transformation of her native land. The intimacy of the program, with its small and attentive group of students engaging professors and each other in direct dialogue, gave Medina the chance to intervene in and help resolve issues that were of profound importance to her. One of the invited seminar professors, Tom Corsellis, who had provided cooperation services in Bosnia and Kosovo through his UK-based relief organization, Shelter Centre, tailored his teaching to her inquiries—as many of the professors would find themselves doing—bringing the students' particular formative experiences to bear on class content.

In lively debates among the participants about what might constitute cooperation in architecture, one of the most successful, eye-opening examples we discussed was the marginalized neighborhood of La Mina, which is located on the outskirts of Barcelona. In 1969 a plan was initiated to clear precarious settlement throughout the city by moving all the inhabitants of these areas into rapidly constructed concrete superblocks. La Mina's overnight conversion from arable land and informal neighborhoods to a housing-project zone gathered 15,000 people from two hundred dispersed shantytowns—each with its own distinct, tight-knit social fabric—into eight eleven-story blocks comprised of twenty-four eighty-family towers. La Mina began its life as a disjointed agglomeration of Andalusians and Iberian Gypsies who had migrated to Barcelona in search of work, all struggling for inclusion and stability. After decades of internal friction and institutional neglect, La Mina neighborhood groups have come to have a voice in improving their environment. Alexander Levi's design seminar encouraged students to get to know a range of La Mina's local activists so they could then propose designs for neighborhood transformation that would meet the individuals' needs and would manifest their collective dreams for a better city.

The students' final design seminar presentation, held in La Mina's civic center, proved to be one of the most rewarding parts of the program. The students received direct, honest feedback on their proposals from involved residents and representatives, who felt that finally someone was giving them the tools to better understand and

Top right
The Camp de la Bota shantytow what is now La photographed i the 1950s

Bottom right
Members of the Adrianas de la an association women-turned-neighborhood-activists, recons the memory of t original shanty h 2004

Left
Completed tent from the seminar "Crisis Relief Strategies"

approach the planners and policy makers who were developing long-term projects that would transform their neighborhood. During the seminar's final presentation, a Gypsy woman, mother of three, commented that it felt liberating simply to imagine the projects proposed by the students. She admitted that before she would not have felt capable of carrying on a discussion about abstract issues seemingly so remote to her.

After the La Mina experience taught the students that Barcelona itself could be seen as a "developing context" in need of careful attention, they felt prepared to investigate Pärnu, Estonia, the site of the master's design studio. The challenge there was to revitalize the city's Mai housing estate, which was built for Soviet workers during the USSR's occupation and administration of Estonia and is still populated by Russian families, many of whom have never learned to read, write, or speak Estonian. The situation in Pärnu shares many similarities with that of La Mina, involving questions of how to improve the lives of resident migrant groups of disparate cultures in neighborhoods undergoing significant social and urban change through a succession of evolving regimes. As part of the design studio's phase of initial immersion, students visited Pärnu for two weeks to learn about the site and meet local residents and planning officials.

For the second graduating class of the program, this time with double the enrollment, we refined the scope of an education in cooperation in architecture. Our primary insight at this point—having experienced firsthand how student interventions in Barcelona and Estonia complemented each other—was that to meet the challenges of a "developing context" one ought to see it as simultaneously global and local. Thus, designers might cooperate in a nearby neighborhood in need, and then apply the finer lessons learned in these local experiences to analogous cases abroad. In this spirit the local La Mina seminar continued to dovetail into a full-fledged design-studio project around the globe. The master's students, most having just arrived in Barcelona, were immediately introduced to real residents in complex life situations and thereby able to peer behind and transcend the dazzling and deceptive market-image fed to tourists and locals alike by the city's and region's promotional machine.

This time around students proposed four design options for the La Mina Laboratory of Social Practice, a program that local activists had been trying to entice Barcelona officials to fund in their neighborhood as a way of turning their struggle against marginalization into a focal point of transformative culture. The site is the last remnant of La Mina's bucolic past and was formerly occupied by a farmstead. The proposal called for a phased implementation, from lighting the public spaces of La Mina, with anticipated events and uses passing without boundaries between indoors and outdoors. Students were asked to develop detailed program and realization strategies as a response to a vision-statement written by local activists. The laboratory would document, archive, and exhibit evidence of ongoing changes in the neighborhood.

In an accompanying seminar, the Argentinean urban planner and environmentalist Ruben Pesci invited the students to envision an ecological greenbelt for Tres Turons, another overlooked area in Barcelona, tucked between the city's first and second ridges of encircling urban hills. The students in Pesci's urban design seminar applied the tools of sustainability and low-cost planning that he employs in environmental projects in Argentina, Brazil, and Uruguay.

Meanwhile, Medina—the student from the program's first year—returned to Sarajevo and became part of the master's design-studio team as faculty, hosting the new group of graduate students—seventeen of them now—in Bosnia. For two weeks the students lived in Sarajevo with local architecture students, teaming up with them to meet with neighborhood groups, designers, and urban planners, and to embark on design. After a preliminary joint presentation of findings with local representatives in Sarajevo, the students worked closely over the next three months—back and forth between Sarajevo and Barcelona—to posit beneficial transformation strategies for Sarajevo city center's left bank, maintaining close contact over the Internet to advance their proposals. A contingent of Sarajevo students and faculty traveled to Barcelona to take part in the final review, attended by the Bosnian ambassador

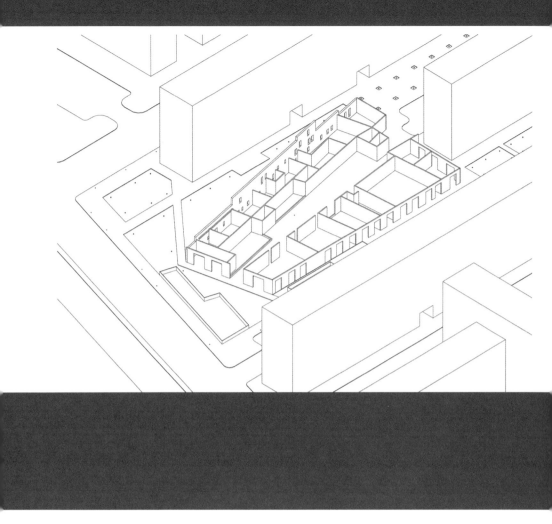

Above and
pages 262–63
Students of
the Master of
International
Cooperation
Architecture
Program
proposed design
for La Mina
Laboratory of
Social Practice,
Barcelona. 2005

to Spain as well as activists from other parts of Europe.

The Sarajevo students, in seeing their own local problems through foreign eyes, were especially animated and refreshed by the openness of an insider-outsider, bottom-up approach to design in their hometown, where a generational authoritarian hierarchy still lingered on their faculties and in their bureaucracy. The Barcelona foreign students, in turn, learned how to propose design solutions as a means to share open-ended discoveries with locals who in the long term would carry on the tough work of being agents for their own change.

Cooperation is an attitude and an aptitude for fomenting positive transformation through open, associative connection.

What students learn in the master's program is how to plug into their native or adopted city as a network for addressing local and far-reaching concerns. In a perpetuation of the ongoing cycle of study and practice, the program and its graduates fortify each other as the latter apply course material to real-life situations, which contributes to the veracity of the program, and to the professional future and personal goals of the graduates. Thus, dichotomies between "near" and "remote," "familiar" and "exotic," "us" and "them" are blurred and transformed into a more complex working notion of social and site-specific design that broadens the scope of architectural design's cooperative reach.

Enhancing Family and Community through Interdisciplinary Design

SAMINA QURAESHI

In order for community-based education to serve communities effectively, universities must challenge many of their entrenched traditions and create a new collaborative paradigm.

As universities across the nation confront traditions of self-directed research and teaching, many search for new relevance in the transmission of knowledge to the public, attempting to break new ground in university-community partnership. But for all the theoretical emphasis on interdisciplinary real-world problem solving, universities too often view place-based learning initiatives as external to traditional tertiary education. Such initiatives must be integrated into the curricular mainstream, or they are doomed to fail. To be sure, such a proposition risks challenging the status quo of funding streams, publication requirements for tenure, and the canonical approach to learning. But if this status quo is not challenged, place-based learning will never rise above a well-intentioned public relations strategy.

In 1999 I began work on a project that I saw as a promising three-pronged approach to teaching and learning. It encompassed comprehensive community development, university-community partnership, and inter-disciplinary tertiary education. My belief that these endeavors can have more of an impact when synthesized remains steadfast; but the process taught me the extent to which each of these components has its own internal contradictions and challenges, which can affect the success of the overall endeavor. Reflecting on the assumptions embedded within each component is a crucial step toward understanding the costs and benefits of this approach and refining the model for future applications.

As an educator my objective was to explore the potential that could be unleashed by rethinking the studio/theory curriculum. As a designer my objective was to assert the primacy of deep, reflective community involvement when conceiving of design interventions in the built environment. The studio/charrette system of responding to exotic design briefs with theoretical architectural solutions does not provide students with the tools or understanding of design opportunities in the real world. If we are to vest the new generation of designers with power to address the deepening inequalities of our society—inequalities that are aesthetic as well as economic and political—we must develop new paradigms of education that involve sustained engagement with a community.

In the blighted zones of American cities, community, family, and human dignity are under assault in a manner that is hard for outsiders to comprehend. The term "inner city" evokes images of poverty, decaying infrastructure, and social breakdown. Decades of social engineering, urban renewal, job programs, and other similar initiatives have not produced the desired degree of revitalization. The disarray has resulted in the collapse of families, the failure of schools, medical systems that do not provide needed care, incomprehension about justice and legal systems, and inaccessible institutions that have commodified the care of the community. In these places history has been bled from the structures of the streets and the memories of the people.

Conventional community development and social service programs are powerless to stem the deterioration of the social fabric in these places, perhaps because there is confusion between real needs and those perceived by social service programs. The people who live in these neighborhoods recognize that these institutions are not helping. Needs are translated into deficiencies and an institutional, "one-size-fits all" approach denies the special circumstances surrounding each human problem.

To many people, there seems to be little or no hope for restoring what has been lost. But a closer look shows that if we set aside our assumptions about what these communities lack, and what is happening in them now, we will be in a better position to address the present and future of community and place.

With these ideas in mind I began work at the University of Miami as the Henry R. Luce Professor in Family and Community, establishing the Initiative for Urban and Social Ecology (INUSE) through the university's Center for Urban and Community Design (CUCD). We began with a call to all departments and schools within the university to join us in an effort to collaborate on a "university-community initiative." Though we were met with skepticism about scheduling, credits, and faculty appointments, we received positive responses from the Social and Behavioral Sciences Department in the Medical School, the School of Law, the School of Communication, and the School of Education. From within the Faculty of Arts and Sciences, the departments of art, photography, and history were responsive as well.

As a first step faculty, students, and community partners jointly identified an at-risk neighborhood adjacent to the university as the focus for our research and practice. West Coconut Grove is an impoverished, historically Afro-Caribbean-American community situated on the Miami–Coral Gables border between the University of Miami campus to the west, and upscale shopping and entertainment areas in Center Coconut Grove to the east. Our hope was to use design strategies to tackle urban challenges within a broad-based, interdisciplinary community-empowerment initiative. By working from the strength of different academic points of view and listening to the words of the people in the community we hoped to serve, we could explore new ways of seeing and responding to their needs and opportunities.

Our preliminary goals were:

• Create new community organizations to work on issues of housing, training, education, healthcare, family estate matters, and to consolidate fragmented improvement efforts.

• Develop a program of commercial revitalization, particularly along the major corridor, Grand Avenue.

• Increase the rate of homeownership.

• Increase the amount of housing, particularly through scattered-site infill development.

• Assist the community in developing a sense of pride in their history and culture.

• Help the community with matters of taxation, inheritance, and ownership.

• Assist the community with matters of healthcare, teen pregnancy, drug abuse, and dog bites (from rabid dogs inhabiting vacant lots that were used as illegal refuse dumps).

The team began by scrutinizing our inclusive rhetoric of "partnership" and "collaboration." An undeniable disparity exists between university and community.

Thus, our work raised a number of questions:

• How can a partnership between the university and the community be managed so that the community leads?

• How can this new partnership engage the resources necessary to implement evolving goals?

• How can we ensure that the ultimate benefits go to the community and its residents, and particularly that potential improvements do not displace residents and businesses?

• How can the community be organized as a unified force best able to take full advantage of the attention brought by its university partners?

• How can the community develop the social capacity to continue building and enhancing itself in the future?

We tried to address the divide between university and community by listening. We set out to get to know the community, mapping its assets and understanding its existing organizations before attempting to arrive at any vision or implement any plan. Some of our early studies included geographical maps of physical and cultural assets; inventories of existing formal and informal community organizations; statistics on home and business ownership, vacancies, and vacant lots; and photographic studies of the people and their habitat. We also tried to be clear about our principles. For us, helping the community rebuild meant restoring a belief in progress, by which we meant access to affordable housing, a renewed sense of history, the promotion of community identity, and the establishment of the proper climate for reinvestment.

Context: West Coconut Grove

West Coconut Grove is one of Miami's founding neighborhoods. It includes among its residents sixth-generation descendants of Bahamians who settled in south Florida in the mid-1800s. Despite this rich cultural legacy, the history of the "West Grove" as a vital, thriving community lives only in the memories of its older residents, not in the reality of today. For the last forty years the community has seen employment decline and poverty rise as it has fought to retain its identity in the face of poor health, drug abuse, and teenage pregnancy.

In stark contrast to surrounding areas where increased affluence has brought many positive changes, West Coconut Grove remains mired in poverty. More than 40 percent of its approximately 3,000 residents live below the poverty level. The median household income in the neighborhood is $14,191, compared to $47,506 in Coral Gables; the median income per capita is $10,308. Nearly 50 percent of the total population is not employed or looking for work, and 50 percent of high school students drop out and never receive a diploma.

In such an economically disadvantaged community the problem of affordable housing is also acute. So far this historic enclave—roughly sixty-five blocks covering half a square mile—has been protected from gentrification by the density and stability of its ethnic population, but it is now under siege from developers. The residents informed us that their priority was staving off displacement, and since ownership is key to stability one of the main initiatives we embarked on was the design and construction of affordable homes. Without strong intervention and long-term goals for improvement, this important and unique Miami neighborhood will inevitably decline to the point where speculative development by outside forces will overwhelm the desires of existing residents and property owners. At that point, its history and potential will be lost forever.

Building Community through University Partnerships

Community building requires a comprehensive, nuanced approach to promote the social, economic, and physical renaissance of the inner city. This rebirth depends on the restoration of a strong, seamless fabric of social connectedness that sustains families and creates a group identity. Social processes and physical settings are needed to help residents evolve out of isolation into comm-unity. These are complex interrelated challenges, and we needed to address them in a holistic fashion.

Each faculty member who participated in the initiative agreed to teach his or her course with West Coconut Grove as the focus. The team planned to meet every two weeks to share findings and learn about each others' projects. Film students in the School of Communication documented the life and personalities of the interconnecting layers of West Coconut Grove's physical and social fabric. Social and behavioral psychology students from the School of Medicine counseled families and children about drug abuse, domestic violence, and public health. Encouraging the citizens of West Coconut Grove to become architects of change in their own right, architecture students held monthly meetings with the community over the course of a year to discuss visions for the future and proposed designs for schools and housing that resonated with the residents' heritage, culture, and everyday needs. The Knight Program in Community Building, which is part of the School of Architecture and grants fellowships to mid-career professionals as part of a forum focused on community building efforts across professions, invited the visiting fellows to attend special workshops. They brought powerful expertise and served as a valuable pool of consultants for advancing the revitalization effort. The Center for Ethics and Public Service (the Law School's community economic development and outreach project) provided counseling for small businesses and community economic development training to residents through workshops and specific counseling sessions. Photography students prepared an exhibition of photographs depicting people and places, patterns and details. History students recorded oral histories of respected members of the community, who contributed valuable background about the neighborhood in more prosperous times. Participating high schoolers in Cityzens, a summer study program (initiated by graduate students in the School of Architecture to inform high-school students about careers in design) proposed a number of exercises in which they examined local architectural styles, details, and cultural patterns in West Coconut Grove.

Through its early stages INUSE has aspired to provide West Coconut Grove residents with an appreciation of their roots and perhaps a new understanding of what community and sense of place can mean to them. These foundational steps—coming to know who they are, what they want, and what they are capable of—help community members launch new economic and technological initiatives with assistance from academic, civic, and business partners.

We heard numerous requests for work-force development training, housing, estate planning, and legal advice for families and, over the next five years, we were able to respond by successfully providing a number of these:

• The film students assembled their footage into a documentary about life in West Coconut Grove and presented it in a public screening on Grand Avenue.

• The photography students organized an exhibition of their photographs as a portrait of the citizens in their community.

• With the help of funding through local first-time homebuyer grant programs, architecture students built four affordable homes on infill sites.

• The CUCD presented vision plans for Grand Avenue and for West Coconut Grove, which are being implemented today.

• Renovation plans were drawn up for a mixed-use abandoned building on Grand Avenue.

• The Cityzens established a "safe walk" through the neighborhood to raise commu-nity awareness about environmental, historical, and safety issues in and around the pedestrian environment of Grand Avenue.

The Bungalow

The Bungalow has the most colorful and lengthy history of the traditional house type. Tracing its origin to simple huts British offices observed in Bengal in India in the 19th century, the Bungalow became the most popular of house types from 1890 to 1930 on the North American Continent.

Typically the Bungalow had no basement, was one or one and a half stories with the upstairs tucked under the roof or dorment of the roof and there is an openness and inter relationship of out door and in door spaces. The strong roof shape served different purposes in different regions but in the South it protected a spacious porch and served as a comfortable covered place to enjoy evenings breezes and neighbors strolling by.

Our modern Bungalow extends its roof to cover a site entrance and carport and efficiency divides the public rooms and private rooms with a wall down the middle of the house.

The Eyebrow

The Eyebrow house was derived from the "I" house, so named due to its narrow profile, one room deep and two stories high. "Eyebrow" because the front windows from the upstairs rooms peer out shielded by a protective roof above. In South Florida such house is also called a "conch House" to distinguish its higher status from a ordinary one story house or "shotgun shack".

Few true "I" houses remain as they, like this example have addition on the back to accommodated a larger family and one which chose to show their importance by presenting a more impressive façade to the street.

To narrowness was also well suited to warmer climates and the need for cross ventilation.
Our modern adaptation uses the "ell" of the bedroom addition to protect a private "parterre" for family gateways or dinning in cooler months.

FIRST FLOOR PLAN

SECOND FLOOR PLAN

bove and
age 270
udents of
e School of
rchitecture,
niversity of Miami
he students
roduced designs
r affordable homes
two vacant lots
nated by the
y of Miami. The
esign intent was
reflect historical
uilding types in the
eighborhood.

The Dogtrot

The traditional Dogtrot house consisted of two rooms separated by a breeze way or hall way covered by a common roof. The open passage was used to protect animals from the elements or allow them to run through the house. It could also be the dinning area situated conveniently between the cooking area and the sleeping area.

The Dogtrot house was described by Mark Twain in Huckleberry Finn "It was a double house, and a big open space betwixt their was roofed and floored and sometimes the table was set there in the middle of the day and it was cool comfortable place!!

The contemporary Dogtrot House the students designed for Coconut Grove has kept the idea of an open space in the center, using it for not only dinning but also cooking and sitting. Three bedrooms and two baths flank the central space and the entire 1300 S.F. house is covered with a large hipped roof which embraces the front back porches as well.

- Assistance in planning a new K-8 charter school and health facilities was provided.

- Legal assistance was offered to neighborhood residents.

- Working with the city, a Neighborhood Conservation District Zoning was adopted to encourage appropriate development.

- A new collaborative organization was created to coordinate community-based organizations.

- A land trust was established to protect against gentrification.

Lessons from the West Grove
Within the community

Building community means drawing upon people with diverse skills, expertise, and levels of engagement in the process. This notion encourages people from various backgrounds to take on issues and activities that, in concert, can create positive outcomes and environments. From these efforts community leaders emerge with the passion and capability to work with diverse groups to develop practical answers to critical concerns. Identifying agents of change with these attributes is the initiative's first priority. However, in any community it is rare to find individuals who can contribute the time it takes to become a leader or sustain an organization. We were fortunate to have as one of the most successful outcomes of our work the creation of a community-based organization, the Coconut Grove Collaborative, which continues to serve as an important meeting ground of most local organizations and enterprises.

Community partnering is another key to success. If the university leads by offering expertise in a high-handed fashion, local community organizations may feel overshadowed. Rather than approaching issues from a top-down perspective, this initiative strove to create a more horizontal, systems approach. The university and community were true partners and stakeholders in development and reinvigoration, and our contribution complemented, but did not replace, the roles of families, local organizations, and other partners. We facilitated honest conversation among all parties, even though this sometimes led to heated debate and disagreements. The key was to communicate honestly and to encourage local leaders to take charge whenever possible.

The purpose of this program was to assist communities in developing a vision plan for revitalization. Our role was to catalyze family and citizen responsibility—to help community members expose and define issues so that they could begin to devise solutions. However, we often found that funding was not available for the tasks necessary to begin making progress. Governmental granting agencies, whether at the city, state, or federal level, must recognize the financial needs of community-based organizations. Nonprofit organizations had to be set up and operating before funds could be put toward community work; securing the money required personnel and expertise that were not immediately available at the time. Certain economic and social problems are intractable and beyond the scope of any one organization.

The initiatives described in this essay were highly appreciated by the community. If there was any resentment expressed regarding the work, it was over the university's lack of support for ongoing neighborhood programs following the conclusion of grants, all of which were obtained from outside sources.

Within the university

Professional schools seek to equip students with the intellectual and practical foundations necessary to pursue professional careers. Research universities are in the business of creating new knowledge. Both kinds of institutions, however, with their wide range of faculty and expertise, can also play a critical role in crafting and delivering comprehensive, integrated approaches to community development.

The university must organize its resources in new ways and find mechanisms for transforming knowledge into praxis. This will require crosscutting educational curriculums that combine thinking and teaching from many departments and opportunities to apply classroom knowledge to real-world concerns. Service learning, courses of study, and fellowship opportunities must be aligned with university-developed resource centers and based on local needs. These core activities should be woven throughout undergraduate and graduate programs.

The University of Miami is beginning to successfully integrate programs in a way that can better help communities meet their needs. For instance, recognizing that students benefit from the building studio experience, the School of Architecture continued the building project as a regular curriculum offering. However, the institution as a whole still faces several major hurdles. Incentives need to be established that attract faculty to embrace this mission in their teaching, research, and writing. Curricular programs must be created that make this approach central, rather than peripheral, to what is expected of students—and to what students expect—by embracing pedagogical approaches that allow for the fluid interaction of students and faculty of various disciplines, both in the development and evaluation of student work. Opportunities need to be provided for constructive interaction between students and community members, and it is imperative that the mismatch in timeframes between academic teaching schedules, student and faculty tenure at the university, as well as the long-term focus that is necessary to immerse oneself in community change, be addressed.

The coordination of these initiatives, inevitably, must be accompanied and sustained by a long-term basis of funding, and a research agenda needs to be developed that will analyze lessons learned to inform future programming. This in turn will help convince funders not to discourage community-based projects. One hurdle the institution faced was the University of Miami's grants administration's inability to understand the value of assisting community-based organizations with scarce assets to grow. However, the assistance of the university development team is vital to fundraising, and much more efficient than leaving each department to apply for separate and distinct grants. Risk management must also instigate policies at universities that indemnify students and faculty from risks of injury and errors and omissions in order to allow them to work in communities. The obstacles of bureaucracy, overhead costs, and access to funding must be surmounted in order to capitalize on the university's interest in assisting on a range of issues from health and child welfare to legal aid and business assistance.

For much of the last century American universities have functioned as if they were in their communities but not *of* their communities. Boundaries between disciplines and between academia and community have created a situation in which universities send specialists into the world with little experience or knowledge of the needs of the community around them. "Service learning" and "project-based education" are terms for pedagogical models that are trying to counteract this trend by encouraging students to assume public leadership as part of their educational curriculum by applying theoretical approaches to actual projects. These models give schools the opportunity to prepare a citizenry that understands the full complexity of today's social problems and can work to create integrated solutions, but most of them have not trained students to have a broad, interdisciplinary perspective on the notion of community.

The designed environment is a reflection of who we are and who we want to be, as individuals and as a society; thus, it is an important component of the cultural and economic well-being of a community and can act as a powerful catalyst for change. As Winston Churchill once said, "We shape our buildings; thereafter, they shape us."

We speak of architecture as a means of building community, but before we can identify how the built environment should be shaped, we must activate the full scope of our interdisciplinary arsenal of strategies to understand the social, cultural, and economic context of the community in question. This means that in our efforts to build cities and communities that work for us—that reach to our collective future while celebrating our individual pasts—we must use every resource at our disposal to understand our origins and how they have contributed to our current set of opportunities and challenges.

For too long we have failed to recognize our interdependencies, our shared social ecology. We must reassess what is to be valued in both the old and new ecologies; we must attempt to re-create attributes of the original system that can sustain the community, and we must identify aspects of new social systems that are valuable and worth adopting. Accepting our rich heritage while taking responsibility for the creation of our current situation is the only sustainable way forward.

All American communities need to place more of an emphasis on a collective identity, a sense of place, a feeling of belonging to something larger and of having a responsibility to that broader context that demands active participation in its sustenance. To bring about these changes we need to make basic alterations in how we live and hold ourselves accountable to our social networks. There are no easy answers; community building must be an evolving process. Universities and their resources are uniquely well situated to help make and sustain these changes. But to address the needs of communities in crisis, and to engage in constructive university-community partnerships, the educational paradigm must allow for truly interdisciplinary collaboration that abandons assumptions about context and is open to learning lessons along the way that were never anticipated in any lesson plan.

Collaboration requires more than an agreement to work together. It requires a commitment of resources, which includes a commitment to understanding the cultural differences between stakeholders. Universities and government agencies must recognize the value of this integrated process and alter the mechanisms for granting and administrating such efforts. Collaborative and reflective capacity-building must be a joint endeavor, one that views community organizing as intrinsic to the cultural suitability and sustainability of any design intervention. Only when we are responsive to this level of flexibility can the effort be more than the sum of its parts. Only then can the power of interdisciplinary design strategies marshal the potential energy of a population toward the greater good.

Breakdown of community, decline of social capital, and chronic poverty are not problems that can be solved without serious engagement at the street level. Though the university has a wealth of resources, it must become better connected across disciplines and less isolated from the world around it if it is to play a constructive role in addressing the disintegration of community. We must learn to cooperate and collaborate better, not only with our academic colleagues, but also with the community at large, providing practical and participatory service and leadership.

> **The designed environment is a reflection of who we are and who we want to be, as individuals and as a society; thus, it is an important component of the cultural and economic well-being of a community and can act as a powerful catalyst for change. As Winston Churchill once said, "We shape our buildings; thereafter, they shape us."**

Building Sustainable Communities and Building Citizens

SERGIO PALLERONI

Student action with communities can have transformative power—for both the students and the citizens they reach.

When I started to teach, I realized we were creating a culture of students in design who had very little experience of the outside world. If I was going to have a significant discussion with my students, I needed to take them beyond the classroom walls.

The initiative to move outside the classroom and even outside the United States to go to other communities in need was a pedagogical priority. It meant taking students out of their usual environment and into a context they did not understand, so that they would let go of some of the predispositions they had. In a new context, a new frame of mind created by their distance from their comfort zone of what was predictable, I reasoned, they could step outside of themselves and significantly reexamine their priorities and goals. How would they effect change? How would they understand their roles as architects and citizens of this world?

I often compare the situation of living in the United States to being in the eye of the storm. When you are standing in the eye of the storm, everything seems calm. But as you step away from the eye of the storm, you realize that this storm you're at the center of is changing the rest of the world dramatically. And I began to realize that the economic policies we are establishing, the social models we are creating, are being emulated and co-opted by the rest of the world. This has tremendous impact, and it is transforming the rest of the world in ways that are irreparable. Tragically, this impact is being felt most acutely by the very poor in squatter communities such as the ones we serve.

The act of building has a larger impact on the environment than anything else we do. If we are not conscious of that, it is not only an environmental issue; it affects cultures and marginalizes communities. So I created a program to address these issues called the BaSiC Initiative.

I am not alone; there are a lot of other educators, in and out of academia, who are concerned with this. They come from many different disciplines, not just the design fields. So some of my strongest collaborators over time have been people in medicine, forestry, ecology, anthropology, and other fields that make up society and universities. They have begun to merge their students with mine,

and we have found that we can use common development projects—a school, a clinic, a center for ecology—as a kind of common ground to begin to teach our students some fundamental lessons that we think are essential to being a doctor, being an architect, or whatever path they choose. But most important, we can also teach them to become citizens, to become collaborators, so that when they leave academia they have established the capacity to pool resources and have come to understand that cooperation can be a powerful tool toward making effective change. Through this collaborative exchange, they have created new models for their own discipline.

The students normally take coursework in their field first. Then, early on in their studies, they choose to join one of our programs. We ask them for a two-year commitment, one year in preparation for the program and then one year for follow-up (on construction, post-occupancy studies, and reflections on their experience). Sometimes that follow-up period creates new projects. For instance, I had some students who went to Cuba and Mexico and then became interested in AIDS. They ended up in Africa building clinics, and now they have established their own program in central Africa to help design and build AIDS clinics.

One thing that happens to the poor is that they are marginalized to the point where they become noncitizens, nonmembers of the economic community. They are excluded from all the decision-making processes that affect their lives. How do you bring people back into decision-making? Our answer is through the act of building, the act of design, the act of creating. This is an important part of our program. Through these acts, marginalized people can come back into the community and reassert their role, their position, their political right.

The other part of the program is that I ask the students to create buildings that are part of the community. We don't want a building that looks like an alien ship that has landed; we want a building that, when people in the community look at it, reflects them in some way—their values, their use of space, their cultural understanding.

We consider every one of our sites, our constructions, and our design/build projects as places in which to learn and exchange knowledge. I always tell the students, following Paolo Freire's great model, that the best way to overcome colonialism, to overcome the rift between rich and poor, is to acknowledge that every walk of life has its own understanding and its own way of seeing the world.

When we show up at sites, there is always some richness there that is easy for us to draw on, such as the way Mexicans make bricks. My students develop this understanding as a result of daily hands-on contact with each project, interacting with craftsmen, interacting with the community. This creates a mutual appreciation and respect. It allows us to integrate new technologies and new ways of seeing the world. You appreciate what the community is doing, and in exchange the community comes to accept the new ideas you are introducing. They feel they have been heard and in turn want to hear what you have to offer, such as new ways of using materials, like compressed-earth building blocks, solar hot-water heating, or composting toilets.

Most recently we have been emphasizing water. Forget oil; water is the biggest crisis the world faces. In ten years we are going to be fighting border wars over water. Three countries—the United States, Canada, and Russia—hold most of the world's fresh water resources. If you step outside of the U.S. and go to any underdeveloped country in the world, the issue of water is huge: drinking water, irrigation, the waste stream. I actually demand that we have a bill of rights that says every client deserves to be able to have drinking water, to treat its own waste in its own site, to be able to walk into its building and have it beautifully lit without turning on a light bulb during the day. The building has to be comfortable and cool. It has to be made of local materials that respect local traditions, and it has to represent local values. And, most important, it has to be a constructed collaboration with the community. We tell students that they are going to have to respect these rights in their designs.

We conduct the design-review process in a public space. Every time we are ready to present a design, we bring all our drawings and other materials out to a local gathering

Below left
Design becomes an
exchange of ideas
and possibilities,
which creates a
site of learning
and empowerment
for both community
and students.
Students and com-
munity members
discuss adding
a garden for the
disabled children
of Jiutepec.

Below
Even an informal
settlement has
important clues for
the students' design
process and its
claim to relevance.
Permanent housing
for a Mexican
squatter community
in Jiutepec.

place, like a tortilla shop in a Mexican village. It becomes a site of exchange at the heart of the community, very active. We always establish a location that is embedded in the neighborhood where people feel they can openly participate in the design process. Most commonly this will happen on the site of our projects, with students discussing a model of their proposal with members of the community.

Part of the design process is to teach students about local culture and history. We also teach them to appreciate the power of the vernacular and the extraordinary capacity to invent from traditions. We also teach them about the spontaneity and trans- itory nature of architecture. Architects tend to create things that are decidedly perma- nent, but some of the most effective uses of architecture are very transitional, like markets in Mexico and many other places around the world. We then require the students to reflect on their experience, at the same time asking them to document the community and its experience organically, as they build not only their homes but the urban fabric of the streets.

When we start the public process of design, we often begin by mocking up the building full scale. We ask people to walk through and we ask them, "Do you get it?" Construction documents do not mean any- thing to the average Mexican or Chinese or Australian. What does mean something is a drawing he or she can understand, a model, tracing the building on the ground and having people walk through it, building a full-scale mock-up. Once you do that the exchange between you and them changes dramatically, because all of a sudden people begin to understand what it is you are proposing. An act of communication is established that makes for better buildings.

Then you start your daily ritual: the draw- ings, building the building. This is the most extraordinary part of the experience because many communities, poor communities particularly, have been approached by their governments and have been given grand- iose plans for housing and schools that fail to materialize. So they are suspicious of our plans. There is nothing like that first day when you are breaking ground, and the building begins to go up, and people start

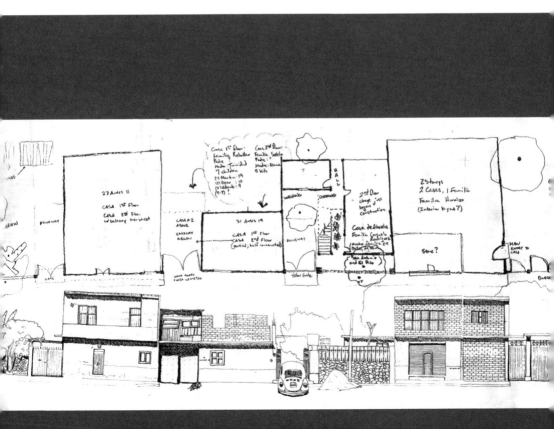

showing up at the site, saying, "Oh my God, they really are going to build this."

The site becomes interesting because the great majority of my students have never built before. On the other hand a lot of the community members in the societies we work with have developed some building experience out of necessity. So the students help them realize buildings they couldn't build on their own by bringing in new ideas, creating a community-based design process, and often providing the funding to get the building built. But the students learn how to build from the community. For instance, the idea of a composting toilet is made possible through the students' appreciation and adoption of the local craft of stucco. As students and community venture into unknown territory, each is awkward in the face of the other's experience. Each makes mistakes, and it is through the common humiliation and appreciation of one another's talents we experience on the site that we actually become a tighter and better group at building.

If there is one thing I have learned, it is that you have to go out there and listen. As Freire said, in the act of listening, you hear yourself as well.

What I am really cultivating in the classroom is the sense of shared citizenship. As Plato would have said, you don't become a citizen unless you act. So I am creating the possibility within the university for students to take all the learning they do in school, and make it real through actions that tell them why that knowledge has any relevance in the first place. The architecture is just a by-product. The main result is the impact it has on the minds of the students and the communities.

Editor's note: This text has been adapted from the transcript of a lecture delivered by the author at the fifth annual "Structures for Inclusion" conference, held on April 2, 2005, in New York City.

ABOUT THE CONTRIBU-TORS

CREDITS AND ACKNOWL-EDGMENTS

ABOUT THE CONTRIBUTORS

Bryan Bell
is the executive director of Design Corps, based in Raleigh, North Carolina, which he founded in 1991 to provide community service through architecture. His other initiatives include the Design Corps Fellowship program, the Design Corps Summer Studio, and the "Structures for Inclusion" annual conference. In 2007 he received a National Honor Award from the American Institute of Architects. www.designcorps.org

Katie Wakeford
received her M. Arch. from NC State University School of Architecture, where she became interested in community design. She began working with Design Corps in 2002, and currently serves as an intern architect with the NC State College of Design's Home Environments Design Initiative, a research and community outreach endeavor focused on affordable and sustainable housing.

Peter Aeschbacher
is an assistant professor in the Departments of Architecture and Landscape Architecture at Penn State University. He is the director of design at the Hamer Center for Community Design, and is a former Frederick P. Rose Architectural Fellow. www.claimingpublicspace.net

Steve Badanes
holds the Howard Wright Endowed Chair at the University of Washington and leads the Neighborhood Design/Build Studio, which constructs community-service projects for nonprofit organizations in the Seattle area. He is a founder of Jersey Devil, an architecture firm perpetuating the tradition of medieval craftsmen. http://online.caup.washington.edu/courses/hswdesignbuild/; www.jerseydevildesignbuild.com; www.yestermorrow.org

Damir Blažević
is the coordinator of Platforma 9.81. He studied in the Department of Architecture at the University of Zagreb and is the initiator of the Invisible Zagreb project.

Gail Peter Borden
has taught at Catholic University, the Boston Architectural College, NC State University, and Harvard. He is on the faculty at the University of Southern California and is a principal in the Los Angeles–based Borden Partnership LLP. He has worked with firms including Gensler and Associates, Frank Harmon Architect, and the Renzo Piano Building Workshop in Paris. www.bordenpartnership.com

Sean Donahue
is principal of Research-Centered-Design and is a member of the faculty at Art Center College of Design in Pasadena, California. His Los Angeles–based design practice consists of professional commissions, self-initiated research, design advocacy, education, and publishing. www.researchcentereddesign.com

Kathleen Dorgan
is trained as an architect and an urban planner and is principal of Dorgan Architecture and Planning in Storrs, Connecticut. She was awarded a Loeb Fellowship at the Harvard Graduate School of Design, a U.S. Department of Housing and Urban Development Community Builder Fellowship, and a Pratt Institute Community Development Fellowship. She teaches in the International Honors Program's Cities in the 21st Century study abroad program.

Deane Evans
is a research professor and the executive director of the Center for Architecture and Building Science Research at the New Jersey Institute of Technology. A registered architect, Evans was the founding director of the U.S. Department of Housing and Urban Development's Partnership for Advancing Technology in Housing.

Roberta M. Feldman
is an architectural educator and researcher who has lectured and published widely in the United States and abroad on socially responsible housing and community design. She is a founding codirector of the City Design Center at the University of Illinois at Chicago. www.uic.edu/aa/cdc

Thomas Fisher
is a professor and the dean of the College of Design at the University of Minnesota, Minneapolis. He has written extensively about the social, environmental, and ethical aspects of architecture over the last twenty-five years, initially as an editor at *Progressive Architecture* and more recently as a writer for several publications.

Mónica Escobedo Fuentes
is a practicing architect who works to help marginalized communities in Sonora, Mexico, obtain housing. A cofounder of the Programa de Vivienda Ecológica of PROVAY, she was also the program's first architect. She continues to practice in the Sonoran Desert and is pursuing a doctorate in architecture at the University of Guadalajara, concentrating on sustainable housing for the poor.

José L. S. Gámez
is an assistant professor of architecture at the University of North Carolina at Charlotte, where he is currently serving as graduate coordinator for the College of Architecture. His research and design efforts focus on the intersections between culture, identity, and social spaces. www.josegamez.com

Deborah Gans
is principal of the Gansstudio in New York City, which has executed projects in industrial design, graphic design, architecture, and other areas. She is currently a participant in a community-based planning-and-design project for New Orleans East. www.gans-studio.net

Ryan Gravel
earned a M. Arch. and a Master's degree in city planning from Georgia Tech in 1999. His thesis project on the Atlanta BeltLine was presented to the city government and in late 2005 the Atlanta City Council, Atlanta School Board, and Fulton County Commission approved a tax-allocation district that will generate $1.6 billion over the next twenty-five years to implement the plan. Gravel works at Perkins and Will in Atlanta.

Amanda Hendler-Voss
is the minister of Christian education at First Congregational United Church of Christ in Asheville, North Carolina, and the faith-communities coordinator of Women's Action for New Directions (WAND).

Seth Hendler-Voss
is a principal landscape architect for the city of Asheville, North Carolina, where he is engaged in public-design and construction projects for parks and recreation facilities. He is also a founding partner and faculty member of the Design Corps Summer Studio.

Gregory Herman
is an associate professor at the University of Arkansas School of Architecture. He has been involved with design/build initiatives since 2001. His recent research has focused on WPA housing in the Arkansas Delta.

Lance Hosey
is an architect and a director with William McDonough + Partners in Charlottesville, Virginia. He has been featured in *Metropolis* magazine's Next Generation program and *Architectural Record*'s "emerging architect" series. With Kira Gould he is the coauthor of *Women in Green: Voices of Sustainable Design* (2007).

Jeffrey Hou
is an associate professor of landscape architecture and an adjunct associate professor of architecture at the University of Washington in Seattle. His areas of interest include design activism and social and ecological multiplicity in the urban landscape. His recent work focuses on insurgent public space and design participation involving minority urban communities and marginalized social groups.

Hsu-Jen Kao
is a senior planner at the Building and Planning Research Foundation, National Taiwan University.

Russell Katz
is a registered architect and has worked for Hans Hollein Atelier in Vienna, Turner Brooks Architect in New Haven, and Deamer + Phillips Architects in New York City. He is based in Washington, D.C, and currently serves on the advisory board to the dean of the University of Virginia School of Architecture. www.momidc.com

Chris Krager
earned degrees in business administration and architecture, and spent five years working in banking and real estate. In 2001 he formed, with Christopher Robertson, the Austin-based design/build company KRDB. www.krdb.com

Elizabeth Martin
opened her design firm, Alloy Projects, in 2001 with offices in Los Angeles and Atlanta. She is the founding director of the A+D Architecture and Design Museum in Los Angeles and is an assistant professor at Southern Polytechnic State University in Atlanta.

Eric Naslund and John Sheehan
are the design principals at Studio E Architects, a firm that specializes in the design of affordable and mixed-use housing projects throughout the southwestern United States. Studio E, based in San Diego, California, has received five National AIA Honor Awards for Architecture for its work in affordable housing. www.studioearchitects.com

Sergio Palleroni
is an associate professor at the University of Texas at Austin and the founder of the BaSiC Initiative, a multidisciplinary fieldwork program that challenges students to apply their education in service of the problems facing marginalized communities throughout the world. He has worked on housing and community development in the developing world since the 1970s. He is the coauthor, with Christine Merkelbach, of *Studio at Large: Architecture in Service of Global Communities* (2004). www.basicinitiative.org

John Peterson
is principal of Peterson Architects and is the founder and chair of Public Architecture, both of which are based in San Francisco. He was a Loeb Fellow at the Harvard Graduate School of Design. www.publicarchitecture.org; www.theonepercent.org

John Quale
is an assistant professor at the University of Virginia School of Architecture, in Charlottesville, where he teaches architectural design studios, building-technology courses, and photography. He initiated and serves as project director for ecoMOD. He and his wife, Sara Osborne, a landscape architect, established Q&O Design in Cobham, Virginia, in 2001. www.ecomod.virginia.edu

Samina Quraeshi
is an educator, author, designer, and artist who has devoted her career to exploring and demonstrating the importance of art and culture in educational, corporate, and governmental environments. She served as director of design at the National Endowment for the Arts from 1994 to 1997, and was the Henry R. Luce Professor in Family and Community at the University of Miami from 1999 to 2005. Her firm, S/Q Design Associates, is based in Boston.

Darl Rastorfer
is a researcher and writer focusing on architecture, civil engineering, neighborhood and community development, and urban and regional planning. He has written and coauthored several books and is a former senior editor for *Architectural Record* magazine. He lives and works in Philadelphia.
www.cdesignc.org

Michael Rios
is an assistant professor in environmental design and landscape architecture at the University of California, Davis. He is past president of the Association for Community Design and former director of Penn State University's Hamer Center, where he also held joint appointments in the School of Architecture and the Department of Landscape Architecture.
www.claimingpublicspace.net

Susan Rogers
is the director of the Community Design Resource Center, a new program at the University of Houston's Gerald D. Hines College of Architecture, where she is also a visiting assistant professor.

Alex Salazar
is an architect who specializes in housing, community/urban design and green building, and a principal of Salazar Design Studio in Oakland, California. He has served on the boards of several nonprofit organizations, including the Association for Community Design, East Bay Housing Organizations and Just Cause Oakland.
www.salazardesignstudio.com

Amanda Schachter
is principal with Alexander Levi of SLO Architecture, based in New York City. She started the degree program for a Master of International Cooperation in Architecture at the Escola Tècnica Superior d'Arquitectura in Barcelona, where she also served as design critic. With Levi, she coauthored *Stanze ribelli: Immaginando lo spazio hacker* (2005).

Laura Shipman
is a member of the Design Corps advisory board. After earning her B. Arch. from Cornell University in 2004, she worked as a Design Corps Fellow with the Community Housing Resource Center in Atlanta. She is currently studying urban design at the Harvard University Graduate School of Design.

Katie Swenson
is the director of the Frederick P. Rose Architectural Fellowship of Enterprise Community Partners and a founding partner of the Charlottesville Community Design Center.
www.cvilledesign.org;
www.urban-habitats.org

Leslie Thomas
practices architecture as a partner in LARC Inc. and LARC Studio in Los Angeles, Chicago, and New York. She edited the book *DARFUR/DARFUR Life/War* (2008) and in 2000 received an Emmy award for art direction on the HBO film *Introducing Dorothy Dandridge*.

Erik Van Mehlman
earned a B. Arch. in English from Tufts University and a M. Arch. from NC State University's School of Design. He has practiced in single-family and multifamily affordable-housing design in Raleigh, North Carolina, for eight years and as a consultant to the city of Raleigh Community Development Department.
www.erik-anna.com

Barbara B. Wilson
cofounded the Austin Community Design and Development Center, and is currently working on her dissertation in the Community and Regional Planning Program at the University of Texas School of Architecture, where she is researching the intersections between regulatory codes and social movements, using the SEED Network as the analytical focal point for her investigation.
www.acddc.org;
www.seed-network.org

Chia-Ning Yang
holds degrees from the Department of Civil Engineering at National Taiwan University, the University of Tokyo, and the University of California, Berkeley. Her research interests lie at the interface of landscape design, engineering, and ecology, with a special focus on stream restoration.

PROJECT CREDITS

The contributing authors would like to acknowledge the following individuals:

Steve Badanes
"Building Consensus in Design/Build Studios"
For list of advisors, sponsors, and all participating students on Noji Commons and Sunhouse, see http://online.caup.washington.edu/courses/hswdesignbuild/projects.html.

Bryan Bell
Preface
2007 Design Corps
Summer Studio
Raised House for Patty Broussard, Biloxi, Mississippi
Students: Robert Briggs, Brett Carlton, Aron Chang, Julia Dalton, Theresa Franzese, Farzaneh Ghassemi, Sarah Green, Kristin Hawk, Max Kim, Jami Primmer, Casie Stone, Ross Wienert, Liqiao Zhang
Design Corps fellow: Vincent Baudoin
Instructors: Bryan Bell, Brad Guy, Sergio Palleroni, David Perkes, Jason Pressgrove
Program credits: BaSiC Initiative, Design Corps Summer Studio, Gulf Coast Community Design Center, Hamer Center for Community Design at Penn State University

Roberta M. Feldman
"Out of the Box"
Double High House
Design Corps designer: Bryan Bell
Consultants: Sean Donahue (graphic designer), Tim Reed (digital renderer)
Manufactured Site
estudio teddy cruz design and research team:
Teddy Cruz with Jimmy Brunner, Giacomo Castagnola, Jota Samper Escobar, Jess Field, Jakob Larson, Mariana Leguia, Scott Maas, Alan Rosenblum, Brian Washburn
MiniMax
studio SUMO design team: Yolande Daniels and Sunil Bald with David Huang and Shai Turner

LaCan Project
David Baker and Partners Architects design team:
David Baker, Taeko Tagaki, Mike Thistle
Packed House
comma design team:
David Khouri, Roberto Guzman, Tim Kincer
house nine
Parallel Design design team:
Ali Tayar with Natalia Echeverri and Prashant Pradhan
Consultant: Attila Rona (structural engineer)
Homes Off the Highway
Taylor and Burns Architects Design team: Robert Taylor, Carol Burns, and Colby Lee, with Cara Mae Cirignano, Kim Parent, Cecilia Ramos
CorPod House
Garofalo Architects design team: Douglas Garofalo, Garry Alderman

Deborah Gans
"Unbearable Lightness"
Project team: Deborah Gans, Matthew Jelacic; Maryjane Starcks; engineers Dr. B. Basily, Dr. E. Elsayad

Amanda Hendler-Voss and Seth Hendler-Voss
"Designing with an Asset-Based Approach"
2005 Design Corps
Summer Studio
Students: Brad Buter, Christina Calabrese, Jeremy Fisher, Chip Howell, Doug Jack, Robin Laney, Robin Koch, Payam Ostovar
Instructors: Bryan Bell, Scott Ball, Seth Hendler-Voss, Amanda Hendler-Voss, Kelly Lowry, Erin O'Brian, JoEllen Wang, Victoria Ballard Bell
2006 Design Corps
Summer Studio
Students: Vincent Baudoin, Jodi Dubyoski, Jessica Fyles, Patrick Jones, Mike Miller, Callie Narron, Megan Williams, Andreas Viglakis
Instructors: Bryan Bell, Seth Hendler-Voss, Amanda Hendler-Voss, Brad Buter

Gregory Herman
"Market Modular"
University of Arkansas student team: Lance Bennings, Matthew Cabe, Mark Horne, Chris Johnson, Andy Kim,

Amy Koenig, John Langham, Chris Lankford, Sheana Mitchell, Eric Pace, Justin Posey, Justin Scott, Lisa Skiles, Denise Thomas, Patty Watts

Jeffrey Hou
"Traditions, Transformation, and Community Design"
Project team: John K-C. Liu, Hsin-Jay Chang, Jeffrey Hou, Shiao-Jun Tsai, Fu-Chang Tsai

Russell Katz
"Finding Balance"
Elevation 314
Green roof consultant: Katrin Scholz-Barth

Eric Naslund and John Sheehan
"Architectural Alchemy"
Indian Wells
Design team: Eric Naslund, John Sheehan, Brad Burke
Landscape architect: Spurlock Poirier
Tesoro Grove
Design team: Eric Naslund, John Sheehan
Landscape architect: Spurlock Poirier (designer), Mohammed Zaki, Delorenzo (landscape architect of record)
Eleventh Avenue
Design team: John Sheehan, Eric Naslund, Brad Burke
Landscape architect: Katherine Stangle

Sergio Palleroni
"Building Sustainable Communities and Building Citizens"
Hogar del Viento
Students: Catherine Craig, Trent Davies, Thomas Diaz, Jia Dong, Julia Ellingwood, Sarah Gamble, Paola Guerrero, Drake Hitchcock, Luciana Misi, Andrea Peterson, Jack Sanders, Andrea Schelly, David Wilson, Peyton Winston
Instructors: James Adamson, Monica Fuentes, Sergio Palleroni, Peter Spruance

John Peterson
"Mobilizing Mainstream Professionals to Work for the Public Good"
Public Architecture:
John Cary, executive director

John Quale
"ecoMOD"
ecoMOD: John Quale,
project director; Paxton Marshall,
engineering director
For list of additional advisors,
sponsors, and all participating
students, see project website
at www.ecoMOD.virginia.edu.

Darl Rastorfer
"The Community
Design Collaborative"
Infill Housing, Allegheny
West Foundation
Project team: Glen Conley,
Christopher Edwards, Ryan
McGrath, Nathan Morgan,
Linda Muronda, Adam Scott,
Rafael Utrera, Jody Beck,
Thomas Crowley, David Schmidt
Cedar Park Renovation
Project team: Dan Garofalo,
Ann Harnish, Robert Lungren,
Laura Raymond
Woolston Child and
Family Center
Project team:
Narintorn Narisaranukul,
Michelle Robinson,
Jennifer Summers

Alex Salazar
"Architecture and
Social Change"
Coalition for Workforce Housing
design team: Gary Struthers,
Noah Friedman, Mark Schiemer,
Jordan Rose

Amanda Schachter
"Teaching Cooperation"
La Mina Laboratory of
Social Practice
Mauricio Cavallini, Kazmy Chi,
Tiphaine Coulardeau, Sam Potts

Erik Van Mehlman
"Competition, Collaboration,
and Construction with
Habitat for Humanity"
Project team: Walt Lewis,
Michael Bustin, Peter Bustin,
Don Corey, Vanese Clough,
Anna Marich Mehlman

Barbara B. Wilson
"The Architectural Bat-Signal"
Rebuilding after Katrina Summer
Design/Build Workshop:
Extra Room for Families in
FEMA Trailers
Students: Virginia Alaxander,
Billy Antozzi, Julia Dalton, Rohit
Eustace, Valerie Giurdanella,

Sabeen Hasaan, Christophe
Ibele, Wade Miller, Lucy Morris,
Ali Tai, Matthew Wolpe
Instructors: Bryan Bell,
Brad Guy, Sergio Palleroni
Engineer: Richard Kaydos Daniels
Program credits: BaSiC Initiative,
Building Goodness Foundation,
Design Corps, Hamer Center
for Community Design at Penn
State University

Chia-Ning Yang and
Hsu-Jen Kao
"The Creek That Connects
It All"
Chih-Jun Liu, senior planner,
Building and Planning
Research Foundation
Shubun Fukudome, president,
Nishinihon Institute of
Technology

ILLUSTRATION CREDITS

Cover, estudio teddy cruz/
Goyo Ortiz
Pages 56–57, Jon Sheridan
Pages 246–47, Richard Shepard

Aeschbacher and Rios:
Peter Aeschbacher, 84
Thomas Dutton, 86 top
Michael Rios, 88–89
Badanes:
Neighborhood Design/Build
Studio, 248, 250, 251, 254–55
Blažević:
Sandro Lendler, Platforma 9.81,
110, 115
Dorgan and Evans:
Kathleen Dorgan, 151, 152
Scott Frances, 155–57
Michael Pyatok, 153
Marvin Rand, 148
Fisher:
© Shehzad Noorani/
MajorityWorld/The Image
Works, 11
Gámez and Rogers:
© Wesley Bocxe/The Image
Works, 20–21
Neighborhood Design/Build
Studio, 22
Gans:
Matthew Jelacic, 50
Gravel:
Ryan Gravel, 140, 142–45
Hendler-Voss and Hendler-Voss:
Bryan Bell, 122–24, 126, 128–31
Herman:
Justin Posey, 184–85, 194,
198–99

Hosey:
Courtesy P. J. and
J. P. S. Hendrikse, 34, 37
Courtesy Vestergaard Frandsen
S.A., 26, 40, 41
Hou:
Jeffrey Hou, 74, 76–77, 80–83
Katz:
Russell Katz, 222, 225, 226
Krager:
KRDB, 220–21, 236, 239–45
Martin and Thomas:
Benny Chan, 118
Lucy Gonzales, 116
Naslund and Sheehan:
Brady Architectural
Photography, 160–61, 163, 165
Ken Guttmaker, 158
Palleroni:
All rights BaSiC Initiative.
Sergio Palleroni, 276
Penelope West, 274
Kristin Will, 279
Palleroni and Fuentes:
Catherine Craig, 47 top
Tad Fettig, 48–49
Sergio Palleroni, 45
Jay Sanders, 47 bottom
Kristin Will, 42
Peterson:
© Mark Darley Photography,
96–97
Quale:
Benjamin Kidd, 206–7
John Quale, 200, 203
Scott Smith, 204, 205
Quraeshi:
Richard Shepard, 264
Rastorfer:
AK Architecture LLC, 104,
108–9
Salazar:
Alex Salazar, 146–47, 176
Schachter:
Las Adrianas de la Mina
photographic archive, 259
Laura Vescina, 256, 258
Shipman:
Tyler Elder, 192–93
Laura Shipman, 186
Rob Williams, 188
Swenson:
Andreas Bacher, 66
Jon Sheridan, 68
Van Mehlman:
Matthew Kesterson, 166
Erik Van Mehlman, 170–71, 175
Wilson:
Virginia Alexander, 33
Brad Deal, 32
Sarah Gamble, 28
Yang and Kao:
Chih-Jun Liu, 58, 62–63, 65

ACKNOWLEDGMENTS

Bryan Bell and Katie Wakeford

We extend our sincere appreciation to each of the contributors in this collection. We admire your work and your commitment to design advocacy and public practice. We are grateful for the enthusiastic and wise guidance of Diana Murphy, our fabulous editor at Metropolis Books, and for the skillful work of copyeditor Claudia De Palma and proofreader Christine Simony. Special thanks to Penny Hardy for her engaging graphic design; she was ably assisted by Elizabeth Oh. Through their dedicated efforts, Virginia Alexander, Juliane Kuminski, JoEllen Wang, and Brent Winter strengthened and enriched this book.

Design Corps is grateful for the support of the National Endowment for the Arts, Deedie Rose, the Edward W. Rose III Family Fund of the Dallas Foundation, the Richard H. Driehaus Foundation, Julia Elsee, and the Graham Foundation for Advanced Studies in the Fine Arts.

We could not have completed this project without our personal support networks. Bryan Bell would like to thank his loving wife and children—Victoria, Sky, and Cole—and his parents, Bryan and Rubie. Katie Wakeford is indebted to her cherished family, especially her wonderful husband, Gregg Cusick.

This book is dedicated to the memory of Robert Gutman.

Project director:
Diana Murphy

Design and production:
PS New York

Separations and printing:
TWP Sdn Bhd, Malaysia

Set in Nimbus Sans and
printed on Nymolla MultiFine

Library of Congress Cataloging-
in-Publication Data

**Expanding Architecture:
Design as Activism**/edited by
Bryan Bell and Katie Wakeford.

p. cm.
ISBN 978-1-933045-78-8
1. Architecture—Social aspects.
2. Architects and community.
I. Bell, Bryan, 1959-
II. Wakeford, Katie.
NA2543.S6E96 2008
720.1'03–dc22

2008020417

Third printing

Metropolis Books is a joint
publishing program of:

**D.A.P./Distributed Art
Publishers, Inc.**
155 Sixth Avenue,
2nd floor
New York NY 10013
tel 212 627 1999
fax 212 627 9484
www.artbook.com

and

Metropolis Magazine
61 West 23rd Street,
4th floor
New York NY 10010
tel 212 627 9977
fax 212 627 9988
www.metropolismag.com

Available through D.A.P./
Distributed Art Publishers, Inc.,
New York.
Proceeds from the sale of this
book will support the work of
Design Corps.